About the Author

Sherman A. Jackson is Professor of Arabic and Islamic Studies and Adjunct Professor of Law at the University of Michigan.

Islam and the Blackamerican

Islam and the Blackamerican

Looking toward the Third Resurrection

SHERMAN A. JACKSON

OXFORD
UNIVERSITY PRESS
2005

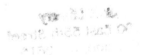

OXFORD
UNIVERSITY PRESS

Oxford University Press, Inc., publishes works that further
Oxford University's objective of excellence
in research, scholarship, and education.

Oxford New York
Auckland Cape Town Dar es Salaam Hong Kong Karachi
Kuala Lumpur Madrid Melbourne Mexico City Nairobi
New Delhi Shanghai Taipei Toronto

With offices in
Argentina Austria Brazil Chile Czech Republic France Greece
Guatemala Hungary Italy Japan Poland Portugal Singapore
South Korea Switzerland Thailand Turkey Ukraine Vietnam

Published by Oxford University Press, Inc.
198 Madison Avenue, New York, New York 10016
www.oup.com

Library of Congress Cataloging-in-Publication Data
Jackson, Sherman A.
Islam and the Blackamerican : the third resurrection / Sherman A. Jackson.
p. cm.
Includes bibliographical references and index.
ISBN-13 978-0-19-518081-7
ISBN 0-19-518081-X
1. African American Muslims—History. 2. African Americans—Religion—History. 3. Black nationalism—United States—History. 4. African Americans—Ethnic identity. I. Title.
BP221.J34 2005
297.8'7—dc22 2004013782

9 8 7 6 5 4 3

Printed in the United States of America
on acid-free paper

To Nadim Abdul-Ahad,
my "Hārūn"

وَنُرِيدُ أَن نَّمُنَّ عَلَى الَّذِينَ اسْتُضْعِفُوا فِي الْأَرْضِ
وَنَجْعَلَهُمْ أَئِمَّةً وَنَجْعَلَهُمُ الْوَارِثِينَ

Acknowledgments

The number of people from whose insights, perspectives, and protestations this book has benefited would defy any attempt at a full accounting. I have enjoyed the advantage of the queries and comments of my undergraduate and graduate students at the University of Michigan, the American Learning Institute for Muslims (ALIM), and the many venues around the country to which I have had the honor of being invited to speak. I also benefited from the many long and often contentious discussions outside of mosques and in coffee shops following Friday prayers and at other Muslim get-togethers. Many of these people had no idea that they were contributing to the present effort. And in many instances I myself would not discover the profundity or relevance of their articulations until long after the fact. In their own way, however, all of these friends, colleagues, and "adversaries" have influenced my thinking. And in so doing, they have all contributed to the present work. While many of their names and even their faces may now escape me, I would like to recognize and express my heartfelt gratitude to them all.

Beyond these more anonymous contributors, a number of colleagues in the academy were kind and patient enough to suffer conversations the sole purpose of which was to test some of the ideas I had been contemplating for this book. I would like to mention in this regard Mohammad Fadel, Umar F. Abd Allah, Aminah B. McCloud, Bruce Lawrence, Charles H. Long, Zareena Grewal,

T. J. Winter, Omar Abd al-Malik, Sulayman Nyang, and Ebrahim Moosa. To all of them, I am deeply grateful.

This book is dedicated to my brother, Nadim Abdul-Ahad (formerly Marvin T. Jackson), whose encouragement, support, and conscientious engagement have been a constant and indispensable source of strength and inspiration. In Nadim, I could not ask for a better, more loving brother. And it is my hope that he will accept this dedication as a small token of gratitude, love, and recognition for all that he has been and done for me over the years.

Finally, I would like to acknowledge and thank my family, Hassan, Shihab, Saphia, Niyyah, and my wife, Heather, for their sacrifice and their understanding in putting up with me—the distracted dad and husband—throughout the writing of this book.

Contents

Islam and the Blackamerican

Introduction

This book traces the ideological encounter between Islam and Blackamericans, from the proto-Islamic black-nationalist spin-off movements of the early twentieth century through the rise and preponderance of orthodox Sunni Islam by the century's end. While such a trajectory might connote a primarily historical emphasis, this book does not aim at a descriptive survey of the places, dates, and personalities connected with the spread of Islam among Blackamericans. Its primary focus is, rather, the ideological dislocations and attempted adjustments that accompanied the shift in the basis of religious authority following the influx of Muslims from the Middle East and Asia after the repeal of the National Origins Act and the Asiatic Barred Zone in 1965.[1] It proceeds in the concentric contexts of: (1) the perduring struggle on the part of Blackamericans to settle upon a self-definition that is both functionally enabling and sufficiently "authentic"; (2) the inextricable power and influence of white supremacy as a seminal feature of the contemporary global *cum* American sociopolitical order; and (3) the hegemonic presumptions and deployments of modern, Middle Eastern and South Asian Islam, particularly as manifested in the collective vision of Muslim immigrants to the United States.

While commonly treated as the most recent chapter in the story of American immigration, prior to 1965 Islam in America was dominated by an indigenous black presence. With rare exceptions, however, the basis of Blackamerican Islam had been the thoroughly

American phenomenon of "Black Religion," essentially a pragmatic, folk-oriented, holy protest against anti-black racism, an orientation shared with many, though not all, Blackamerican Christians and Jews.[2] But following the settling of critical masses of Muslims from the Muslim world, the basis of religious authority in Blackamerican Islam shifts to the sources, authorities, and interpretive methodologies of historical Islam. On this development, given their presumed mastery over this intellectual legacy, immigrant Muslims came into a virtual monopoly over the definition of a properly constituted "Islamic" life in America. Meanwhile, Blackamerican Muslims found themselves increasingly unable to address their cultural, political, and social reality in ways that were either effective in an American context or likely to be recognized as "Islamic" in a Muslim one. Like Blackamerican Christians of an earlier era, struggling to find their voice in the context of a Christianity dominated by white Americans, Blackamerican Muslims found themselves struggling to reconcile a dignified black, American existence with the super-tradition of historical Islam, on the one hand, against the presumed normativeness of a historically informed and culturally specific Immigrant Islam, on the other.

All of this would be complicated by the uneasiness with which Blackamerican Muslims related to their own status as Westerners in general and as Americans in particular. On the one hand, their corporate experience as a marginalized racial minority bred a certain diffidence if not hostility toward the idea of embracing America or the West. In fact, the anti-Western sentiment permeating much of Immigrant Islam appeared at first blush to reflect a shared historical perspective between the two groups. This would soon dissipate, however, under pressure of a mutually contradictory relationship to American whiteness. At the same time, the two groups' sociocultural interactions, for example, in mosques and Islamic centers, exposed the incongruence of the immigrant claim (and directive) to privilege universal religion over particularistic culture. Ultimately, this would obviate to Blackamerican Muslims their indebtedness to a cultural and historical legacy that was emphatically domestic, even as they continued to grapple with aspects of the dominant culture in America.

While Immigrant Islam's failure to confirm the impartiality of its vision may have destroyed its claim to unquestioned authority, Blackamerican disaffection could not be expressed via a simple *marche arriere* to classical Black Religion. To begin with, the overwhelming majority of Blackamerican Muslims were now orthodox Sunnis. As such, even if aspects of the agenda of Black Religion remained valid, Black Religion itself could no longer be invoked as the sole or even primary basis of authentication. More importantly, while immigrant Muslims might boast a certain chronological seniority, Blackamericans had established their relationship with Islam independent of and long before the post-1965 immigrant wave. This relationship went back, in fact, to the beginning of the twentieth century and the proto-Islamic movements of Noble Drew Ali and, especially, the Honorable Elijah Muhammad. Despite their tenuous connection to the sources and Tradition of historical Islam, these movements had the seminal effect of transforming Islam itself, at least as an idea, into the cultural and ideological "property" of Blackamericans as a whole. In this capacity, these movements conferred upon Blackamericans a sense of *ownership* in Islam. Over time, this would evolve into a visceral/psychological attachment on the part of Blackamerican Muslims to the legacy and achievements of Islam in history. In such a context, to abandon the super-tradition of historical Islam to immigrant Muslims would be to forfeit this prized ownership and, in so doing, confirm immigrant superiority in American Islam.

This essentially romantic attachment to Sunni Tradition would not be enough, however, to preempt the role and influence of Black Religion. For one, the cumulative legacy of American racism operated to preserve the latter's strength and relevance. In addition, Blackamerican mastery of Sunni Tradition remained more an ideal than a reality. As such, Black Religion continued to inform the perspective and sensibilities of Blackamerican Muslims by default. So too, however, would Immigrant Islam, and precisely for the same reason. Ultimately—and this would become *the* defining feature of Blackamerican Islam by the end of the twentieth century—by this single default, that is, non-mastery of Sunni Tradition, the critical posture of Black Religion and Immigrant Islam toward America and "the West," respectively, would combine to create a Blackamerican Muslim self-definition that was practically dysfunctional, enabling Blackamerican Muslims neither as blacks nor as Americans nor, ultimately, as Muslims in America. The challenge, as such, for Blackamerican Muslims has become how to negotiate a dignified, black, American existence without flouting the legitimate aspects of the agenda of Black Religion or vesting the latter with too much authority, and without falling victim to the ideological claims, prejudices, and false obsessions of Immigrant Islam.

This book will argue that the answer to this challenge lies in Blackamerican Muslim mastery and appropriation of the Sunni super-tradition, a development that I refer to as the "Third Resurrection." In this new relationship, however, both mastery *and* appropriation are critical to success. Otherwise, to recognize the authority of Sunni Tradition without acquiring competence in it would be to become a tool of one's own domination. To master it, on the other hand, only to apply it to situations or in ways that reflect the perspective of immigrant or overseas masters would promote the same end. As such, as an ideal, the Third Resurrection refers not simply to the period during which

Sunni Tradition gains recognition among Blackamerican Muslims but to the era in which Blackamerican Muslims emerge as self-authenticating subjects rather than dependent objects of and in this tradition.

My use of the term "Third Resurrection" is neither gratuitous nor idle. It reflects, rather, my belief in the inextricable link between the spread of Sunni Islam among Blackamericans and the proto-Islamic movements of the early twentieth century. This is not to make the demonstrably false claim that all Blackamerican Sunnis trace their roots to these movements. It is merely to affirm that Islam owes the legitimacy and esteem it enjoys in the black community as a whole primarily to these proto-Islamic beginnings. In other words, the phenomenon of *communal conversion* among Blackamericans—which sets Islam apart from, say, Buddhism or even Judaism in America—is genetically linked to these early developments. As such, the past, present, and future of Islam among Blackamericans can only be understood in the context of a historical trajectory that begins with and proceeds from them. While these movements may be of little or, in some instances, no significance today (as, for example, with the Moorish Science Temple), this should neither obscure nor negate their overall historical impact.

When the Honorable Elijah Muhammad died in 1975, his followers came to refer to the period before his death as the "First Resurrection," during which blacks were said to have been delivered from the darkness of their slave mentality into the light of their true Blackamerican selves. The period immediately after his death, under the divided leadership of Imām W. D. Muhammad and Minister Louis Farrakhan, came to be known for a time as the "Second Resurrection." Under both of these "dispensations," it was the charismatic leader rather than any objective method of scriptural interpretation that made and unmade religious doctrine. But subsequent difficulty adjusting to the "new" criterion associated with historical Islam would produce a palpable lull (if not a crisis) in Blackamerican Muslim leadership. Today, as the era of charismatic leadership draws to an end, whatever future Islam has in black America will be one in which the authenticating agent is almost certain to be the structured discourse of Sunni Tradition. This will be the era of the Third Resurrection, as a reality if not as an ideal. Mapping the evolution and modeling the parameters of this development is the subject of this book.

Sunni Tradition: Relevant Features

The Third Resurrection is not a romantic, iconoclastic, antimodernity impulse that seeks refuge in the material lifestyle of the medieval past. Its primary interest lies, rather, in certain *structural* features of classical Muslim ecumenicism whose function it was to reconcile the competing interests of interpretive integrity and intrareligious pluralism. Given the breadth of its geographical expansion and its conscious decision *not* to adjudicate doctrinal disputes through a centralized ecclesiastical authority, classical Sunnism was forced to develop alternative mechanisms for this purpose. These mechanisms provided the ability to adjust to changing circumstances as the religion moved through space and time. It is primarily these mechanisms, rather than any body of fixed medieval doctrines, that the Third Resurrection seeks to enlist into the cause of Blackamerican Islam.

It was not theology but law that achieved primacy in classical Sunni Islam. Islamic law, however, was not the creation of the early Muslim state. Rather, private Muslims during the first two centuries after the death of the Prophet Muhammad (632 C.E.) succeeded in gaining recognition for their interpretive efforts as representing the most reliable renderings of divine intent. By the early decades of the third/nineth century, a full-blown interpretive methodology (*uṣūl al-fiqh*) had emerged, with the Qurʾān, Sunna (normative practice and supplemental commentary of the Prophet Muhammad) and the Unanimous Consensus (*ijmāʿ*) of the jurists as primary *sources* and analogy (*qiyās*) as the main *method* of extending the law to unprecedented cases. During this same period, the jurists began to organize themselves into formal interpretive communities or schools of law, known as *madhhabs*. By the fourth/tenth century, the *madhhab* had emerged as the exclusive repository of legal authority, and from this point on, all interpretive activity, if it was to be sanctioned as "orthodox," would have to take place within the boundaries of a recognized school. By the end of the fifth/eleventh century, based on the principle of survival of the fittest, the number of Sunni schools would settle at four. These were the Ḥanafī, Mālikī, Shāfiʿī, and Ḥanbalī schools, all equally orthodox, all equally authoritative. This would be the number at which the Sunni schools would remain all the way down to modern times.

Parallel to these developments, Sunni Islam would also embrace a doctrine of prophetic infallibility (*ʿiṣmat al-anbiyāʾ*). According to this doctrine, the Prophet Muhammad (like all prophets) was deemed to have been protected from sustaining errors in interpreting revelation.[3] Even more important than the substance of this doctrine, however, was its corollary: namely, that *only* the Prophet Muhammad was infallible. On this understanding, from the time of his death up until the coming of The Hour, no individual, including the Caliph, would be able to claim interpretive infallibility. For Sunnism, this divine favor passed not to any individual but to the interpretive community as a whole.[4] On this understanding, only those interpretations upon which the interpretive community unanimously agreed could be deemed infallible and thus binding on the entire community. Where, on the other hand, their collective effort resulted in disagreement, competing views simply had to be left standing. To be sure, this was not an exercise in relativism. In fact, most medieval Muslim jurists would agree with Stanley Fish's distinction between relativism and pluralism: "[T]he absolutely true . . . exists, and I know what it is. The problem is that you know too, and that we know different things, which puts us . . . armed with universal judgments that are irreconcilable, all dressed up and nowhere to go for an authoritative adjudication."[5] In sum, for the Muslim jurist, in the absence of Unanimous Consensus or the Prophet Muhammad coming back and declaring this or that view to be correct, there was simply no fair and objective basis for binding the community to one over another view.[6]

This synergy between the doctrine of Prophetic infallibility and the principle of Unanimous Consensus laid the foundation for intra-Muslim pluralism. As long as a jurist's view showed itself to be grounded in authoritative sources and based on recognized principles of interpretation, no one could legitimately deny him the right to express it—regardless of substance—as long as it did not violate a pre-existing Unanimous Consensus.[7] Concomitantly, while there might be many views that could justifiably claim to represent *an* Islamic position, the only views that could be said to represent *the* Islamic position were those that were backed by Unanimous Consensus.

This system produced a stunningly massive body of legal, theological, and religious doctrine, some worthy of consideration in a modern context, others emphatically not. In negotiating its way to a dignified American existence, the Third Resurrection will look to the classical legacy as the *starting point* rather than the end of its contemplation. More importantly, the structural features of classical Islam will confer upon Blackamerican Muslims both the right and the responsibility to develop their own body of concrete doctrine. This is not to convert the classical Tradition into an ideological flea-market or a license to abandon the value and/or concept of orthodoxy. Indeed, Blackamerican Muslims will be able to purchase the advantages of the classical system only by paying the cost of recognizing its constraints. Still, given their role as independent *agents*, as opposed to passive recipients, in the process of formulating doctrine, the classical Tradition will function as both a brake *and* as an accelerator.

Islam(s) and Race: Against the Tyranny of the False Universal

This simultaneous invoking of the classical Tradition while restricting my focus to the relationship between Islam and Blackamericans is almost certain to raise the suspicion if not ire of many Muslims, especially but not exclusively immigrants, who see in it a violation of Islam's universality. Equally critical, however, will be a growing contingent of non-Muslim intellectuals who have come to look upon race as an outmoded and dangerous category that divides rather than unites us as humans. From the cultural Right, for example, Allan Bloom has lamented that "just at the moment when everyone else has become a 'person,' blacks have become blacks."[8] From the Left, in an effort to undo all racialized identities, Kwame Anthony Appiah declares, "The truth is that there are no races."[9] My response to these critics is that their universalism is ultimately neither as transcendent nor as enabling as they might like to imagine. In fact, both "human" and "Islam," as undifferentiated categories, constitute not true but false universals that only serve the psychological and or material interests of those who define them. On this understanding, part of the whole point of the Third Resurrection is to expose and thwart the power and pretensions of false universals.

By false universal, I am referring to the phenomenon of history internalized, normalized, and then forgotten as history. This invariably leads to the tendency to speak in universal terms but from a particular cultural, ideological, or historical perspective. In this process, the cognitive mass of the universal category eclipses the contribution of the particular perspective from which the speaker speaks. "Human," "Islam," "justice," and the like are all taken, thus, to represent not particular *understandings* but *ontological realities* that are equally esteemed and apprehended by everyone, save the stupid, the primitive, or the morally depraved. From this vantage point, only those who subscribe to specific concretions of these ostensibly universal categories are justified in laying any claim to them. In this capacity, and precisely because it is so imperceptible, the false universal turns out to function as a powerful tool of domination.

All of this is evocative, of course, of the postmodernist assault on Enlightenment universalism. While postmodernist discourse has deepened my appreciation for these matters, it is not the actual source and beginning of my critique.[10] This goes back, rather, to Sunni Tradition, specifically the writings of the Hanbalī jurist and theologian, Taqī al-Dīn Ibn Taymīya (d. 728/1328), who mounted a devastating critique of the early Greek and later Muslim doctrine of ontological universals. Over the course of this campaign, Ibn Taymīya defends the integrity of primordial, natural reason (*fiṭra*) against the aspersions cast upon it by the rationalist proponents of formal definitions and logical syllogisms. Given the tendency of the founders and proponents of modern rationalism—from Kant to Hegel to Blumenbach—to use reason to validate white domination of blacks,[11] Ibn Taymīya's critique seemed particularly relevant to an analysis of the Blackamerican predicament. This seemed all the more so, given his 'protestant' leanings and his deep aversion to privileging interpretive calisthenics over simple piety and devotion. As is known, Islam has achieved its greatest success in the United States among the Blackamericans masses. The subtle prejudices of their socioeconomic betters notwithstanding, this has been key to the religion's resilience in black America. Though a genius in his own right, Ibn Taymīya understood the importance of preserving religion's accessibility to the masses, whose integral role in religious history has been summarized by the German theologian and historian of religion, Ernst Troeltsch, in the following terms:

> The really creative, church-forming, religious movements are the work of the lower strata. Here only can one find that union of unimpaired imagination, simplicity in emotional life, unreflective character of thought, spontaneity of energy and vehement force of need, out of which an unconditioned faith in a divine revelation, the näiveté of complete surrender and the intransigence of certitude can rise. Need upon the one hand and the absence of an all-relativizing culture of reflection on the other are at home only in these strata.[12]

Ibn Taymīya's opposition to "Islamicized" Greek thought should not be seen as some sort of fideistic opposition to reason per se. His complaint was, rather, that rationalist forces had succeeded in identifying their particular system of reasoning with reason itself, such that only those who paid homage to the former could lay any legitimate claim to the latter. This had the effect of either binding believers to doctrines that defied their perception of the world and the fundamental dictates of scripture or of disabusing them of their otherwise demonstrably sound beliefs.

Ibn Taymīya insisted that formal definitions (*ḥudūd*/ sg. *ḥadd*) (as the foundation of logical syllogisms) were arbitrary and self-serving in that they posited distinctions between "essential" and "accidental" qualities that were not objective but indebted to the perspective of the definer. Thus, for example, while the standard definition of "human" as a "rational animal" singled out rationality as the *essential* quality, Ibn Taymīya pointed out that humans are no more distinguished by the attribute of reason than they are by that of laughter. As such, it should be no less legitimate to define humans as "laughing animals" than it would be to define them as rational ones. Ibn Taymīya's point was that the priority of reason over laughter was not an ontological reality but a mental (read ideological) one. Yet, once this definition gained recognition as a plain and simple dictate of 'reason,' this priority would be placed beyond critique as an objective reflection of the external world.[13] On this construction, the views and actions of those who were deemed to be more adept at *systematic* reasoning would earn greater recognition than the views of those whose strength lay in humor, compassion, religious devotion, or even natural reason, even if scripture itself warranted no such advantage.

This tendency to project mental realities onto the world was also identified as the source of the fallacy of ontological universals. Here Ibn Taymīya insisted that while the mind looks out at similar specimens (e.g., squirrels, humans) and abstracts from these noetic categories, that is, "squirrelness" or "humanity," the latter do not correspond to any *ontological* realities in which all squirrels and humans participate. "Squirrelness" and "humanity" exist, rather, only in the mind. This was a *grundnorm* for Ibn Taymīya, the full dimensions of which have been summed up in the following terms:

> In the external world only individuated particulars exist, particulars that are specific, distinct, unique. Each individual exists in the context of a reality (*ḥaqīqa*) that is different from other realities. The uniqueness of such realities renders the individual what it is in so far as it is an individual (*huwa bi-hā huwa*) It is one of Ibn Taymiyya's cardinal beliefs that externally existing individuals are so distinct from one another that they cannot allow for the formation of an external universal under which they are all subsumed. . . . Accordingly, man *qua* man, or the absolute man or human, exists only as a mental concept. From this it follows that all universals, be they natural, logical, or mental have only mental existence.[14]

This is not to deny the common attributes observed among things in the external world. Ibn Taymīya was not implying that the world is an illusion and that we do not actually see the common attributes that we think we see. Squirrels exist, are mostly gray, and have bushy tails. And these common attributes are absolutely real. Ibn Taymīya's point, however, was that these attributes have no existence apart from individual squirrels themselves. As such, were all the squirrels in the world to perish, there would remain no universal "squirrelness" out there hovering about in the universe waiting to be instantiated in a real squirrel, even if the *idea* of a squirrel might remain in the minds of people.[15]

This denial of ontological universals has direct and far-reaching implications for our understanding of both Islam and race. As for Islam, it implies that there is no "real," "true," or "authentic" Islam apart from the historical instantiations (read interpretations) of the religion in the world. Even if the

Qur'ān and the Sunna were to remain physically in the world, there would be no *doctrine* of Unanimous Consensus or Five Pillars or jihad in the absence of Muslims, for these are products of human understanding rather than ontological givens. And while this does not imply that any particular doctrine or school is *ipso* false, it does mean that none is transcendent. Muslims, in other words, whenever and wherever they happen to be, are ensconced in historical situatedness, and this endows them with a perspective from which they speak. Where their uncoordinated efforts result in unanimous agreement, this may serve as the functional equivalent of a transcendent view, inasmuch as the agreement itself shows the view to be impervious to the dictates of any particular perspective. But where there is disagreement (assuming due diligence) no particular perspective can be justified in projecting itself onto the world as a universal standard for all. It is here that my critique of what I have been referring to as "Immigrant Islam" begins.

Immigrant Islam embodies the habit of *universalizing the particular*. It enshrines the historically informed expressions of Islam in the modern Muslim world as the standard of normativeness for Muslims everywhere. In fact, it equates its *understanding* of Islam itself with a simple, unmediated *perception* of an undifferentiated ontological reality. On this approach, "true Islam" can only assume one form anywhere it goes. And in this process, Immigrant Islam's interpretations are effectively placed beyond critique via the tacit denial that they are in fact interpretations. In short, Immigrant Islam does not interpret; it merely *transfers* "true" Islam from one location to the next.

This essentialism is reinforced by the mental habit of trying to subsume Old and New World realities under a single articulation of Islam. Even when Immigrant Islam purports to address specifically American issues, half its audience remains the teeming throngs and popular clerics of the Middle East and Asia. As one Muslim immigrant writer recently boasted, his column in a Western newspaper was also run in the Muslim world, enabling him to speak to both audiences simultaneously.[16] But on such an arrangement, with rare exceptions, the real object of his ruminations could be neither the concrete realities of New York or Karachi or Cairo but, rather, an empty abstraction hovering somewhere over the Atlantic. Yet, because these declarations carry the *imprimatur* of having issued from an individual from the Muslim world and because non-Western critics located in the West are able to present their cultural inheritance as bona fide and useful knowledge, these prescriptions routinely pass for a genuine engagement of "the West" in the name of Islam.

In all of this, the classical Tradition plays a misleading and profoundly problematic role. On the one hand, it rarely informs the actual substance of the doctrines of Immigrant Islam, at least not directly. This is because most immigrant Muslims are themselves only slightly less removed from the classical Tradition than are their Blackamerican counterparts. On the other hand, the classical Tradition is *presumed*, by natural inference, to be the basis of immigrant articulations, in which capacity it actually confers authority upon the latter. Because, however, Immigrant Islam is not *really* based on the classical Tradition, it cannot transfer the latter's power of self-authentication to Blackamerican Muslims. As a result, the latter are forced to proceed without the power or possibility of self-authentication, which leaves them to process their black, American reality through the prism of the real and/or imagined expectations of immigrant and overseas possessors of "true Islam."

Having said this much, I should add that Immigrant Islam is *not* synonymous with immigrant Muslims, especially those of the second and third generations, many of whom are actually opposed to its hegemony. Thus, while a successful Third Resurrection will necessarily attack the false pretensions of Immigrant Islam in general, this does not mean that it must target immigrant Muslims. The Third Resurrection is aimed at ideas not at people. Still, in the absence of a viable, American alternative, most immigrant Muslims are likely to remain at least provisional supporters of Immigrant Islam, for, if nothing else, the latter goes a long way in preserving their sense of authenticity, identity, and ownership. In this context, it remains to be seen how disaffected immigrant Muslims will relate to the Third Resurrection and vice versa.

As for race, while the concept of race should not be projected onto the world as an *ontological* reality, this does not justify the denial of the concrete attributes and "situatednesses" observed among individuals and groups in society. Just because there is no such thing as ontological "squirrelness," it does not follow that squirrels themselves do not exist. In his critique, Professor Appiah seems to think that because the notion of *biological* race is untenable, so too is the notion of race. He never tells us why we should accept this privileging of science, but I suspect that Ibn Taymīya would know the reason: Modern science, like medieval Aristotelian logic before it, has become the most expedient means of feigning objectivity and implying universality while hiding perspective. As such, by proving that there is no *scientifically* justified notion of race, we can pretend to prove, in an ideologically neutral fashion, that race period does not exist. To my mind, however, this is like saying that because there is no scientifically justifiable definition of love or emotional pain, neither love nor emotional pain is real.

For my purposes in this book, the scientific validation of the notion of race is irrelevant. Rather, by race, I have in mind something similar to the view of W. E. B. Du Bois that Professor Appiah set out to refute. According to Du Bois, a race is

> a vast family of human beings, generally of common blood and language, always of common history, traditions and impulses, who are both voluntarily and involuntarily striving together for the accomplishment of certain more or less vividly conceived ideals of life.[17]

Rather than biology, what Blackamericans have in common is a shared set of sociopolitical and historical circumstances, a common condition of circumscription, reaction, and contingency, all predicated upon the color of their skin. The Blackamerican, in short, is not a biological reality; he is a sociohistorical one. And no amount of scientific theorizing will undo him as an ontological, sociohistorical fact.

To my mind, the campaign to deracialize the Blackamerican goes well beyond the dictates of disinterested reason or science. It is reminiscent, rather, of Jean Paul Sartre's characterization of earlier European attempts to deny the Jew his Jewishness. As Sartre points out, the ultimate aim of the French anti-Semite was

> to persuade individuals that they exist in an isolated state. "There are no Jews," he says, "there is no Jewish question." This means he wants to separate the Jew from his religion, from his family, from his ethnic community, in order to plunge him into the democratic crucible whence he will emerge naked and alone, an individual and solitary particle like all the other particles.[18]

While Professor Appiah affirms that races *do not* exist, Professor Bloom suggests that blacks *should not* exist as a race. But Sartre reminds us that the efforts of outright racists may be ultimately no less destructive than those of liberal humanists. Speaking again in behalf of that other "problem people," he notes:

> The former wishes to destroy him as a man and leave nothing in him but the Jew, the pariah, the untouchable; the latter wishes to destroy him as a Jew and leave nothing in him but the man, the abstract and universal subject of the rights of man and the rights of the citizen. . . . Thus there may be detected in the most liberal democrat a tinge of anti-Semitism; he is hostile to the Jew to the extent that the latter thinks of himself as a Jew.[19]

To my mind, rather than contributing to resolving the problem of racism in America, deracializing Blackamericans will only exacerbate it. On the one hand, it can only add to the power and efficiency of white supremacy as "the invisible institution" that circumscribes the lives of all non-whites, even as it holds out ever-elusive standards of sociocultural and civilizational redemption. Ibn Taymīya was right: The absolute human exists only as a mental concept. But the masterful conflation of this absolute human with the perspectives of the dominant group is what has established and sustains the power of white supremacy. Indeed, it is precisely our inability to see whiteness as an idiosyncrasy with the same immediacy with which we see blackness or Hispanicness that preserves the former's status as a neutral, objective benchmark. And it is ultimately this false universal that perpetuates the contingency, subjunctiveness, and liminality of black life. On the other hand, a deracialized black population will only ensure that no serious, organized resistance to American racism emerges, as individualized blacks, "naked and alone," are placed before the overwhelming prestige, power, and resources of the dominant culture and the American state. My commitment to the conservation of race is, thus, not an attempt to revert to the racist mentality of the so-called First Resurrection. It is in recognition, rather, of the reality of race as a set of sociocultural and political facts and as a tool for combating the debilitating hegemony of the most intractable American false universal.

The American Context

This positive valuation of race as a category is less indebted to the dictates of Islam per se than it is to the peculiar character of America as a nation. As Matthew Frye Jacobson recently noted, "It is America that produced the distinctly *racial* understanding of 'difference.' "[20] In this context, American whiteness has always reigned as the most prized public asset a citizen could own. Beyond the different ways in which they relate to the historical legacy of Islam, their mutually conflicting relationship to American whiteness has contributed much to Blackamerican–immigrant Muslim relations. America, in other words, has not simply functioned as a neutral territory on which mutually conflicting perspectives, proclivities, and ambitions are brought into shared space. American sociopolitical reality has contributed much more directly to the Blackamerican–immigrant Muslim divide.

By 1965, U.S. immigration law had rendered Muslim immigrants from the Middle East and Asia legally white. On this development, coming to America represented not simply a chance for a better material life but a chance to participate in whiteness—real whiteness, like that of the colonial masters, as opposed to the mere "light-skinnedness" the term connoted in the Muslim world. By this time, however, American whiteness had become a sanitized and undifferentiated category. Armenians, Greeks, Italians, Jews, and countless others had all gained admission and exerted a palpable homogenizing effect. Epithets such as "hymie," "wop," "polack," and "mick" had lost much of their currency and by now meant little to nothing to the new arrivals. But the Muslim immigrants all understood (or soon learned to understand) the term "nigger." And they would all take great pains, and comfort, to distance themselves from this negative category. In short, from the very moment of their arrival, the American sociopolitical landscape almost guaranteed the deepening of any anti-black prejudice that might have accompanied immigrant Muslims to their new home.

For their part, while Blackamerican Muslims had preceded their immigrant co-religionists by several centuries, they found themselves unable to integrate and climb the socioeconomic ladder as quickly or effectively as the new arrivals. From their perspective, while American whiteness operated to authenticate and enhance the position of immigrant Muslims, it continued to exert the nearly opposite effect on them. Yet, the putatively universalist, race-blind discourse of historical/Immigrant Islam showed itself to be helpless before this reality, where not actually accommodating of it. Indeed, if, as has been suggested, to approach American society without the clue of race is to produce nursery rhymes, the new "Islamic" discourse of Immigrant Islam constituted a painfully vacuous melody. This would remain the case, at least for most immigrant Muslims, all the way until the events of September 11, 2001, which resulted in an anti-immigrant Muslim backlash that carried unmistakably racial implications. Today, as the "legal whiteness" of immigrant Muslims proves incapable of offsetting the negative effects of a newly acquired, post-9/11 "social nonwhiteness," it remains to be seen if they will join Blackamerican Muslims in a Third Resurrection that seeks to confront the problem of white supremacy in America without degenerating into reverse racism and without hiding behind the empty platitudes of "Islamic" utopianism.

Yet, even beyond issues of race and ethnicity, America contributes to the rise and substance of the Third Resurrection in yet another way. While one may generally think of immigrants from Muslim countries as an undifferentiated category, the immigrant Muslim community in America is quite distinct from its counterparts in other parts of the world. As a British convert once remarked to me, "You in America attracted the Muslim aristocrats, while we in Europe got the plebeians." Inevitable differences and exceptions notwithstanding, this perspective was actually confirmed by what I observed personally in Australia. There, rather than being dominated by the vision, sensibilities, and profile of doctors, engineers, and Internet-technology specialists, the Muslim community included sizable numbers of unskilled laborers, semieducated hopefuls and displaced refugees. This translated into a noticeable Muslim presence on the Australian welfare roles and in Australian prisons. From the perspective of an American convert for whom "immigrant Muslim" translated almost invariably into "educated" or "professional," this was simply shocking.[21] More importantly, the Australian Muslim community, unlike its immigrant American counterpart, was unable, given this profile, to create the kind of utopian image of the Muslim world that could impute to Muslim Tradition the kind of prestige that might render either a source of attraction to new converts. As a result, I cannot recall meeting a single indigenous convert throughout my (admittedly brief) stay in Australia.[22]

My point in all of this is that, for quite deliberate reasons, America tended to attract far greater proportions of wealthy, ambitious, educated immigrant Muslims. This contributed greatly to the prestige of the Muslim world and Muslim Tradition among Blackamerican converts. Had America's immigrant Muslim population resembled that of Australia (or perhaps Britain), Muslim Tradition may have never (or would have much more slowly) acquired the status it has come to hold among Blackamerican Muslims. In this light, the American context, through the sheer caliber of the immigrant Muslims America attracted, must be seen as having contributed significantly to the rise and substance of the Third Resurrection.

Finally, the explicitly American context of American Islam is also what prompted me to vex my reader with the neologism, "Blackamerican," a term I picked up from the late C. Eric Lincoln but which, to my knowledge, he never explained. My use of the term is based on the following considerations. On the one hand, to speak simply of "black Americans" as the counterparts of "white Americans" is to strengthen the hand of those who wish to deny or hide white privilege. On the other hand, to speak of African Americans is to give short shrift to almost half a millennium of New World history, implying that Blackamericans are African in the same way that Italian Americans or Greek Americans are Italian or Greek. I emphatically recognize, wholly embrace, and celebrate the African *origins* of Blackamericans. But in my view, the force of American history has essentially transformed these erstwhile Africans into a new people. This is especially so with regard to their *religious* orientation. Of course, I could have opted for the hyphenated convention "Black-American." But, as I indicate in chapter 4, the whole point of the hyphenated American is that the right side of the hyphen assumes the responsibility of protecting the cultural, religious, and other idiosyncrasies of the left side. As Blackamericans have rarely if ever enjoyed this protection on a par with other ethnic Americans, it would be misleading, in my view, to cast blacks as just another hyphenated group in America.

Among the great Western democracies, America is unique in that the largest single group of its Muslims consists of indigenous converts. Thus far, however, no one has convincingly explained why Islam spread among Blackamericans in this fashion. While we have been left to assume that there is some African connection to all of this, the historical record simply does not bear this out. My contention is that Islam owes its momentum among Blackamericans to the phenomenon of Black Religion. This is the subject of chapter 1, in which I also discuss the positive and negative implications of this connection and the extent to which Black Religion has had and continues to negotiate its relationship with other sources of Islamic religious authority.

In chapter 2, I deal with the transition from Black Religion to historical Islam as the basis of religious authority in American Islam. This is the beginning of the Third Resurrection, but only descriptively. That is to say, while the basis of religious authority shifts, Blackamerican Muslims remain objects rather than subjects in this development. I look at the causes of this and the nature of the dislocations it engendered. I also hazard a suggestion about the basis upon which the Blackamerican–immigrant divide, particularly regarding the two groups' mutually conflicting relationship to American whiteness, might be ameliorated. I frame this chapter in a comparative vein around the contention of the nineteenth-century black Presbyterian, Edward Blyden, who argued that if white European and American missionaries in Africa did not transfer religious authority to African Christians in a timely fashion, the latter would ultimately regurgitate Christianity.

Among the major achievements of the proto-Islamic movements was their successful use of Islam as a means of developing an alternative modality of American blackness. Islam, in this context, connoted a racial/cultural 'orthodoxy' as well as a strictly religious one. This heightened the sense of competition between Islam and other Blackamerican movements, secular and religious. But as long as Blackamerican Muslims were perceived as remaining true to the agenda of Black Religion and the dictates of Blackamerican cultural orthodoxy, the Arab/Muslim world (as a constituent of the Third World) occupied a positive place in the collective Blackamerican psyche. When, however, Blackamerican Muslims began to show signs of being culturally and intellectually overrun by immigrants, they began to draw the charge of cultural apostasy. This gave rise to a phenomenon I refer to as of "Black Orientalism," essentially an attempt to undermine the authority of Islam in the black community by casting the Arab/Muslim world as precursors and imitators of the West in the latter's antiblackness. This is the subject of chapter 3.

In chapter 4, I model the likely shape of Blackamerican Muslim thought under the Third Resurrection as a *prescriptive* ideal. It is here that I appeal to Muslim Tradition in an effort to reconcile blackness, Americanness, and adherence to Islam. I discuss the rejectionist impulse of Blackamerican Muslims as well the challenge of coming to terms with such features of America as pluralism, the U.S. Constitution, and the separation between church and state. All of this is set against the parallel necessity of avoiding the trap of what Stephen Carter refers to as the "domestication" of religion, whereby religion is moved from a position where it can resist or challenge the state and the dominant culture to a position where it can only applaud these.

Given its historical roots and routes, the major preoccupation of Blackamerican Islam has been the public square and the secular interests of subverting white (and then Arab/immigrant) supremacy. While I argue that these interests are not inconsistent with the teachings of Islam, I maintain that an exclusive focus on these matters exposes the religion to the danger of degenerating into just another secular ideology, subtly oblivious to matters of personal piety, obedience, and service to God. In such a context, even a successful effort to realize these secular aims cannot hope to lead to the ultimate goal of salvation. In the final chapter, chapter 5, I discuss the necessity of avoiding the trap of secularization and of developing in Blackamerican Islam a tradition of personal piety and spirituality. I consider traditional Sufism as a possible starting point in this regard.

Every book has its limitations, and I would like to say a word in closing about three conspicuous limitations of the present work. First, this book deals with an area of study that is widely recognized as being "undertheorized." The negative effects of this scholarly neglect are most clearly manifested in the lack of available documentation on various trends and attitudes in American Islam. On this deficiency, there are a number of areas, particularly in chapters 1 and 2, where I took the liberty of relying on my more than twenty-five years of intimate involvement in the Muslim community, Blackamerican and immigrant, rather than refer my reader to documented evidence. I chose to include these personal insights and cumulative experiences on the belief that to exclude them would be to perpetuate the inadequacies of existing scholarship and in so doing raise various aspects of our present ignorance about Islam in America to the level of a science. In defending this approach, I should like to remind my reader that this book purports to represent neither sociology nor history as formal disciplines. Moreover—and this is especially true when dealing with the Blackamerican community—just because there is no documentation on a trend or attitude, this does not mean that it does not exist. Everyone in the Muslim community in America knows, for example, of the influence of Salafism[23] over the past two decades or so. Yet, this is hardly reflected in the scholarly literature on Islam in America. In the final analysis, it may be the Muslim response to this aspect of the book that will serve as the most reliable confirmation or corrective. In the interim, I shall simply beg my readers' indulgence.

Second, I have all but ignored the gendered side of the story of Islam and the Blackamerican. The twentieth-century "feminization" of Christianity (through its ordination of women and gays, its new, soft, antiviolence rhetoric and its sociopolitically domesticated tone) against the stereotype of a hypermasculine, patriarchal, lascivious, and violence-sanctioning Islam has been one of the ways in which the modern West has sought to signal its moral superiority over the religion of Muhammad. Ironically, it has been precisely through this "hypermasculinity" that Islam has appealed to the masses of Blackamericans, especially Blackamerican men. Black masculinity being historically threatening to and threatened by American white supremacy (note, e.g., the stereotypes about black male sexual prowess and the practice of lynchings, respectively), Islam has represented a haven of sorts for black manhood. This has serious implications for gender relations between Blackamerican Muslim men and women; if Blackamerican Muslim women see their interest as residing in an antipatriarchal, demasculinized Islam, this can only put them at odds with what has sustained the religion's appeal among Blackamerican men. On the other hand, at least in the present context, a hypermasculine Islam can only experience great difficulty in sustaining its appeal among Blackamerican women, particularly the more educated and socioeconomically advanced. This is a topic that deserves serious attention. But a full treatment of it would have required more extensive backgrounding, theorizing, and nuancing than I felt possible in a work of this length. This is a topic, however, to which I hope to be able to return in a later effort.

Finally, while I have limited my focus to the challenges and efforts of Blackamerican Muslims, the issues and approaches covered in this book have obvious implications for nonblack Muslims as well. This is particularly so regarding white American Muslims, who must also find ways to come to terms with racism and other American realities without exposing themselves to the charge of "cultural or ethnic apostasy." Given my fear of falling into one or another false universal of my own, I have chosen to allow these communities to speak for themselves and from their particular perspective. This should not be taken, however, to imply any belief on my part in the impossibility of an ecumenical American Islam as the preferred alternative to the proliferation of monadic Blackamerican, white American, and Hispanic Islams.

Over the course of this book, I have found it necessary to characterize positions, impute motives, and challenge the views of a number of scholars. This has all been done in what I hope will be taken as a spirit of scholarly exchange. Throughout this endeavor, I have tried to be fair and respectful. In the end, I can only hope—and this is my solemn prayer—that my pen did not get the better of me.

1

Islam and Black Religion

Several attempts have been made to establish the number of Muslims in America. While total estimates vary from four to as much as eight million, strong representation by Blackamericans remains a constant. One estimate, for example, made over a decade ago, put the number of Muslims in America at six million. Of these, 42 percent were said to be Blackamericans. The second largest group, the Indo-Pakistanis, came in at 29 percent, followed by the Arabs, who posted between 12 and 15 percent.[1] The remaining 14 to 17 percent represented a cross-section of races and ethnicities, including a growing number of white and Hispanic Americans. Whatever the truth of these numbers, it is clear that Blackamericans constitute a major segment of America's Muslim population. Equally important, however, if not always recognized in these terms, Muslims make up the largest block of non-Christians in black America. Indeed, in numerical terms at least, the relationship between Blackamerican Muslims and the Blackamerican community at large is rapidly approaching the relationship between Blackamericans and the rest of America.

This apparent attraction between Islam and Blackamericans has been the subject of numerous speculations, some explicit, others implied. A recent body of literature has sought to explain it in terms of the success of the early propaganda attributed to the Nation of Islam in which the latter attempted to shame Blackamericans away from Christianity by declaring the latter to be "the white man's religion."[2] Islam, by contrast, at least on this depiction, was said to be the black man's religion, complete with deep and verifiable roots in the African motherland. In a far more sinister but clearly cognate thesis, the nineteenth-century German Orientalist Carl Becker pointed to the attraction between blacks and Islam as a sign of the latter's inferiority. Christianity being too sophisticated for primitive, simple-minded folk, Islam was the most that one could expect of blacks. Only an inferior religion could hold such attraction for such a clearly inferior people.[3] A third explanation, albeit more tacit, begins with the image of Islam as the friend and liberator of the oppressed. Blacks being the quintessential oppressed people of the world, it is only natural that Blackamericans should gravitate towards Islam, or so the explanation goes.

In all of these explanations, blackness, like oppression, is essentially stripped of its historical specificity and treated as an abstract universal, a veritable super-category at the center of which lies some putative essence in which all people with black skin (however we define and measure that) are presumed to participate. On this understanding, whether we are talking about Blackamericans, black Nigerians, or blacks in Surinam, the relationship to Islam is essentially the same: Blacks relate to Islam as blacks or "oppressed people." And there is nothing unique or special about the relationship between *Blackamericans* and Islam.

To be sure, this view is deeply indebted to the tendency (among politically correct whites and ideologically driven blacks) to play down if not ignore the distinctions between blacks or Africans on the one hand and Blackamericans on the other. This is predicated upon a certain refusal (or inability) to recognize that it is neither blood nor biology but history that makes "a people" and that it matters little whether that history is subjectively chosen or imposed by some other from without. On this refusal, Blackamericans continue to be viewed (and to view themselves) as displaced Africans rather than as a distinct and genuine people whose "peopleness" was fired in their centuries-long crucible in North America. The Western, or what Ali Mazrui once referred to as the "Afro-Saxon,"[4] identity of Blackamericans is commonly treated as a proposition to be overcome, apologized for, or explained away rather than a fact to be acknowledged and probed for insights. This persists despite the fact that, as Charles H. Long so eloquently points out,

> It would be difficult, if not impossible, to make the case for the non-Western identity of the black community in America, though several make this claim. The element of truth in this claim is that though we [Blackamericans] are Westerners, we are not Westerners in the same way as our compatriots, and thus we afford within America an entree to the *otherness* of humankind.[5]

This is neither a new nor wholly marginal view among Blackamerican thinkers.[6] James Baldwin, for example, would go so far as to proclaim that "Negroes do not . . . exist in any other [country]."[7] At the other end of the spectrum, Amiri Baraka (LeRoi Jones) would speak of the transformation of black Africans into a "Western people."[8] Even the ever-critical Harold Cruse would insist that "the American black is a specific product of Americanization . . . not an African . . . an Afro American."[9] Yet, for all its currency among Blackamerican scholars and thinkers, this view exerts little influence over the general understanding of Blackamerican history. Whereas Copts, Phoenicians, Assyrians, and other groups in Egypt and Syria, for example, could *become* Arabs in a matter of a few centuries,[10] and Germans, Francs, Slavs, Poles, and countless other Europeans could become "Americans" or even "whites" in an even shorter span of time, nearly half a millennium of American history has failed to gain recognition as having exerted a similar effect on the sons and daughters of Africa. This entrenched myopia has promoted a sustained marginalization, if not discounting, of important aspects of American history. Indeed, with the single exception of American slavery, America is often the last place one looks in attempting to explain any number of tendencies and phenomena among Blackamericans.

Over the remainder of this chapter, I shall challenge this tendency and argue that the past, present, and future of Islam among Blackamericans can only be understood in the context of the relationship between Islam and Black Religion. In this context, Islam among Blackamericans will be seen as constituting a distinctly American phenomenon, not unlike the Black Church, Afrocentrism, or the Civil Rights movement. By Black Religion, however, I am referring neither to the Black Church nor to what scholars generally identify as the religious orientation of Africans prior to their induction into the transatlantic slave system.[11] Nor is Black Religion, as I use the term, necessarily the religious orientation of all Blackamericans. Cumulatively speaking, however, the hegemonic influence, if not always dominance, of Black Religion has spread more steadily among Blackamericans than any other religious orientation over the past two centuries. This influence, moreover, is directly linked to its emergence and continuing relevance as an almost *sui generis* response to a distinctly American reality. In this capacity, Black Religion constitutes a fundamental break with its would-be African antecedents. Indeed, as I use the term, Black Religion might be more accurately referred to as "Blackamerican Religion."

I shall begin with a brief (but I hope adequate) refutation of the notion of the universal black/oppressed and his or her relationship to Islam. From here I will move to a description of Black Religion and its essential characteristics as a religious orientation. I will then trace the early relationship between Black Religion and Islam (or proto-Islamic movements) in the early part of the twentieth century and go on to look at some of the positive and negative aspects of this relationship as manifested among contemporary Blackamerican Muslims. Finally, I will offer some thoughts on the future of Islam and Black Religion, including the question of whether the latter remains inextricably woven into the fabric and future of Blackamerican Islam and the extent to which it has had and continues to negotiate its place alongside other sources of Islamic religious authority.

The Black/Oppressed vs. the Blackamerican

In one of her essays recollecting her experience as a foreign student in America back in the 1970s, the Moroccan Muslim feminist Fatima Mernissi recalls her surprise to find that Islam was spreading among Blackamericans. This was strange, according to Mernissi, because while Blackamericans seemed to be finding in Islam a message of equality and social justice, inequality and exploitation of the disenfranchised had always operated in her experience as accepted norms.[12] Having lived and traveled throughout the Muslim, and especially the Arab, world, Mernissi was well acquainted with the rigid class divisions and social stratification that characterized Muslim societies. This, in fact, was the source of her amazement. For if societies that held up Islam as the ideal could see no contradiction between that ideal and sustained inequities and exploitation, how was one to explain the tendency among Blackamericans to turn precisely to that ideal as a basis for alleviating their sociopolitical woes?

Of course, as a feminist, the inequity uppermost in Mernissi's mind was that affecting women. Color discrimination, while alive and well in the Muslim world, has not yet produced a "discreet and insular class" that identifies itself as "a people."[13] And even if such a class did exist, they would not likely go under the designation "blacks." For the black–white dichotomy so central to Western social discourse has little functionality in Middle Eastern and Asian Muslim contexts.[14]

The same cannot be said, however, of other parts of the world where Islam has had a significant presence. And when we turn to these communities, we find that not only have oppression and inequity been tolerated in the name of Islam but that this has taken place in contexts where black people bore the brunt of such injustices. The example I have in mind is that of South Africa, where a Muslim community, first Malay and then Indian, existed from the middle of the seventeenth century. This community was lamentably slow, however, in coming to condemn anti-black apartheid. In fact, for the better part of its history the Muslim community in South Africa saw no contradiction at all between apartheid and the faithful practice of Islam. Thus, as late as 1964, the South African Muslim Judicial Council (MJC) could defend its de facto collaborationist position in the following terms:

> Has the [apartheid] government forbidden the worship of Allah? Has the government closed down or ordered the demolition of any mosque in a declared white area? If our government has ordered our Muslims to desert the faith of our forefathers, then our *ulema* [religious scholars] would have been the first to urge us to resist, even to the death.[15]

While this may not have been the position of all nonblack Muslims in South Africa, it was by all appearances the dominant view up until the 1970s.[16] This, no doubt, goes a long way in explaining the extremely slow and limited spread of Islam among black South Africans. More importantly, however, it raises serious questions, as does the experience of Mernissi cited above, about the presumed affinity between Islam, blackness, and oppression. For if oppression and blackness are supposed to promote conversion to Islam, mass conversion should have occurred among oppressed blacks in South Africa.[17] But this did not occur, which brings us back to the question: Why have oppressed blacks in South Africa (among other places) failed to locate in Islam what Blackamericans across the Atlantic would come to identify as the very essence of the religion?

Of course, the easy answer to this question would be that the Indian and Malay monopoly over the meaning of Islam in South Africa prevented South African blacks from coming to see in Islam any utility in addressing their plight. Under Indian and Malay authority, in other words, Islam was not presented—and thus could not be seen—as holding meanings that rendered it an effective antidote to the apartheid system. While there is a certain value in this view, it cannot serve as a full response. For the fact is that a similar, if not identical, situation obtains in America today, where immigrant Muslims claim superior, if not ultimate, authority to define Islam and the Muslim agenda. Thus, for example, during the 2000 presidential elections, the major Muslim American political organizations, all run by immigrants, issued a public endorsement of Republican candidate George W. Bush, despite the Republican Party's historically strained relationship with the Blackamerican community and without so much as attempting to secure a mandate from Blackamerican

Muslims![18] Yet, there is no evidence that this has slowed, let alone stopped, the spread of Islam among Blackamericans.

The real difference between South African (and other) blacks, on the one hand, and Blackamericans, on the other, lies in the absence among the former of two things: (1) an indigenously rooted vehicle via which they could successfully *appropriate* Islam; and (2) charismatic figures who could harness and make effective use of that vehicle. The vehicle to which I am referring in the case of Blackamericans is Black Religion. The charismatic figures are none other than the early twentieth-century Blackamerican "Islamizers," namely Noble Drew Ali and, especially, the Honorable Elijah Muhammad.

It is important to understand in this context the meaning and function of "appropriation" as I use the term. By appropriation I am referring to the act of enlisting the aid of a set of nonindigenous ideas or doctrines in one's own existential or ideological struggle. What renders an act one of appropriation as opposed to simple borrowing is that the appropriator does not recognize any "property rights" of the original owners. Instead, the whole point of appropriation is both to claim the idea or doctrine for oneself and to assume the right to define, interpret, and tailor it according to one's own psychological and existential needs, with little or no deference to how the original owners or their heirs might have gone about this enterprise. It is here, in fact, that the importance of the vehicle via which appropriation is made possible comes to the fore. For it is precisely the function of this vehicle to enable the appropriator to make believable the claim that he or she is neither surrendering to any "other" nor attempting to plagiarize or "piggy-back" on the latter's identity. Rather, the new idea is adopted, or so it is implied, because it enables the appropriator and his or her followers to become truer, more authentic selves. A black adopts Islam or Christianity, in other words, not in order to become an honorary Arab or white but in order to become a truer, more authentic "black man"! In order to be able to do this, however, and make it believable, he must first be able to claim Islam or Christianity as his own. This is ultimately what the vehicle of appropriation enables him to do.

The importance of these vehicles of appropriation is generally overlooked in analyzing the process of religious conversion. This is because religious conversion is most often viewed from the perspective of the proselytizer or missionary. Most of the time, religious conversion is seen in terms of the success of the proselytizer in getting the convert to "come over" to the new religion rather than in terms of the success of the convert at getting the new religion to validate his past and inspire in him a vision of a new tomorrow. As we shall see, however, the latter is precisely the advantage that Black Religion conferred first upon Blackamerican Christians in the eighteenth and nineteenth centuries and then upon the Blackamerican proto-Muslim "Islamizers" at the beginning of the twentieth century, as a result of which the latter were able to appropriate Islam. By finding in Islam the means to an ostensibly more perfect expression of American blackness, the Blackamerican "Islamizers" were able to co-opt, legitimize, and even popularize the religion among the Blackamerican masses. Indeed, had it not been for this historical act of appropriation, it is doubtful that Islam would have ever come to enjoy the success that it has among Blackamericans.

Black Religion

As I enter my discussion of Black Religion proper, I must preface it with a more substantive reiteration of an earlier caveat. Black Religion, as I use the term, is emphatically *not* a synonym for "African-American religion," a super-category into which all expressions of God-consciousness among Blackamericans can be fit. Rather than constituting a motherset, Black Religion would be more properly understood as a subset of the aggregate of black religious expression in America. By capitalizing this designation, my aim is not to connote Black Religion's universality or even its preeminence. It is simply to underscore its distinctiveness as a religious orientation among Blackamericans. In sum, Black Religion is but one, albeit by far the most hegemonic, of several religious orientations among Blackamericans.

The central preoccupation of Black Religion is the desire to annihilate or at least subvert white supremacy and anti-black racism. As widely diffused a sentiment as this may be among Blackamericans, this has not been the driving force behind any number of Blackamerican religious experiences and articulations, from slavery down to present times. In *God Struck Me Dead: Voices of Ex-Slaves*, for example, Clifton H. Johnson provides testimonial upon testimonial in which the conversion and quotidian religiosity of former slaves are virtually devoid of any racial preoccupation.[19] In fact, in one testimonial, suggestively entitled, "Slavery Was Hell Without Fires," the most lamentable fault an ex-slave could find with her former master's family was that they "did everything but say their prayers."[20] At another point, the same woman recalls the cruelty of a neighboring slaveholder who used to "walk through the field and, seeing a [black] baby crying, take his stick and knock its brains out and call the foreman to come and haul off this nasty, black rat."[21] Her response, however, was simply to aver her belief in ultimate divine justice: "I don't believe a just God is going to take no such man as that into his kingdom."[22]

With certain modifications, a similarly deracialized religiosity could be said to characterize the thought of the celebrated Howard Thurman.[23] Thurman (1899–1981) lived through the era of black power, black consciousness, and Black Theology. Yet, to the end he remained more a mystic/spiritualist than a revolutionary, stressing *human* realization and fellowship over specifically *black* liberation. As he noted in his essay on segregation,

> The fact that the first twenty-three years of my life were spent in Florida and Georgia has left its scars deep in my spirit and has rendered me terribly sensitive to the churning abyss separating white from black. . . . Nevertheless, a strange necessity has been laid upon me to devote my life to the central concern that transcends the walls that divide and would achieve in literal fact what is experienced as literal truth: human life is one and all men are members of one another. And this insight is spiritual and it is the hard core of religious experience.[24]

Thurman's articulations, like those of the ex-slaves cited by Johnson, reflect the extent to which black religiosity, even as it recognized the evils of racial subjugation, was not always an externalizing reflex that sought to change individual experience by changing the world. Black religiosity could also be an emphatically internalizing reflex that aimed at spiritual transformation from within, even as the world without remained corrupt. Black Pentecostalism, for instance, is another, supreme example of this. This was a movement about which it has been written, "The radical social impulse inherent in the vision of the disenfranchised was transformed into social passivity, ecstatic escape, and finally, a most conservative conformity."[25] Rather than working to overthrow the evils of white supremacy, enrapture in glossolalia ("speaking in tongues") became a central goal and ultimate manifestation of Pentecostal faith. This is all the more important in the present context, given that many scholars hold American Pentecostalism, black and white, to have been founded or at least co-founded by a black man, William J. Seymour (1870–1922).[26]

As these examples indicate—and one could cite more, from the early Conjurers[27] to the mood and priorities of early twentieth-century black Catholics, Episcopalians and Congregationalists[28] to the likes of Father Divine and Daddy Grace[29]—waging war against white supremacy and anti-black racism has not been an integral feature of *all* religion among Blackamericans. As such, "Black Religion" and "African-American religion" must be understood to connote two distinct, though interrelated, realities in Blackamerican life.

Having said all of this, my original point regarding the status and influence of Black Religion remains valid and critical to an intelligent understanding of

Blackamerican religious history in general and the history of Islam among Blackamericans in particular. While Black Religion may have never been the *only* religious orientation among Blackamericans, it has emerged over time as the *most hegemonic*. This is what Albert Raboteau, for example, seems to have in mind when he writes in his general description of African-American religious history: "Before and after the Civil War, African Americans drew religion to its moral and prophetic calling, making it the center not only of African-American culture but of a challenging ethic of equality and dignity throughout American society."[30] By the mid- to late 1960s, the influence of Black Religion, as "a challenging ethic of equality and dignity," would become so ubiquitous that it would be difficult for many to resist the temptation to retroject its status and impact back through the whole of Blackamerican history. While such retrojection waxes in many instances historically anachronistic, it would be equally unjustified to deny the existence of the Black Religion impulse as the most steadily growing hegemony in the black community for at least the past two hundred years.

Having imposed these limits on the scope and degree of Black Religion's influence, we may now turn to a more substantive description of Black Religion itself. To date, there is no scholarly consensus on the precise definition of Black Religion. Nor is there even complete uniformity in the use of the term.[31] There is, however, general agreement that the central and most enduring feature of Black Religion is its sustained and radical opposition to racial oppression. At bottom, Black Religion is an instrument of holy protest against white supremacy and its material and psychological effects. While it is an inextricably religious orientation, it refuses to separate the quest for otherworldly salvation from the struggle for temporal liberation and a dignified existence. Its point of departure is American slavery and, as the late C. Eric Lincoln put it, had it not been for American slavery, there would have been no Black Religion.[32] Nevertheless, as we shall see, Black Religion is emphatically distinct from the older "invisible institution" of what Albert Raboteau referred to as "slave religion."[33]

Black Religion has no theology[34] and no orthodoxy; it has no institutionalized ecclesiastical order and no public or private liturgy. It has no foundation documents or scriptures, like the Baghavad Ghita or the Bible, and no founding figures, like Buddha or Zoroaster. The God of Black Religion is neither specifically Jesus, Yaweh, nor Allah but an abstract category into which any and all of these can be fit, the "God of our weary years," the "God of our silent tears." In a real sense, Black Religion might be profitably thought of as the 'deism' or 'natural religion' of Blackamericans, a spontaneous folk orientation at once grounded in the belief in a supernatural power outside of human history yet uniquely focused on that power's manifesting itself in the form of interventions into the crucible of American race relations.

In its attempt to proscribe black consciousness and restrict it to a universe of meanings that promoted feelings of inferiority and the propriety of Blackamerican servitude to whites, American slavery, in tandem with a consciously preserved ideology of white supremacy, engendered in Blackamericans what Charles H. Long refers to as a "lithic consciousness," a state of mind which in confronting a reality bent on domination invokes *a will in opposition,* a veritable cosmic "No."[35] As Houston A. Baker Jr. observes (in another context), "It has always been necessary for black people in America not only to comprehend the space of their identity-in-difference but also energetically to refigure this space by employing expressive *counterenergy.*"[36] In a similar vein, Cornel West notes that "Black striving resides primarily in movement and motion, resilience and resistance *against* the paralysis of madness and the stillness of death."[37] In another essay descriptively entitled, "*Subversive* Joy and *Revolutionary* Patience in Black Christianity," West speaks of an "existential freedom," which he describes as "a mode of being-in-the-world that *resists* dread and despair."[38]

All of these articulations point to a distinctly "negative" predisposition in the collective psyche of Blackamericans. If, as Amiri Baraka and others have argued, Blackamericans are essentially a "blues people," their blues are ultimately an exercise in resistance and protest. Blackamericans, in other words, are quintessentially a "protest people." Black Religion reflects this in the sustained sentiment of protest and resistance that lies at its core. This is not to deny or downplay the mellow and even heroic element in Black Religion, as reflected, for example, in its general resistance (inevitable exceptions notwithstanding) to the urge to embrace reverse-domination or supremacy, and its dogged, almost happy, pursuit of a dignified existence in the face of overwhelming odds. Still, at bottom, Black Religion remains, in its abiding commitment to protest, resistance, and liberation, ultimately more committed to a *refusal* to be the object of another's will than it is to a positive *affirmation* of any particular philosophy of life. Subversion, resistance, protest, opposition: These are all key to the constitution of Black Religion.

Early America and Black Religion

That such sentiments should find expression in religion rather than in some other construct is preeminently a function of Blackamericans' African past. As the noted African scholar John Mbiti points out, "Africans are notoriously religious!"[39] This primordial religiosity alone, however, would contribute little to the actual substance of Black Religion. Rather, it would be the early New World experience that would inform this new orientation and ultimately define its essence. This would be effected by way of four important early American realities.

First, even before the transatlantic slave trade began, the Aristotelian–Neoplatonic tradition, which undergirded medieval European rationalism, had made extremely limited inroads into West Africa. In fact, what little success this tradition had south of the Sahara was almost certainly due to the influence of Islam. The Ashʿarite school of Muslim theology (which embraced major aspects of Aristotle) was ubiquitous among learned West African Muslims. Muslims, however, during the period of the slave trade were a minority in West Africa, and, consequently, a minority among those taken to America. In his important study, *African Muslims in Antebellum America*, Allan Austin puts the number of Muslims at forty thousand of a total of eleven million slaves in the territory making up the United States by 1860.[40] On these numbers, this rationalist tradition, to the extent that it existed, would be both weak and further weakened as African slaves were wedged away from its geographical source. More importantly, once in America, the onerous restrictions on black literacy and education would annihilate any remnants of such a tradition and ultimately result in an effective barrier emerging between the slave population and the new intellectual *zeitgeist* of the day. Through the twin elements, in other words, of forced exodus and forced illiteracy, the early American experience would deny the masses of Blackamericans access to the rationalizing forces of the European Enlightenment as these swept across the American plain effecting major shifts in religious thought and sensibilities. In this context, to use the now passé depiction of the nineteenth-century French philosopher, August Comte, the masses of Blackamericans remained in a religious state of consciousness while white Americans "moved on" to a rational and then a scientific one.[41] This is partly what Cornel West seems to have in mind when he observes that "[t]he paradox of Afro-American history is that Afro-Americans fully enter the modern world precisely when the postmodern period commences."[42] In sum, early America reinforced the primordially religious orientation of her enslaved Africans by doubly denying them access to a rationalist tradition on the basis of which they might transcend that orientation and or negotiate a new relationship between religion and the exigencies of life.

Second, the shock of exile alongside the dehumanizing brutalities of American slavery engendered a cosmic mood swing, as Africans were torn from a palpably intimate connection to the cosmos in Africa to a cold and nagging New World tragic realism.[43] On the American plantation, the African found himself in a world in which the ancestors and "living dead" could be neither appealed to nor appeased.[44] Trees and rivers remained, but none of these were sacred and none belonged to them. A cosmic alienation set in, as America's most-wanted unwanted confronted a maddening helplessness and victimization in a world that offered access to no higher authority than the victimizers themselves. The Africans were powerless, friendless, and, to all intents and purposes, godless. Yet, even without familiar gods or spirits, an indefatigable hope would set in, and a primordial belief in the inevitability of divine justice would buoy them. Endurance, or what Cornell West would call "revolutionary patience," would come to constitute their silent prayer to a yet unknown God whose wrathful vengeance was sure to bring salvation.

This set the stage for early America's third contribution to Black Religion, namely Christianity, or more specifically Protestantism. On the one hand, the introduction of Christianity would lead to a number of concrete transformations in the African religious orientation, for example, from a primary focus on the ancestors and the "living dead" to a primary focus on God. At the same time, it would provide a vehicle by which a distinctly Blackamerican religious orientation could be developed and expressed. This was the beginning of the great transformation from what Albert Raboteau refers to as the "invisible institution" of "slave religion" to the highly visible and consciously *Protestant* phenomenon of Black Religion.

During the seventeenth and eighteenth centuries, as part of its struggle to stem the hegemonic advance of Renaissance and Enlightenment paganism and stop the extension of Catholic ecclesiastical authority, America was increasingly a Protestant country. It lived in the aftermath of the Protestant Reformation and produced a First and Second Protestant "Great Awakening" of its own. In this context, traditional African religion, with its magic and conjuring, its multiple gods and intermediaries, its spirit world and attachment to the "living dead"[45] was too conspicuously alien and too easily dismissed as primitive, pagan heathenism. It was not just Christianity, however, that passed this negative judgment against African religion; it was more specifically *Protestant* Christianity. Had America been a Catholic country, the early African Americans would have retained much more of their traditional African religious orientation. As Raboteau points out, traditional African religion survived much more in Latin America than it did in the United States precisely because Catholicism was more accommodating to the African religious ethos than was Protestantism:

> Catholic devotion to the Blessed Virgin and to the saints offered a rich context for syncretism with the gods of Africa. The use of sacramentals (blessed objects) such as water, rosaries, vestments, and relics in Catholic ritual was more akin to the spirit of African piety

than the sparseness of Puritan America, which held such objects to be idolatrous.[46]

In sum, American Protestantism functioned as the *feuerbach* through which African and then slave religion would pass en route to a new Blackamerican identity. In this capacity, Protestantism would become an integral and inextricable ingredient in the formation of Black Religion. If, as Mbiti insists, Africans were notoriously religious, African Americans would become notoriously "Protestant," even in cases where they affiliated with non-Protestant groups and denominations. Indeed, to this day, one can detect a palpable Protestant mood and predisposition running through the warp and woof of Blackamerican religious expression.

Finally, there was the impact of demographics. As David W. Wills points out, "Numerically significant Christianization of the slave population only began after 1760 and did not really come to full tide until after 1830, by which time most American blacks were native born."[47] In other words, the aforementioned weakening of the African religious impulse (through shrinkage in the number of imported slaves) coincided with the spread of Christianity among blacks born and reared in Protestant America. This increase in conversion rates was almost certainly related to Protestantism's ultimate triumph as the most effective vehicle by which to wage any principled campaign against American slavery. It was also aided, however, by the fact that the two main groups who proselytized to African Americans—the Baptists and the Methodists—were themselves Protestant *dissenters* from European Christianity, both of whom had embraced and emphasized belief in the equality of all believers before God. As we shall see, nineteenth-century native-born Blackamerican Christians were far less tolerant of the status quo, far less deferential to clerical authority, and far more assiduous in their search for instruments of protest than were their African-born predecessors. As more and more native-born Blackamericans entered Christianity, Black Religion would achieve its first major feat of appropriation. Armed with the imprimatur of Christianity, it would secure both a coherent voice and a righteous indignation that resonated even among white Americans. No longer limited to yelling and screaming in tongues at the horrors of American slavery, Black Religion now spoke with clarity and a modicum of legitimacy.

Christianity and Black Religion

It should be noted, however, that the "marriage" between Black Religion and Christianity was just that—a marriage, not a dissolution of the former into the latter. As such, while Christianity may have been taken as the last name (and thus we speak of the Black *Church*) Black Religion retained its original character and identity, including the spirit of protest and palpable, however attenuated, vestiges of the affective and frenzied traits of African religion. In time, an increasingly influential strain of black Christianity would come to consist of a core that was essentially Black Religion and an outer shell that was the theological and liturgical teachings of white Christianity. While this is not at all to suggest any lack of sincerity on the part of early Blackamerican Christians, it is to note that increasing numbers of Blackamericans were developing a different appreciation of and agenda for Christianity. It was not of freedom from the oppression of sin or of the bonds of the flesh that these early Blackamericans sang in their spirituals; it was of liberation from the bitter plight of bondage and racial subjugation. Indeed, the callous and self-serving use to which many white American Christians put their religion would breed a certain contempt, cynicism and even sarcasm towards the ideals of white American Christianity:

> Our Father, who art in heaven
> White man owe me 'leven, and pay me seven,
> Thy kingdom come, thy will be done
> And ef I hadn't tuck that, I wouldn't a got none.[48]

From this perspective, the corporate Blackamerican approach to Christianity would be, to say the least, patently unique. White missionaries and church leaders were relentless in voicing their frustration at what they deemed to be the superficiality of Negro conversion. As one such writer put it: "Most of the time the Negro outwardly accepts the doctrines of Christianity and goes on living according to his own conflicting secular mores."[49]

Nevertheless, the marriage between Black Religion and Christianity continued into the nineteenth century. In fact, the first decades of the that century saw Black Religion take on a more openly radical character and reach the apogee of its success in appropriating Christianity. Contrary to the view, still popular in many circles, that Christianity functioned invariably as an opiate that lulled Blackamericans into accepting their condition of subjugation, the early nineteenth century was a watershed of protest by Blackamerican Christians who used both the pen and the sword to prosecute their cause. In 1802, Gabriel Prosser mounted his violent revolt in Virginia. This was followed by the bloody assault by Denmark Vessey in South Carolina in 1822. In 1829, Robert Alexander Young published his pamphlet, *The Ethiopian Manifesto, Issued in Defense of the Blackman's Rights, in the Scale of Universal Freedom*, in which he called for militant action and revolution. That same year saw the publication of David Walker's scathing *Appeal to the Coloured Citizens of the World* in which he spoke of the innate devilishness of whites and their status as the "natural enemies" of blacks. Meanwhile, in 1831, Nat Turner's "visions" led him to unleash holy terror on the white citizens of Southhampton, Virginia, in the largest and most significant slave revolt in American history. All of this activity was carried out in the name of Christianity. This was a Christianity, however, emboldened by the spirit of Black Religion.[50]

Revolution, however, was not the only contribution that Black Religion made to Black Christianity. At least two other features figured prominently in this amalgamation. The first was Black Religion's notoriously atheological approach to religion. This was manifested in the almost complete neglect of the theological intricacies of white Christology. Rather than focus on the divinity, sonship, or vicarious substitution of Christ, most Blackamerican Christians tended to identify with Jesus as a "fellow sufferer . . . the little child . . . the companion . . . the man who understands."[51] Jesus for most Blackamerican Christians was not so much the God of heaven, though that he was too, as he was the more immanent—and more intimate: "Lord who befriends us and is concerned about our problems."[52] White churchmen were constant in criticizing their black bretheren for their confused and vague understandings of Christ. Meanwhile, even learned leaders of the Black church, men like Richard Allen, would devote little effort to developing a Christology of their own. Rather, they would simply go along—at least apparently—with the catechism handed down by the white mother church.

To be sure, this combination of theological apathy and conservatism was connected to what we said earlier about the rationalizing forces of the European Enlightenment having bypassed the masses of Blackamericans. Even without the "higher criticism" that sparked the Fundamentalist backlash in white American Christianity in the nineteenth and twentieth centuries, Blackamerican Christians would remain doctrinally "fundamentalist,"[53] all the way up to the rise of Black Theology in the 1960s.[54] Aspects of this theological conservativism would appear in both Noble Drew Ali and the Honorable Elijah Muhammad, both of whose theologies constitute radical innovations in the context of Muslim orthodoxy but reveal themselves to have clung rather slavishly to Christian categories and antecedents.[55] Not only would Blackamerican obliviousness to European/American liberalism promote *theological* conservatism, it would sustain a palpably conservative *social* ethic as well, including an unabashed patriarchal impulse, a no-nonsense folk morality, and a stark gender differentiation that militated strongly against andrognyny, especially in the form of the emasculation of Blackamerican men. Beneath the surface, this grassroots conservatism continues among the masses of Blackamericans, even as its potency has been diluted by the liberal tendencies of Blackamerican political leadership following the marriage between Liberalism and the Civil Rights movement in the 1960s and by the intellectual hybridization that has accompanied increased black participation in the Western academy.[56]

A second additional contribution of Black Religion to Black Christianity is reflected in the latter's focus on Africa as the locus of its longing and belonging. Not America but Africa was home to the Blackamerican. And there was a deep and abiding sense that the image of Africa had to be guarded, clung to, and zealously preserved, for to lose Africa would be to suffer the ultimate defeat. It would mean being rendered a stepchild of history, a creature of men—white men!—rather than a creature of God. This obsession with the image of Africa is reflected in the names of many of the independent Black churches that emerge from the latter part of the eighteenth century, for example, the African Methodist Church or the African Methodist Zion Church. It would go on to influence quasi-religious movements in the twentieth century, from Marcus Garvey's back-to-Africa enterprise to Maulana Karenga's Kwanzaa to Molefe Asante's Afrocentricity. Like all romanticisms, this particular feature of Black Religion was especially given to excess. But this should not seduce one into dismissing its importance or its influence. No religious movement that hoped to gain a following among Blackamericans could afford to ignore the image of Africa. Indeed, even Islam would ultimately benefit from its perceived "African connection," which would enable it to appeal to Blackamericans in a way that, say, Buddhism or even Judaism never could.

These, then, for our purposes, are the main features of Black Religion. Taken as a whole, Black Religion might be thought of as a form of "Radical Conservatism": radical in its rejection of racial subjugation and white supremacy, conservative in its theology and its social ethic. Probably from the early decades of the nineteenth century, and perhaps because of demographic changes that saw the majority of Blackamericans born in the United States, Black Religion came to be increasingly esteemed as the most authentic and genuine form of religious expression for and among Blackamericans. Hailed as the religion of the masses,[57] it would become *the* religious orientation—indeed, *the* orientation, period—to which any successful sociopolitical movement among Blackamericans would have to pay homage.[58]

Islam and Black Religion

As we move into our discussion of the relationship between Islam and Black Religion, four key facts must be born in mind. First, the spread of Islam among

Blackamericans was a twentieth-century phenomenon. Second, it was a northern phenomenon. Third, it was an urban phenomenon. And, finally, it was largely a working-class and underclass phenomenon.

That there were African Muslims among America's slave population is incontrovertibly known and well documented.[59] My point in limiting the spread of Islam among Blackamericans to the twentieth century is simply to emphasize that prior to that time Islam was unable to sustain and perpetuate itself on North American soil. The reasons for this, if we think about it, are quite simple. While non-Muslim slaves had to contend with the overriding stigma of color, Muslim slaves had to weather the much older and more deeply rooted stigma of religion. Whereas, according to scholars like Theodore Allen, whiteness as a racial category uniting first land-owning and then ultimately all Europeans (particularly against blacks) was not invented until the late seventeenth century,[60] the negative image of the Moor and the Muslim went back more than half a millennium. The First Crusade began in 1095. Dante's *Divine Comedy*, with its horrific portrayal of the Prophet Muhammad, was completed in 1321. Grenada, the last great independent Muslim principality in Spain, fell to the Christian *conquistadores* in 1492. Even the discovery of America that same year was ultimately a reaction to Islam. Christopher Columbus was prompted to seek his alternate route to India not by a spirit of discovery or adventure but by fear of the dreaded Muslim masters of the Red and Mediterranean seas. In sum, as Norman Daniel[61] and others have demonstrated, fear and hatred of Islam existed in the West long before the transatlantic slave trade began. And when these sentiments joined forces with white supremacy and the dehumanizing brutalities of American slavery, it became virtually impossible for African Muslim slaves to perpetuate their faith in America. Metaphorically, this is poignantly reflected in the complete absence, prior to the twentieth century, of a single standing African-built mosque in all of North America,[62] the mosque (along with the Call to Prayer [*adhān*]), being the quintessential public symbol of Islam.[63] Or, on a more personal level, one might look to the career of the North Carolinian slave, Umar b. Said (d. 1864). As demonstrated in the Arabic manuscript samples preserved of this West African Muslim, Umar begins with a failed attempt to reproduce portions of the Qur'ān (in Arabic), which he can no longer remember correctly. He ends by producing a grammatically and substantively correct Arabic version of the Lord's Prayer![64]

To all intents and purposes, then, Islam begins its relationship with Blackamericans in the early decades of the twentieth century. None of the distinct and palpable features of African Islam show up in the formative period of Blackamerican Islam, for example, the African penchant for Sufism (mysticism) or African Islam's staunch commitment to the Mālikī school of law.[65]

Nor are any of the major African Muslim figures (e.g., Ahmad Bābā, Uthmān Don Fodio, Aḥmadu Bamba) known among more than a smattering of Blackamerican Muslims. Indeed, as Sylviane Diouf notes in her important study of African Muslims in the Americas, "there is no indication so far that the African American Muslims of today inherited Islam from the Muslims of yesterday."[66] In fact, she notes, it is extremely doubtful that the last African Muslims in the Americas would have even recognized, let alone endorsed, the early proto-Islamic movements.[67]

Rather than any African connection, two factors, both connected to the Black Church's estrangement from Black Religion, would pave the way for Blackamericans to establish their relationship with Islam. The first of these was connected to the uneasy place Blackamericans occupied within Christianity as a whole. The second was connected to the Black Church's problems in adjusting to the realities of its new home in the post-Reconstruction North.

While the process of Blackamerican appropriation of Christianity had been underway for more than a century and had produced a number of important and palpable results (e.g., the establishment of independent black churches), it remained incomplete, inasmuch as full Blackamerican partnership in Christianity remained an ellusive ideal. Given their peculiar place in Western civilization, Blackamericans simply could not assume the status of ultimate authorities on, as opposed to mere consumers of, Christian priorities and thought. These remained, rather, the zealously guarded preserve of white Americans. As the frustrated nineteenth century black Presbyterian Edward W. Blyden complained in his classic, *Christianity, Islam and the Negro Race,*

> Christianity . . . came to the Negro as a slave, or at least as a subject race in a foreign land. Along with the Christian teaching, he and his children received lessons of their utter and permanent inferiority and subordination to their instructors, to whom they stood in the relation of chattels.[68]

Thus,

> His [the Negro's] subordinate position everywhere in Christian countries has made him believe that what his foreign [white] teachers think is the only proper thing to think and that what they say is the only right thing to say. He is, therefore, untrue to the natural direction of his powers, and attempts to soar into an atmosphere not native to his wing.[69]

Even if we allow for a certain exaggeration on Blyden's part, the reality for most Blackamericans in the nineteenth and early twentieth century was that *as Christians* someone other than themselves enjoyed ultimate authority and, as such, stood in permanent judgment over them. This would quietly erode Blackamerican Christian self-confidence and their sense of belongness to the "white man's religion." As Blyden would go on to insist, speaking now specifically of black Christians in the United States,

> From the lessons he everyday receives, the Negro unconsciously imbibes the conviction that to be a great man he must be like the white man. He is not brought up—however he may desire it—to be the companion, the equal the comrade of the white man, but his imitator, his ape, his parasite. To be himself in a country where everything ridicules him, is to be nothing—less, worse than nothing. To be as like the white man as possible—to copy his outward appearance, his peculiarities, his manners, the arrangement of his toilet, that is the aim of the Christian Negro—this is his aspiration. The only virtues which under such circumstances he develops are, of course, parasitical ones. Every intelligent Negro, in the lands of his exile, must feel that he walks upon the face of God's earth a physical and moral incongruity.[70]

This uneasiness about their place within American Christianity would predispose sizeable elements within the Blackamerican community, especially the poor and uneducated classes, to an almost frantic openness to alternative modalities of religious (and cultural) expression as Blackamericans. This tendency would be sharpened by developments in the early twentieth century when Blackamericans began to move out of their traditional environment in the South to the Northern metropolis, where their racial *and* cultural minority status would be much more deeply felt.

The marriage between Christianity and Black Religion had been a southern-dominated affair. While a number of black churches flourished in the North, the overwhelming majority of Blackamericans lived in the South. The 1900 U.S. Census placed approximately 90 percent of America's nearly nine million blacks in the South, with only 25 percent of these residing in urban areas.[71] The South, moreover, was home to Blackamerican folk culture. After slavery and Reconstruction, the evils of racial discrimination continued to circumscribe black life in both the North and the South. But because black southerners shared with their white counterparts many features of a common culture, for example, food, language, "southern pride," integration (as the antidote to segregation) did not necessarily imply assimilation, or surrendering to the ways of an alien dominant culture. As such, as long as the majority of

Blackamericans remained in the South, Black Religion could function, *mutatis mutandis*, pretty much as it always had. At least it could express itself, to the extent that circumstances allowed, in a voice and in cultural patterns genuinely felt to be its own. But when, on the eve of World War I, massive industrialization and job opportunities led Blackamericans to migrate en masse to the northern city, the Black Church found itself in a new cultural millieu where it confronted challenges and opportunities that forced it out of its traditional posture. Faced with the stigma of a slave past, writ large under the patronizing eye of an economically advanced and culturally more sophisticated North, the leaders of the Black Church, invariably middle class and often light-skinned if not mulatto, strove with all their might to assimilate into white America. Here, however, in what one might characterize, following the lead of H. Richard Niebuhr, as a classic case of "bourgeoisification," the line between integration and assimilation became hopelessly blurred.[72]

Meanwhile, the masses of Blackamericans, consisting largely of poor and uneducated Negroes (derogatorily referred to by their middle class betters as "low-type coons") remained "unavailable both socially and culturally to any talk of assimilation from white man or black."[73] True to the spirit of Black Religion, these were the people who would ultimately come to exercise the greatest influence over the meaning and personification of American blackness. Psychologically, socially, and culturally dislocated, they would grow increasingly alienated from the Black Church.

This alienation did not extend, however,—at least not to the same degree—to Black Religion. In fact, in many ways, the mission of Black Religion became more rather than less meaningful. As E. Franklin Frazier implies in his treatment of the "secular rebellion" of the early Gospel Singers, even where the Black Church was no longer felt to be the place where one could freely express or "find" oneself, the themes, moorings, and sentiments of Black Religion remained an important part of what one wanted to express.[74] Even Alain Locke's "New Negroes" occasionally reveal their lingering commitment to the religious sentiments and aspirations of the folk:

> Oh when I think of my long-suffering race,
> For weary centuries, despised oppressed
> Enslaved and lynched, denied a human place
> In the great life line of the Christian West;
> And in the Black land disinherited,
> Robbed in the ancient country of its birth,
> My heart grows sick with hate, becomes as lead,
> For this my race has no home on earth.

Then from the dark depth of my soul I cry
To the avenging angel to consume
The white man's world of wonders utterly;
Let it be swallowed up in earth's vast womb,
Or upward roll as sacrificial smoke
To liberate my people from its yoke![75]

This was the context out of which men like Timothy Drew (later Noble Drew Ali) and Elijah Poole (later the Honorable Elijah Muhammad) would emerge. Both half-educated southerners who migrated North, they stepped into a vacuum created by the misfortunes of the Black Church. Noble Drew Ali's Moorish Science Temple was established around 1913; Elijah Muhammad assumed leadership of the Nation of Islam in 1934. This, according to Joseph R. Washington Jr., was roughly the period during which Black Religion's relationship with the Black Church was falling out of kilter:

> Since the 1920s, black religion, the religion of the folk, has been dysfunctional. From this period on the once subordinate and latent stream of white Protestant evangelicalism has been dominant and manifest, relegating the uniqueness of black religion to verbal expression from the pulpit in such a way that action was stifled.[76]

Writing in the early 1960s, Washington could not see that Black Religion had found a new home in Islam.[77] In fact, he all but ignores Islam, relegating it to the ranks of the small and desparate "cults" of the northern metropolis. He restricts the number of recognized religions in America to five: Protestantism, Judaism, Roman Catholicism, secularism, and the "religion of the Negro," or Black Religion.[78] During the period under consideration, however, as the disembodied spirit of Black Religion floated about in search of new accomodations, it would be Islam, at this point more imagined than real, that offered asylum.

The detailed histories of the early "Islamizers" have been treated by numerous scholars, and I will not repeat them here.[79] For my purposes, however, it is important to recognize that these men were not so much *interpreting* Islam as they were *appropriating* it. There was little or no attention devoted to the manner in which previous Muslim communities had understood or practiced Islam. And there was only the most perfunctory attempt to integrate even the most basic Islamic doctrines and rituals into the religious life of the community, from the Five Pillars to the finality of prophethood resting with Muhammad of Arabia. In fact, there is little evidence that Noble Drew Ali or Elijah Muhammad knew much at all about Islamic doctrine.[80] Rather, these men were appealing to Islam as a means of raising the concerns and spirit of Black Religion to a new level of respectability among Blackamericans, just as Christianity had facilitated the appeal to white America in earlier times. As in the latter case, Black Religion functioned as the core, with the trappings (namely vocabulary) of Islam serving as the outer shell. Also as in the case of early Black Christianity, it was Islam that was being appropriated and pressed into the service of Black Religion rather than the other way around. For it was Black Religion, now bereft of its former relationship with Christianity, that needed the legitimation and historical weight that a great world religion like Islam could confer.

Having said this much, there does appear to have been something felicitous about this early relationship between Islam and Black Religion, a relationship bordering on the proverbial "marriage made in heaven." First, Islam was "African," or at least "Eastern," complete with its own non-European language, language being perhaps the most important and deeply missed of all the casualties of the American slave experience. Second, it was independent of white people (or at least Europeans), the latter having no authority to define its ethos or its substance. Third, it had a well-established reputation for resistance and armed struggle and a vocabulary easily put to the task of dividing the world into "us" and "them." Fourth, it was tied to a grand and glorious civilization in which people of color (or at least non-Europeans) stood center stage. Fifth, it had a deep fraternal spirit—all Muslims are brothers. Sixth, it had clear atheological potential, its basic creed, "There is no god but God," glaring in simplicity next to the Trinity and other intricacies of Christology. Seventh, it loaned itself easily to the conservative social ethic of Black Religion, the more sensationalized aspects of its moral and legal code (e.g., covered women, no-nonsense approach to crime) adding legitimacy and historical weight to that ethic. Eighth, the old-school retributive justice that had catered to the tragic realism of African American slaves and sustained hope in the early Blackamerican Christians was abundantly expressed in the Qur'ān, with Moses, for example, being the most oft-cited prophet in the holy book and God's accounts of His destruction of the wicked abounding therein.[81] Even Islam's apparent disadvantages, for example, being the object of Western hatred and fear, now translated into positive attractions, as the disillusionment of displaced and now more radicalized, lower-class blacks in northern cities evolved into an unabashed separatist platform. Finally, Islam, in its majority Sunni expression, had no organized ecclesiastical hierarchy capable of imposing restrictions on who could speak in its name. This sat well with the proletarian origins of the early Islamizers, neither of whom had gone beyond a primary education. Indeed, this absence of institutional hierarchy facilitated their claim of having the authority to appropriate Islam according to their own lights and priorities.

Proto-Islam Between Conversion and Appropriation

For their part, Sunni Muslim observers (Blackamerican and immigrant) have been generally shocked and dismayed by the theological and doctrinal excesses, omissions and outright blasphemies of the "proto-Islamic" Islamizers: God is a man, God is black, Elijah Muhammad is a prophet, Noble Drew Ali is the author of another revelation, the white man is the devil, and so forth and so on. While certainly condemnable from the standpoint of Muslim orthodoxy, these infelicities are actually no more outlandish than some of what we encounter in the early history of the Muslim world, where, incidentally, the people knew Arabic and had direct access to Muslim scripture (Qur'ān *and* hadith) and Muslim scholarship.[82] This is clearly demonstrated in the famous heresiographical work, *Maqālāt al-islāmīyīn*, by the renowned Abū al-Ḥasan al-Ashʿarī (d. 324/935), eponymous founder of the Ashʿarite school of Muslim theology. In this work, al-Ashʿarī records the views of numerous early groups who associated themselves with Islam. While he clearly does not consider many of these views to be orthodox, he does seem to see in them a reflection of the efforts of these early groups to "find themselves" in Islam. This is perhaps why he entitles his work *Doctrines of Those Who Associate Themselves with Islam* (*Maqālāt al-islāmīyīn*) rather than *Doctrines of the Muslims* (*Maqālāt al-muslimīn*), on the one hand, or *Doctrines of the Muslims and Heretics* (*Maqālāt al-muslimīn wa al-mulḥidīn*), on the other. The following is a tiny sample among the many contained in this work:

1. A group called the Bayānīyah held that God existed in the image of a man, and that He would perish in His entirety, except for His face.[83]
2. A group called the Mughīrīyah held that a man named al-Mughīrah b. Saʿīd was a prophet and that he knew the Greatest Name of God (*ism Allāh al-aʿẓam*) and that the one they worshipped was a man made of light who wore a crown on his head and had all the limbs and organs of a man.[84]
3. A group called the Khaṭṭābīyah held that all of the [Shiite] Imams were prophets and messengers of God and that there would always exist two of them, one vocal, the other silent. The vocal one was Muhammad (upon him be peace) and the silent one was ʿAlī b. Abī Ṭālib.[85]
4. A group going under the general designation of "Murji'ah" held that deeds were irrelevant to the constitution of Belief and that Belief is

purely a matter of having knowledge of God and Unbelief is purely a matter of being ignorant of God. Moreover, they held, the statement "God is the third of three (*thālith thalāthah*)" does not constitute Unbelief.[86]

5. A group called the Azāriqah (a subgroup of the Khārijites) held that every major sin (e.g., adultery, wine-drinking) is an act of Unbelief, and that the territories of those Muslims who disagree with them are non-Muslim, enemy territories (*dār kufr*) and that those who commit major sins will dwell in the Hellfire forever.[87]

The point in all of this is not to vindicate the doctrines of the early Blackamerican *Islāmīyīn*. My point is simply to place these irregularities in the context of what I said earlier about the enterprise of religious conversion, namely that it entails a process by which the convert seeks to get the new religion to validate his past and speak effectively to his present and future. This is often a messy undertaking that entails numerous misses (at least from the standpoint of orthodoxy) en route to complete assimilation. Yet, it is in most instances a necessary process if the religion is to be successfully integrated into the life of the convert community and the latter is not to end up in virtual paralysis via a process of being force-fed theological and other doctrines it neither understands nor feels, finding itself in the meantime alienated from its historical self and thus incapable of tapping into its own historical legacy for tools and insights through which it can confront and effectively redirect reality on the ground.

This is precisely the pitfall the proto-Islamic Blackamerican Islamizers of the early twentieth century were able to avoid. Because they assumed ownership over what they perceived to be Islam and because their manner of appropriation did not sever their relationship with traditional Blackamerican culture, they were able—and this is especially true of the Nation of Islam—to redefine both that culture and its relationship to the dominant culture, forging in the process a new, alternative modality of blackness that was both identifiably "Islamic"[88] *and* American. With its members' bow-ties and two-piece suits, their soldier-like demeanor and Ivy-League vocabulary, the Nation of Islam was able to create a deeply-felt and publicly recognized "Muslim" identity without importing any of its material features from outside the United States. Moreover, and this is especially clear in the career of the redoubtable Malcolm X, they clearly and effectively appropriated Islam to a new vision of the Blackamerican past, present, and future. Indeed, the Nation's success at connecting "Islam" with the masses of Blackamericans via its creation of a long-sought alternative modality of American blackness can be seen even more clearly in their influence among *non-Muslim* Blackamericans. From the rejection of the Afro hairstyle to the vicious assault on pork consumption to the spread of Arabic names (including those bastardized versions of the "*a-ee-a*" pattern, for example, Tameeka, Shameeka, Lakeesha), Blackamerican popular culture was profoundly reshaped. Indeed, though seldom recognized for it, the Nation of Islam's impact on Blackamerican culture in the second half of the twentieth century constitutes one of the most masterful feats of "dual appropriation" in American history.[89]

In sum, the impact of the early Blackamerican 'Islamizers' on the spread of Islam in black America was both seminal and far reaching. Their ignorance and excesses notwithstanding, through their marriage of 'Islam' with Black Religion, men like Noble Drew Ali and the Honorable Elijah Muhammad succeeded in appropriating Islam for Blackamericans and in so doing created a psychological space through which millions of Blackamericans would subsequently enter the religion. This is what blacks in places like South Africa failed to produce or to avail themselves of. Moreover, as Richard Brent Turner reoveals in his treatment of the Ahmadiyah Mission to America, which dates back to the formative period of the 1920s,[90] had immigrant Muslims, orthodox or heterodox, rather than Black Religion, been the conduit through which Islam was introduced to the masses of Blackamericans, it is almost certain that Islam would have never gone on to realize the success that it has come to enjoy in the Blackamerican community.

Black Religion and Blackamerican Sunni Islam

Few would challenge the foregoing depiction of the relationship between Islam and Black Religion as long as we are talking about proto-Islamic groups such as the Nation of Islam or the Moorish Science Temple. But, contrary to the impression one gets from academic writings on Islam in America, proto-Islamic groups like the Nation of Islam have constituted an infintessimal minority (considered heterodox by the majority) for more than a quarter century. In this light, Blackamerican Sunni Muslims (the overwhelming majority) might object to my associating Islam with these proto-Islamic movements, for the major Blackamerican Sunni groups emerged in the 1960s and 1970s, largely in *conscious opposition* to the Blackamerican *Islāmīyīn*. From this perspective, Blackamerican Sunnis might argue that it is inaccurate, if not remiss, to speak as if that which can be said about the Moorish Science Temple or the Nation of Islam provides a reliable basis for making general statements about Islam in black America.

These are legitimate objections. My contention, however, is that the differences between the proto-Islamic *Islāmīyīn* and the orthodox Sunni majority do not rise to the level of negating their common orientations. This contention is grounded, moreover, in a conscious rejection of the tendency to assume that Black Religion (like most things black in America) is inherently retrograde, or that it is necessarily inconsistent, in all its aspects, with the mood and principles of Islam, or that in bringing this orientation to their practice and understanding of Islam Blackamericans would be doing something different from what other Muslim communities have done in other times and places. My argument, in other words, is not that Blackamerican Sunni Islam is synonymous with or simply another species of Black Religion but that Black Religion remains, if only by default,[91] an orientation shared by the masses of Blackamericans. As such, Black Religion influences the manner in which Blackamerican Sunnis approach, process and prioritize the data of Islam. This is clearly manifested in a number of positive and negative tendencies exhibited by Blackamerican Sunni Muslims.

Blackamerican Sunni Groups: A Brief Synopsis

There are essentially six major Blackamerican Sunni groups. These are (1) the Salafī movement; (2) the Dār al-Islām movement; (3) the American Society of Muslims; (4) Jamāʿat al-Tablīgh; (5) Sufi groups; and (6) "Independents." Given the limitations of space, I can only give a thumbnail description of each of these groups, though each deserves a full-length study of its own. In considering these descriptions, one should note that these are only "groups," not "sects." They are not racially "closed," members move freely from one group to another, and, their doctrinal and ideological differences notwithstanding, they all recognize each other as Sunni Muslims.

(1) *The Salafīs*: The Salafīs might be described as *the* protestant reformers of modern Islam, at least as regards their subscription to a modified version of the principle of *sola scriptura*. Their name comes from their devotion to going back to the way of the early Pious Ancestors (*salaf*) of the first three generations following the death of the Prophet Muhammad, as a means of undercutting what they deem to be unsanctioned accretions and innovations (*bidʿah*) that accrued over the centuries. They do not clothe the traditional schools of law (*madhhabs*) with authority but insist that all arguments go directly back to the Qurʾān, the Sunna (normative practice and instruction of the Prophet) and the way of the Pious Ancestors. Having abandoned (in principle or by default) the highly developed interpretive tradition of the classical schools and having failed in the meantime to produce a viable alternative, Salafī inter-

pretations tend toward fideism and to ignore the space–time differentials between the time of the Prophet and modern America. Similarly, they tend to be far more suspicious of the idea of compatibility between Islam and American social, political, religious (e.g., interfaith), and even educational institutions. Salafīs emphasize the importance of theology (*ʿaqīdah*) and are adamantly opposed to Sufism, often seeing in the latter unsanctioned practices and superstitions that compromise Islam's commitment to monotheism (*tawhīd*). Their movement is genetically linked to the Wahhābī movement of Muhammad Ibn ʿAbd al-Wahhāb (d. 1792), and Saudi Arabia is the capital of Salafism worldwide. The Blackamerican contingent has produced, however, its own leadership of sorts, as Blackamericans began to enter the movement in the 1970s when many of them went to Saudi Arabia to study, often on scholarships provided by the Saudi government. In the United States, Salafism is largely an East Coast phenomenon. Its influence goes far beyond its numbers, however, as its staunchly "protestant" approach resonates with the generality of Blackamerican Muslims.[92]

(2) *The Dār al-Islām Movement*: This movement was founded in New York in 1962. It grew out of the Islam Mission Society founded by the West Indian immigrant, Shaykh Daud Faysal, in 1934. It is presently led by Imām Jamīl al-Amīn (formerly H. Rap Brown). Ideologically, the Dār is influenced by the teachings and writings (via translation) of the Indian and later Pakistani thinker, Abū al-Aʿlā al-Mawdūdī (d. 1979). Like the Salafīs, the Dār emphasizes adherence to the Sunna of the Prophet and the avoidance of assimilating non-Islamic influences. This translates into a sustained suspicion, if not hostility, toward American social, political, religious, and educational institutions. Dār members are generally not Sufis and do not subscribe to any particular school of law (though, through their connection to the Indian subcontinent, the Hanafī school tends to influence their practice). Unlike the Salafīs, however, they are neither opposed to the traditional schools of law nor Sufism per se, and they do not place quite the same emphasis on theology. They are tightly organized and display a high level of organizational discipline. One of their distinquishing features is the emphasis they place on the Pledge of Allegiance (*bayʿah*) to the group's leadership. They are more highly concentrated on the East Coast, but have communities in the South, the Midwest and on the West Coast.[93]

(3) *The American Society of Muslims*:[94] This is the group until very recently headed by Imām Wārithuddīn Muhammad, who took over leadership of the Nation of Islam following the death of his father the Honorable Elijah Muhammad in 1975.[95] Imām Wārithuddīn courageously moved the movement away from its heretical, race-based theology and guided it into Sunni Islam. Today,

its members are universally accepted as Sunni Muslims. At least two features distinquish the American Society of Muslims. On the one hand, it benefitted from the "dual appropriation" effected by Elijah Muhammad, as a result of which it could embrace, *inter alia*, the value of Western secular education. Its members tend thus to be more fomally educated than those of the Salafī, Dār al-Islām, or the Jamāʿat al-Tablīgh (see below) movements. Its Clara Muhammad school system has graduated students who go on to enroll in elite American universities, including Harvard, Yale, Princeton, the University of Pennsylvania, the University of Michigan, and others. On the other hand, it has had only a tenuous ideological connection to the Muslim world, as a result of which it has been slow in producing members with intimate knowledge of traditional Islamic discourse.[96] This has cost them over the years, as the other groups have tended to outpace them in making the transition to more authentically Islamic sources of religious authority. Like the Salafīs and the Dār, its members are neither Sufis nor committed to any particular school of Islamic law. Unlike the former two, however, the American Society of Muslims tends to be more positively predisposed to American cultures and values.[97]

(4) *Jāmāʿat al-Tablīgh*: Unlike the groups cited so far, the Jamāʿat al-Tablīgh (also known as Tablīghī Jamāʿah) is one in which Blackamericans are a minority and in which there is no clear Blackamerican leader (though some look to Maulana Zubayr in Detroit). In America, the majority consists of Muslims from the Indian subcontinent, where the movement began in 1927, as part of an effort to purify and reinvigorate the Faith. Yet, the Jamāʿat has exerted significant influence on Blackamerican Muslims, often being the channel through which many enter Islam. Its overall ethos is that of the traveling mendicant, emphasizing spiritual purification and the renunciation of worldly delights. Though far from being antinomian, its members tend not to stress issues of Islamic law and focus, rather, on the life of the spirit. Of all the groups, the Jamāʿat is perhaps the most consistent in their avoidance of Western dress. They are also among the least politicized of Sunni Muslim groups.

(5) *Sufi groups*: There are two main Sufi groups among Blackamericans. These are branches of the Naqshabandīyah and the Tijānīyah orders. Blackamericans began to enter the Tijānīyah order as far back as the 1970s; they began to enter the Naqshabandīyah order in the 1980s. The latter includes at least one Blackamerican *muqaddam* or spiritual leader. Both of these orders are "orthodox" in that they eschew antinomianism and insist on adherence to the provisions of Islamic law. Worldwide, the Naqshabandīyah are commonly found in the Balkans, Turkey, Central Asia, India, and parts of the Middle East. The Tijānīyah are commonly found in North and subsaharan Africa. In fact,

there is reportedly a Tijānīyah Qur'ān- school in Senegal supported by Blackamerican Tijānīyah. Sufi groups, however, are a small minority among Blackamerican Sunni Muslims.[98]

(6) *Independents*: This group is the most difficult of all to define. They are not necessarily opposed to any of the above groups but do not subscribe to any of the latters' ideological platforms and do not hold formal membership in any of them. Independents are often former members of these groups who consider themselves to be "graduates" who have not yet settled into a new home. Or, they may have been introduced to Islam by immigrants, who themselves have no affiliation to any particular Islamic movement. Independents' nonaffiliation with other groups should not be taken to imply any sort of "new age" disaffection with "organized religion." Indeed, they are often just as ideological as any other group and do not subscribe to the notion of limiting religion to private life. Their numbers include numerous Muslims who have studied abroad. And they are just as likely to be influenced by modern ideologues, such as Sayyid Quṭb (d. 1966) or Abū al-Aʿlā al-Mawdūdī (d. 1979), as they are by modernized representatives of the classical Tradition of Islamic law and jurisprudence.[99] They run the gamut in terms of levels of political involvement and attitudes toward American cultures and values. And they are just as likely as members of any other group to be Imāms or leaders of mosques.

Blackamerican Sunni Islam and Black Religion: Negatives and Positives

Negatives

Like all human constructs, Black Religion embodies a number of deficiencies, false obsessions, and unexamined biases. Being grounded in "Negro folk culture," it tends to reflect certain fears, prejudices, and limitations born of its folk roots. For example, the traditionally exalted place of the Blackamerican preacher over his uncultured flock yielded a certain authoritarianism in the context of which critical activity was stifled and the more educated were perceived to be a threat to legitimate authority. This remains a part of Black Religion and is the reason it has been slow in developing a tradition of systematic thought or theology and remains more deistic than theistic, relying more on general notions of God and "the good" than on God's revelation. Similarly, given its distrust of and sense of being threatened by the dominant culture, Black Religion has tended to seek refuge in fraternalism and separatism rather than in strategic planning or reconciliation. But perhaps most important of all,

Black Religion tends to display an almost single-minded obsession with issues of race, having little or nothing to offer nonblacks or to say on issues unconnected to race. As one black critic of Black Religion put it,

> Race is everything to black religion; nothing else really counts. And on issues other than race the followers of black religion have little time to think. In fact, on every issue besides race, they are dependent upon their white brethren.[100]

All of the aforementioned Blackamerican Sunni groups display, albeit in varying degrees, these obsessions and drawbacks associated with Black Religion. Their leaders tend towards authoritarianism and anti-intellectualism, which continues to deprive them of any role in Blackamerican—let alone American—intellectual life. They are far more comfortable with protest and social critique than they are with identifying and capitalizing on opportunity. Indeed, their socioreligious ethic remains largely negative, fixated almost entirely on the avoidance of vice with little attention to promoting a positive vision that includes not only moral and strictly religious concerns but aesthetic, cultural, and economic ones as well. They remain wedded to a self-defeating, separatist impulse, which, while most often justified in terms of avoiding un-Islamic influences, tends to manifest itself in the curious desire to separate from white non-Muslims but not from black ones, even when this means remaining in crime-ridden, crack-infested neighborhoods with failing schools and depleted infrastructures. Even the term "*kāfir*," which should mean simply "non-Muslim," is commonly used as a veiled reference to "the white man."

All of these tendencies are indebted to Black Religion's siege mentality or "will in opposition," which aims primarily at resisting or removing evil from the world rather than contributing good to it. Ultimately, this leads Black Religion to its most serious and inextricable paradox: Black Religion remains relevant almost entirely to the extent that the evil it seeks to remove from the world remains in the world. To the extent that it succeeds in stifling or eradicating the evils of racism, Black Religion threatens to render itself obsolete.

This has serious implications for Blackamerican Sunni Islam. For America has seen significant changes in race relations since the rise of the Civil Rights Movement. And to the extent that improved race relations diminishes the relevance of Black Religion, one can only assume that Blackamerican Islam will be similarly affected. This is perhaps the most serious of all the liabilities attending the continued relationship between Islam and Black Religion in its classical form. For not only does this fixation upon race jeopardize the credibility of Islam's claim to universal truth, it falsely assumes that a concrete economic, social, cultural, and political vision will emerge automatically out of a visceral commitment to one's race.

As America strides towards its ever-elusive dream of eradicating the negative significance of race, or as other national concerns such as the catastrophe of September 11, 2001, force race and related matters to the margins of the national discourse, Blackamerican Sunnis are likely to find themselves increasingly irrelevant to American public life. Moreover, on every issue besides those connected to race, it will be the voices of immigrant, white American, Native American, and Hispanic Muslims that America will hear. In a tragic repetition of history, through their own self-imposed marginalization, the blind rejectionism of Blackamerican Sunni Muslims may lock them in the position of simply meandering through yet another American reality over which they exercise little influence and no control.

Positives

Not everything, however, in the relationship between Black Religion and Sunni Islam is negative. The inextricable place occupied by God in Black Religion, alongside the dogged, albeit vague, belief in an order beyond this world, provides Blackamerican Islam with added insulation against the forces of American secularism. On these basic beliefs, one is not likely to find, as one does among segments of the Jewish and Christian population, "atheist" or "agnostic" Blackamerican Muslims, who simply practice "Islam" for its cultural or civilizational content. For Blackamericans, being a Muslim will always entail a conscious sense of responsibility toward, if not commitment to, the religion, and more specifically the religious law, however imaginatively these might be interpreted.

Second, it might be argued that the negative element reflected in Black Religion's greater commitment to a refusal than to a positive affirmation confirms the orientation reflected in Islam's Testimony to Faith (*shahāda*): "There is no god but God." Islam has always recognized the negation of false claimants to divinity to be the more important and difficult task, belief in and commitment to the one true God flowing naturally out of this. As social beings, that is, in a state of society as opposed to a state of nature, this is what Islam assumes to be *the* human challenge. In this context, negation can be seen to be not simply the antithesis of affirmation but the necessary and inextricable complement to the latter.

Third, Black Religion's "will to opposition" tends to promote what James Baldwin once described as a visceral distrust of the dominant intellectual and cultural tradition. This is not the same as, and should not be construed to imply, blind anti-Westernism; indeed, Blackamerican Muslims (perhaps more so than other Blackamericans[101]) are becoming increasingly aware of their own constitution as Westerners. But Blackamericans have never been Western in the same way as other Americans, and this makes for a much more cautious and studied approach to the dominant cultural and intellectual tradition. This has the potential to slow if not frustrate not only the process of unwarranted assimilation, whereby Muslims frantically scour scripture and tradition for justifications for the latest intellectual or cultural fad, but also what Stephen Carter refers to as the domestication of religion.[102] Ultimately, this provisional distrust may render Blackamerican Sunnis more likely to develop into genuine "Muslim intellectuals" as opposed to mere proponents of the dominant cultural and intellectual trends who happen to bear Muslim names.[103]

Fourth, the conservative side of Black Religion's "radical conservatism," filtered through the rules and principles of Islamic law, might show Blackamerican Muslims the way to an alternative to both the liberalism of the Civil Rights establishment and the Black conservatism championed by the likes of Clarence Thomas, Thomas Sowell, or Shelby Steele. Indeed, perhaps enough time has passed on the death of Malcolm X that his legacy can be reshaped into the basis for a new Blackamerican Muslim "radical conservatism,"[104] a conservatism that avoids moral prudishness, pseudo-Stoicism, and the tendency to cede to those who claim to be the ideological heirs of the Founding Fathers the exclusive authority to define either "American culture" or "Conservative values." Like Jewish Conservatives—and unlike black Conservatives—Blackamerican Muslim Radical Conservatives will not allow those who have victimized them to undermine their cause by simply charging them with embracing victimology. Like any conservativism, however, Muslim radical conservatism will have to avoid a number of liabilities, particularly regarding issues affecting women. But assuming, as I have, that the "radical conservative" impulse is not limited to Blackamerican men, many of these liabilities should be offset by women's participation in the actual shaping of that conservative alternative. In this context, perhaps more clearly than in any other, women's inclusion in the intellectual life of the Blackamerican Muslim community reveals itself to be essential to the latter's health and success.

Finally, inasmuch as Blackamericans at large remain essentially a "protest people," Black Religion remains an important source of legitimacy and a bridge to the broader Blackamerican community. Moreover, the raison d'ētre of Black Religion, namely racism, or more precisely, white supremacy, is still alive and well in America. As such, there is still a place, albeit different from the past, for the vigilant, holy protest of Black Religion. Indeed, as the late C. Eric Lincoln put it:

> any religion of Blacks in America which did not in some fundamental way address the prevailing issues of racialism would be improbable if not grotesque.[105]

Even if Blackamerican Islam's approach to America's social, economic, and political realities fail to avoid completely the negative aspects of Black Religion, we should not be too quick in calling for an end to their relationship. For as Reinhold Niebuhr so powerfully reminds us, "Contending factions in a social struggle require morale; and morale is created by the right dogmas, symbols, and emotionally potent oversimplifications."[106] Black Religion, for its part, has always been rich in powerful oversimplifications, and its rejectionist instinct has always served to insulate it from the anesthetizing forces of accommodationism, domestication, and intellectualism, all of which tend to mollify rather than address the demand for change. This is almost certainly what Joseph R. Washington Jr. had in mind when he stated that "Independent Negro [Christian] congregations and institutions are ineffective among Negroes because they have failed in faithfulness to Black religion."[107] On such an observation, it may be that Blackamerican Muslims might only ignore the power and efficacy of Black Religion to their own eventual disadvantage.

Blackamerican Islam in Transition: The Third Resurrection

Today, however, Blackamerican Islam is and for more than three decades has been in a state of transition. While Black Religion continues to influence the thinking and sensibilities of Blackamerican Muslims, it no longer enjoys the near monopoly it once did. Rather, in terms of authority, that is, the ability to command compliance on the belief that it is right to comply, there has been a fundamental shift in Blackamerican Islam. Rather than to Black Religion, it is to the sources and authorities of historical Islam that Blackamerican Muslims now appeal in order to authenticate their views and actions and earn these recognition as Islamic. This shift in the basis of authority in Blackamerican Islam constitutes a fundamental break with its past and marks the beginning of the "Third Resurrection."

Yet, for reasons discussed more directly in chapter 2, the sources and tradition of historical Islam remain more of an ideal than a reality for the majority of Blackamerican Muslims. As a result, Black Religion retains much of its authority and influence by default. Still, there can be no doubt that the latter has ceased to function as the sole or ultimate authority. As such, gone are the days when Blackamerican Muslim leaders can instruct their followers through appeals to racial or class-based fraternalism without grounding these in the Qur'ān, Sunna, or Muslim Tradition. Gone, too, are the days when Blackamerican Islam can be profitably studied by scholars who know nothing about Islamic law, Sunni orthodoxy, or the history of the Muslim world. For there is now a new, dialectical synthesis between Black Religion, Modern or Modernized Islam,[108] and aspects of the critical Western tradition that lies at the heart of Blackamerican Islam.

Today, virtually every major city in America has a contingent of Blackamerican Muslims studying the Islamic sciences in the Muslim world. At the same time, there is a growing number of Blackamerican Muslim Ph.D.s who hold positions in Arabic, Islamic studies, and related areas in major U.S. institutions. Over the coming decade, as more and more Blackamerican Muslims master Arabic and the Islamic religious sciences, alongside what they deem useful of the critical Western tradition, Blackamerican Muslims are likely to return to a position of full partnership (if not leadership) in the intellectual life of American Islam. This will be an American Islam, however, whose primary influence is no longer classical Black Religion but an amalgamation of "reformed" Black Religion, aspects of the critical Western—especially American—tradition and the super-tradition of the Islamic religious sciences calibrated to the realities of the New World.

There are those who would argue that Christianity was effectively imposed on Blackamericans. Whatever the truth of this claim may be, the relationship between Islam and Blackamericans bears no such parallel. Blackamericans received Islam neither in a state of bondage nor from white Americans. Nor did Muslims choose Blackamericans. It was rather Blackamericans who chose Islam. At its roots, Blackamerican Islam is a thoroughly American phenomenon that grew out of the efforts of Blackamericans working through the agency of Black Religion. In this context, the real and enduring significance of the early Blackamerican *Islāmīyīn* who effected the marriage between Islam and Black Religion is that they gave Blackamericans a sense of ownership in Islam. Through them, Islam was appropriated and made the "property" of Blackamericans so that for a Blackamerican to become a Muslim entailed neither racial nor cultural apostasy nor violated any of the "rules" of American blackness. Indeed, the early Blackamerican *Islāmīyīn* made significant contributions to the very definition of American blackness itself. It is in large part their rootedness in this tradition—directly or indirectly—that explains why, despite all of the challenges and difficulties facing contemporary Blackamerican Muslims, including their often strained and frustrating relationship with the immigrant Muslim community, they have not abandoned Islam but have doggedly clung to the religion.

Yet, for all the benefit that Black Religion has brought to Blackamerican Islam, the relationship between the two remains problematic. And perhaps the real question is whether Blackamerican Muslims will ultimately transcend their Black Religion roots, transform Black Religion itself, or simply integrate it more effectively and selectively into their understanding and practice of Islam. Whatever the future of Blackamerican Sunni Islam might be, this renegotiation is certain to be at the heart of it. Meanwhile, a major element in this process of renegotiation will be the relationship between Blackamerican and Immigrant Islam, along with the "new" basis of religious authority introduced and largely presided over by the latter. It is to this relationship that I shall now turn.

2

The Third Resurrection and the Ghost of Edward Wilmot Blyden

The death of the Honorable Elijah Muhammad in 1975 marked a watershed in the history of Islam among Blackamericans. By 1976, by which time Elijah's son and successor Imām Wārithuddīn Muhammad[1] had publicly abandoned the creed of his father and redirected the movement into Sunni Islam, the classical Nation of Islam had ceased to be a contender in the ongoing competition to define Islam in America. Instead, with the exception of a small contingent led by the very capable Minister Louis Farrakhan (who refused to follow Imām Wārithuddīn) the overwhelming majority of Blackamerican Muslims were now orthodox Sunnis who dismissed Elijah's (and subsequently Farrakhan's) movement as a pseudo-Islamic heresy.[2] Still, Elijah's departure was crucial in that it coincided with the early stages of a massive influx of Muslims, especially Arabs and Indo-Pakistanis, from the Muslim world. This introduced major changes not only in the ethnic make-up of the Muslim-American community but also in the basis of religious authority by which a properly constituted Islamic life could be thought about, authenticated, and practically pursued. As long as Black Religion, formally or by default, remained at the core of Blackamerican Islam, the latter's priorities, obsessions, aspirations, and vision remained grounded in American reality. This single-minded commitment to the black cause, together with the legacy of the Nation of Islam's success at reforming America's unwanted, had earned Islam a place of respect in the collective Blackamerican psyche. By the 1970s, this had permutated into a certain image of Islam as a religion inherently suited to the plight and sensibilities of Blackamericans. But Elijah's death, alongside the rapidly changing racial and ethnic constitution of the Muslim community, signalled the beginning of the end of this emphasis on America, these mental associations between Islam and Blackamericans, and, most importantly, the ability of Blackamerican Sunnis to employ Islam in ways that promoted a dignified existence for themselves and lived up to the expectations of the broader Blackamerican community. Instead, the new eyes, the new faces, and the new prism brought by immigrant Muslims would drastically alter both the focus and the image of Islam in America.[3]

To be sure, Sunnism, albeit on a limited scale, had established itself among Blackamericans as far back as the 1930s.[4] In fact, prior to the 1970s, Blackamericans dominated the American Sunni scene, at least in terms of those who actively identified themselves as practicing Muslims. Prior to that time, Sunnis from the Muslim world tended to play down if not conceal their religious identity, a fact reflected in such name changes as that from Muḥammad Jumʿah to Michael Friday or Maryam Ṭaḥḥan to Mary Miller. In 1965, however, the government repealed the National Origins Act and the Asian Barred Zone legislation. As a result, by the late 1970s, immigration from the Muslim world was fast outpacing Blackamerican conversion, and by the late 1980s, while still the largest single block, Blackamerican Sunnis would be reduced to an overall minority, an estimated 42 percent of the whole. These demographic changes, in tandem with a number of unexamined assumptions about those who purportedly knew Islam versus those who were presumably learning it, laid the foundations for an effective "immigrant supremacy," according to which the priorities, insights, perspectives, historical experience, and understandings of the Arabs, followed by those of other immigrant Muslim groups, were established as both normal and normative, the "Islamicity" of Blackamerican (and other American) Muslims being measured in terms of how intimately they identified with these. On this development, "the good," "the true," "the beautiful," even "the important" were increasingly perceived as having origins that were neither black nor American. The growingly obvious manifestations of this new *weltanschauung*, reflected, for example, in the grossly attenuated relevance of Islam to the plight of Blackamerican (versus immigrant) Muslims or the lack of Blackamerican representation in the major Muslim-American organizations,[5] led some to conclude that Blackamerican converts from Christianity had simply moved from the back of the bus to the back of the camel. In more recent years, this perspective has gained popularity even within Blackamerican Sunni circles. This intrareligious perspective parallels in many ways that of the nineteenth-century black Presbyterian Edward W. Blyden who, in his classic work, *Christianity, Islam and the Negro Race*, complained and warned of the dangers of white supremacy that informed the attitudes of white missionaries in their dealings with their African co-religionists. Ironically, it would be Islam that Blyden would hold up as the model of how a religion could be both indigenized and safeguarded by native converts without the original carriers having to resort to mental colonization or paternalistic micromanagement.

In this chapter, I shall attempt to describe in more specific terms the encounter between Blackamerican Sunni Muslims and Immigrant Islam, with particular reference to both entities' contribution to the establishment of a régime of religion-based domination predicated upon immigrant supremacy. As we shall see, the immigrant impact on Blackamerican Islam during the last quarter of the twentieth century has been no less significant than the earlier contribution of Black Religion. As such, neither the present nor future of Islam among Blackamericans can be understood or predicted without an ample account of the depth and nature of this influence. At the same time, not only will the Muslim, and especially the Blackamerican Muslim, response to these developments determine the status of Blackamericans in Islam, it will also have an enduring impact on the status of Islam among Blackamericans. For this response will ultimately reveal Islam to be either an agent of positive change and enrichment or a tool of paralysis. As such, following my description of the nature and evolution of the aforementioned religion-based domination, I shall offer what I believe to be a practical and religiously mandated basis for ameliorating the Blackamerican–immigrant divide.

Before proceeding, however, I would like to return to Edward Blyden's classic, *Christianity, Islam and the Negro Race* (CINR), in order to establish what I believe to be a useful framework within which to ponder the encounter between Immigrant Islam and Blackamerican Muslims. Specifically, Blyden's depiction reminds us that while, on the one hand, a people's acceptance or rejection of a religion may be informed by the status or reputation of the religion's carrier people, on the other hand, its effectiveness and ability to sustain its efficacy and appeal among the target community can only be preserved by the target people themselves. As such, there is an exceedingly delicate balance to be maintained between carrier and target peoples. For where the transfer of religious authority from the former to the latter occurs too quickly, syncretism and heretical appropriations are likely to proliferate. Where it occurs too slowly, cultural and intellectual stagnation and paralysis are bound to set in. If it never occurs at all, religion-based domination results, and what began as the anticipated indigenization of the religion ends up as the latter's inglorious twilight among the convert population.

Edward Wilmot Blyden

Edward Wilmot Blyden was born in St. Thomas in the Virgin Islands in 1832. He attended primary school in Venezuela and very soon attracted the attention of a certain John Knox, a white minister, who encouraged him to enter the ministry. In 1850, at the behest of Knox, Blyden traveled to the U.S. mainland to enroll in Knox's *alma mater,* Rutgers Theological College. Rutgers turned him down on grounds of race, and seven months later, in December of 1850, Blyden left for Monrovia, Liberia, at the invitation of the controversial American Colonization Society (ACS), an organization established by a group of Presbyterian ministers in 1816 to encourage and aid free and newly manumitted Blackamericans to migrate to West Africa.[6] By 1858 Blyden had received his ordination as a Presbyterian minister and begun a series of prominent and influential positions in Liberia, including professor of classics (Liberia College), president of Liberia College, secretary of state of Liberia, commissioner to the United States and Great Britain, minister of the interior and ambassador to the Court of St. James (Great Britain). He also studied (and later taught) Arabic and traveled to Egypt and Syria in pursuit of language skills. After an unsuccessful run for the presidency of Liberia in 1885, he moved to neighboring Sierra Leone. The following year, he left the Presbyterian Church to become a "Minister of Truth." The year after that, he published his controversial, *Christianity, Islam and the Negro Race.* He died in 1912.[7]

CINR was a collection of essays written over a period of at least sixteen years. A work of iridescent prose, it shows Blyden to have mastered several languages, including Hebrew, Arabic, French, German, and Latin, and to have been a keen student of the history of religions. To understand the overall aim and thrust of the work, three things about Blyden must be born in mind. First, Blyden believed deeply in the mission of the ACS, the vice presidency of which he assumed in 1884.[8] He made several trips to America and looked to Blackamericans to play a major role in "civilizing" Africa. Second, Blyden was deeply committed to Christianity, which he equated with civilization and saw as the key to the ACS's civilizing mission. This attachment to Christianity has been somewhat obscured by his tendency in CINR to praise Islam and criticize Christianity, the fact that he was once addressed by an African Muslim as "ʿAbd-ul-Karim,"[9] and his ultimate departure from the Presbyterian Church. It should be noted, however, that all but two of the essays that deal most directly with the status of blacks in Christianity versus Islam carry dates prior to the time of Blyden's departure from the Presbyterian church.[10] In fact, in one of the undated essays, "The Mohammedans of Nigritia," which internal evidence shows to have been written in or after 1886,[11] Blyden openly expresses his wishes for Africa in the following terms: "Arm the Negroes, in the name of Christ, if Africa is to be conquered for Christ."[12] As for Blyden's being given an Arabic Muslim name, this is commonly done for many reasons, such as ingratiating non-Muslims with Islam or as a gesture of appreciation for acts of kindness or friendship. It is by no means a definitive indication of conversion. Indeed, as police commissioner of New York, none other than future president Theodore Roosevelt would acquire the nickname "Hārūn al-Rashīd Roosevelt."[13] Finally, Blyden was deeply committed to the upliftment of blacks in Africa and elsewhere and to demolishing commonplace nineteenth-century theories of black inferiority. Part of the whole point of CINR is to argue that the native talents, genius, and proclivities of blacks should neither be overlooked nor feared as retrograde pollutants destined to corrupt or undermine the integrity of the Christian faith.

Blyden's major concern in CINR was the effects of European missionary activity on the spread and standing of Christianity in black Africa. In Blyden's view, the deeply entrenched racism of the nineteenth century had so thoroughly infected the European (and by extension the white American) psyche that it informed both their teaching and practice of Christianity. This had the effect of alienating indigenous Africans, whose conversion to Christianity inevitably inducted them into a system of religion-based domination. This invariably undermined African genius and self-esteem and promoted a feeling among Africans that they could not "be themselves" as Christians. This, Blyden feared, if left unchecked, would ultimately cause the African to regurgitate Christianity and thwart the religion's spread throughout the continent.

According to Blyden, Africans who converted to Christianity were not afforded the freedom to interpret their own reality and to determine the polarity and status of various aspects of their pagan heritage and how urgently or casually or fully or partially these should be modified or eschewed. Rather, this was all judged by their European teachers, who invariably viewed these things through the prism of their "superior" European culture and civilization, which they equated, of course, with *Christian* culture and civilization. According to Blyden,

> The Christian Negro has, hitherto, as I have tried to show throughout this volume, rarely been trained to trust his own judgment or to think that he has anything to say which foreigners will care to hear. . . . The faulty estimate which he himself entertains of the true field for his energies is not corrected by his guides, who familiar with and strong on their own ground, can conceive of no other. . . . It is

> difficult for the European to put himself in the place of the Christian Negro. But it is evident that there can be hope for the future improvement of the African only as he finds out his work and destiny and, as a consequence, learns to trust his own judgment.[14]

The problem, according to Blyden, began with the European's assessment and understanding of his place in the world in general and in Christianity in particular. On the one hand, he held his race to be superior to all others. On the other hand, his race among all the races had established a special relationship with Christianity. The European (and by extension the American, Canadian, Australian, and New Zealander) assumed the status of custodian of Christianity, looking upon himself as *the* purveyor of the religion and thus the guide and teacher of Christians everywhere. Armed with this self-endowed religious authority, he set out to remake the entire Christian world in his image. As the nineteenth-century German theologian, Ernst Troeltsch, summarized the matter: "Christianity and Western culture are so inextricably intertwined that a Christian can say little about his faith to members of other civilizations and the latter in turn cannot encounter Christ save as a member of the Western world."[15]

For his part, Blyden accepted the propriety and even necessity of discipleship, that is, of learning from the masters in order to become in turn a master oneself. But discipleship and imitation were two different things, and what Europeans imposed upon their African brethren was imitation, not discipleship.[16] Ultimately, Christianization of the African amounted to a destructive process of Europeanization.[17] In this process, "The African mind [wa]s regarded as a great blank, or worse than a blank, filled with everything dark and horrible and repulsive. Everything [wa]s to be destroyed and replaced by something new and foreign."[18] Under such tutelage, the African Christian soon found himself looking upon his heritage and people in quiet contempt. For, to his European teachers, nearly everything about him was new and strange and utterly despised for being so un-European. Try as he may, "the European never g[ot] over the feeling of distance, if not repulsion, which he experience[d] on first seeing the Negro."[19] Instead,

> with the earnest vigour and sanguine temper which belong to youth he preaches a crusade against the harmless customs and prejudices of the people—superceding many customs and habits necessary and useful in the climate and for the people by practices which, however useful they might be in Europe, become, when introduced indiscriminately into Africa, artificial, ineffective and absurd. The "thin varnish of European civilisation," which the native thus receives, is

mistaken for a genuine mental metamorphosis, when as a rule, owing to the imprudent hurry by which the convert's reformation has been brought about, his Christianity, instead of being pure is superstitious, instead of being genuine is only nominal, instead of being deep is utterly superficial, and, not having fairly taken root, it cannot flourish and become reproductive.[20]

The denouement of this monopoly over religious authority was a certain cultural and psychological dislocation that put the African Christian off balance in virtually every aspect of his life. This cultural and intellectual confusion and moral hesitancy was summed up in a letter Blyden cites from an African clergyman from Sierre Leone in 1872:

> The result [of European monopoly of religious authority] has been that we, as a people, think more of everything that is foreign, and less of that which is purely native; have lost our self-respect and our love for our own race, are become a sort of non-descript people, and are, in many things, inferior to our [pagan] brethren in the interior countries. There is evidently a fetter upon our minds even when the body is free; mental weakness, even where there is physical strength, and barrenness even where there appears fertility.[21]

To be sure, Europeans were not alone in bringing this germ of black inferiority and psychological dislocation to Africa. Blyden also implicates Blackamerican missionaries in this process. At one point, for example, he expresses concern about mentally colonized black clergymen from America coming to Africa and operating (wittingly or not) as surrogates and promoters of European civilization. These Blackamericans may have been mere imitators of their white American sponsors, but, precisely because they were black, their activity was doubly effective in confirming white superiority and placing greater distance between Christianity and native African sensibilities.[22] From this station, subsequent generations of Africans would inherit no sense of ownership in Christianity, such that they would be empowered to develop expressions of the religion that enabled them to remain both Christian and African *naturally*.

All of this stood in stark contrast to the situation of Islam in Africa. According to Blyden,

> The Mohammedan Negro is a much better Mohammedan than the Christian Negro is a Christian, because the Muslim Negro, as a learner, is a disciple, not an imitator. A disciple, when freed from leading-strings, may become a producer; an imitator never rises above a mere copyist. With a disciple progress is from within; the

> imitator grows by accretion from without. The learning acquired by the disciple gives him capacity; that gained by an imitator terminates in itself. The one becomes a capable man; the other is a mere sciolist. This explains the difference between the Mohammedan and the Christian Negro.[23]

The fundamental reason behind this difference, according to Blyden, was simple: Islamization in Africa did not entail Arabization. "Mohammedan conquests mean subjugation to the Koran and not to Arab or Turk."[24] In short, Blyden's experience had convinced him that the process of Islamization in Africa was one in which religious authority was neither hoarded nor monopolized by Arab (or other) carriers but transferred in a timely fashion to the native Africans, who in turn successfully indigenized the religion by broadening and deepening its institutions in a manner that rendered it suitable to the African, while sacrificing nothing essential to its doctrinal integrity. In contradistinction to Christianity, "Mohammedanism, in Africa, left the native master of himself and of his home."[25]

> Their local customs were not destroyed by the Arab influence introduced. They only assumed new forms, and adapted themselves to the new teachings. In all thriving communities in West and Central Africa, it may be noticed that the Arab superstructure has been superimposed on a permanent indigenous substructure; so that what really took place, when the Arab met the Negro in his own home, was a healthy amalgamation, and not an absorption or an undue repression.[26]

For Blyden, only by reversing the status quo and establishing a similar reality for African Christians would Christianity be able to preserve itself and flourish in West and Central Africa. Otherwise, the gains made to that point would be short lived, as the disparity between being African and being Christian grew to unbearable proportions and subsequent generations of black Africans saw no alternative but to revert to their "natural," non-Christian state.

Blackamerican Muslims and Immigrant Islam

Authority Old and New: The Great Migrations of the 1970s and 1980s

Between the situation described by Blyden in West and Central Africa and the encounter between Immigrant Islam and Blackamerican Muslims in the

United States lies one important difference. Whereas Europeans (along with Western blacks like Blyden and other ACS members) had been the primary carriers of Christianity to West and Central Africa, Islam—both proto- and Sunni—had already established itself among Blackamericans *before* the immigrant wave of the 1970s. As such, unlike the situation confronting West and Central African Christians, religious authority was not imposed on Blackamerican Muslims *ab initio* from without. Rather, an indigenous régime of religious authority had already existed and was subsequently displaced by a régime that fell under the control of another group. While immigrants played a key role in this process, in truth, this substitution cannot be reduced to a simple matter of immigrant arrogance or will to dominate. Rather, Blackamerican Islam harbored from its very inception a critical weakness that would be both exposed and exacerbated by the mere coming of the immigrants.

This weakness was Blackamerican Islam's inability to authenticate itself on the basis of any criterion that enjoyed recognition *outside* the black community. Even where Blackamerican Muslims invoked the Qur'ān and Sunna, there was no recognized, authoritative tradition or method of interpretation that would guarantee the acceptability of their interpretations among non-Blackamericans. In this context, *the mere coming* of the immigrants would pose a major challenge. For, from this point on, not only would Blackamerican Muslims' ability to self-authenticate their views drastically decline, their very "Islamicity" would be judged on the basis of a criterion that anteceded Blackamerican Islam, was alien to the Blackamerican experience and was the presumed intellectual property of non-Blackamericans.

The Crisis within Blackamerican Islam

Meanwhile, theological and ideological conflicts within Blackamerican Islam would accelerate the transition to the "new" criterion. Even before Elijah Muhammad's death, Imām Wārithuddīn Muhammad (at the time Wallace D. Mohammed) had begun to question the "orthodoxy" of his father's teachings. His openness in this regard had resulted in several "suspensions," the first occurring as early as 1963, the last one ending as late as 1974.[27] In 1963, he went so far as to establish the short-lived Afro-Descendent Upliftment Society.[28] His return to the fold following the assassination of Malcolm X in 1965 was probably grounded, at least in part, in his recognition of the Nation's utility as an organizational structure.

Wallace's differences with his father were both substantive and longstanding. The cumulative record of his activities clearly reflect his perduring desire to find an alternative theological foundation in which to anchor his

Islam. Thus, on one level, it is clear that the original impetus behind his courageous redirecting of the Nation into Sunni Islam began with him and was not the result of any outside influences. On another level, however, Imām Muhammad was nudged not only by immigrant encouragement and pressure but by a long-standing antagonism with the "Old Guard" of Blackamerican Sunnis (referred to at the time as Orthodox Muslims). In the latters' minds, Sunnism had always connoted a certain opposition and hostility towards the Nation. And though they were fewer in number and far less organized, they looked upon Imām Muhammad with suspicion if not contempt. Even after he publicly abandoned the creed of his father, the Old Guard continued to view themselves as Islamically superior to him and his *nouveau islamiques*.[29] This perduring and fractious competition, alongside the fact that Imām Muhammad had sought theretofore to authenticate his movement almost entirely on the basis of Black Religion, not to mention palpable vestiges of black Christianity, would magnify the utility of an alternative basis of authority to offset this rapidly increasing authenticity deficit. Not to be outdone, meanwhile, the Old Guard would hasten to confirm their status as the premier Blackamerican upholders of Sunni orthodoxy, in some ways even exaggerating their commitment thereto.

The friction between Imām Muhammad and the Old Guard (which included the Dār al-Islām movement, The Islamic Party, The International Islamic Brotherhood,[30] *Jamāʿat al-Tablīgh*, numerous Independents, and, later, the *Salafīs*) had been based partly in theology and partly in ideology. Theologically, the Old Guard had always recognized and strived to stay within the boundaries of what they perceived to be the general scheme of Sunni orthodoxy. They recognized the Qurʾān and Sunna, at least in theory, as the primary, indisputable sources of the religion. Similarly, they accepted as Islamic almost any doctrine or practice whose provenance was assumed to go back to the Muslim world, which functioned in their understanding as a proxy for the Tradition of historical Islam. Given their limited direct exposure to historical Islam, their reliance on the latter was often far more imagined than real. But this did not detract from their perception of what they were doing or of what it meant to be a Sunni Muslim. Ultimately, this orientation would set the Old Guard off fundamentally from Imām Wārithuddīn and his followers. For the latter had emerged from a tradition in which the Qurʾān and Sunna were marginal at best and the hermeneutic and juridical traditions of historical Islam were not recognized at all.

Ideologically speaking, Imām Muhammad and his followers were the heirs to the Honorable Elijah Muhammad's masterful appropriation of American middle-class and genteel manners and customs. This engendered a self-perception that welcomed the best of America as part and parcel of their religious and ethnic identity. Proper diction, the pursuit of education, and sartorial neatness ceased to be signatures of bourgeois whites or Uncle Tom Negroes and became part and parcel of what was required to be authentically black and Muslim! Having appropriated these values, the followers of this tradition would gradually realize a modicum of upward mobility, which, in turn, reinforced the efficacy of these values and generated a certain contempt for those who failed to display them. By contrast, the Old Guard remained uninterested in any attempt to appropriate middle-class (let alone genteel) American ways. On the contrary, their construction of what it meant to be black and Muslim sought to undermine the propriety of identifying with these by equating such identification with assimilating the ways of Unbelievers. On this approach, while they might pride themselves on a certain "doctrinal correctness," the Old Guard remained alienated from their indigenous American heritage and possessed of no indigenous cultural basis upon which to construct a religious identity. This would add significantly to their sense of identification with immigrant Muslims on whom they could rely to confirm their outward looking approach to Muslim-American identity-formation.

The disparity and competition between the Old Guard and Imām Wārithuddīn over the meaning of Islam and its relationship with America would find its *terminus ad quem* in the coming of the immigrants. Prior to the introduction of Immigrant Islam, there was no universally recognized Islamic authority that could arbitrate the conflicts and disagreements between the various Islamic and proto-Islamic groups. By dint of incumbency, however, immigrant Muslims would be immediately vaulted into this role. Unlike the various Blackamerican groups, no one could question their status as Muslims; for if they were not Muslims, who was? Almost immediately, this translated into the authority to sit in judgment over everyone in America who claimed to be Muslim. In the mid-1970s, when Imām Muhammad was still in the early stages of instituting the basic teachings and practices of Sunni orthodoxy (from the authority of Prophetic Sunna to the obligation to perform the five daily prayers) he and his movement would be the most vulnerable to this new, unassailable authority. But even the Old Guard would ultimately find themselves in a new position of dependency. For their recognition of the Qur'ān, the Sunna and Muslim tradition left them with no alternative but to recognize the added authority of those who could only be assumed to have superior knowledge of these. In the end, no group of Blackamericans who hoped to establish or sustain their status as Sunni Muslims would be able to sidestep the self-authenticating authority of Immigrant Islam. This would lead to the displacement of Black Religion as the unacknowledged though primary basis of legitimacy and religious authority, inaugurating the Third Resurrection in Blackamerican Islam.

Authority Half-Lost, Authority Half-Acquired

The introduction of Immigrant Islam into the collective space of Blackamerican Muslims resulted in the latter's loss of their interpretive voice as well as their monopoly over what had functioned as a bona fide, indigenous tradition of proto-Islamic and Islamic thought and exegesis. By the late 1970s, this tradition found itself rapidly receding in the face of approaches originating in the Muslim world. This was a pivotal development in American Islam, one that put Blackamerican Muslims at a marked disadvantage. From this point on, virtually every indigenous insight, proclivity or ambition would be impugned or marginalized via a *prima facie* presumption that all that was alien or meaningless to the immigrant Muslim was alien or meaningless to Islam.

Prior to the immigrant waves of the 1970s and 1980s, when Black Religion was the primary prism through which Blackamerican Muslims understood Islam, the meaning of being a Muslim was relatively simple. A man who had spent his entire adult life religiously aimless, womanizing, drinking, selling drugs, and committing violent crimes suddenly (or gradually) replaced these activities with acts of religiosity and moral rectitude. He changed his name, and his language underwent some modifications. He modified his dress and adjusted the way he carried himself. Endowed with this new Islamic outlook, he needed little instruction on how to function as a husband, a father, a son, or a neighbor. Nor did his commitment to racial justice and a dignified existence for Blackamericans require much re-thinking. For these were easily Islamicized by simply applying, *mutatis mutandis,* what he had always accepted as proper to these enterprises. His social ethic remained mildly conservative. His political orientation was mildly revolutionary. His cultural proclivities and tastes remained pretty much what they had always been, being tempered only by his understanding of the religion's ban on the most obvious forms of vice. As for his religious identity, he either chose what he imagined to be Islamic, borrowed whatever customs he may have happened upon from the Muslim world or carved this out of his indigenous heritage (which by the 1960s included a conspicuous African element). All of this was done, however, in a fashion that placed him, in his own mind, in a distinct and elevated position among his people, seldom taking him beyond what they recognized as the boundaries of the collective cultural fold. To be sure, as a Muslim, he remained ever aware of numerous aspects of his indigenous culture that were inconsistent with Islam. But only the most obvious and egregious of these were immediately discarded, the more benign and less obvious being tacitly tolerated and gradually transcended at a rate commensurate with his growth as a Muslim.

All of this changed, however, beginning in the 1970s. While this is not the place for an exhaustive demographic survey of Muslim immigration, a few well-known facts will help shed light on the scope and instrumentalities of immigrant hegemony and influence. First, the new waves of Muslims from overseas tended to settle in those major metropolitan areas of the United States that also boasted sizable concentrations of indigenous Muslims. In this regard, it has been asserted that roughly 70 percent of the American Muslim population was concentrated in ten states: California, New York, Illinois, New Jersey, Indiana, Michigan, Virginia, Texas, Ohio, and Maryland.[31] To this list must be added states such as Pennsylvania and Georgia, the Philadelphia Muslim community, for example, being among the most significant in the country. At any rate, these demographics facilitated direct interaction and shared space between immigrant and Blackamerican Muslims.

Second, the post-1965 immigrant population was dominated by students and professionals whose cumulative resources far outstripped those of their Blackamerican coreligionists. This provided the immigrant community with the ability to establish new and superior institutions. In 1963, a group of immigrant students founded the Muslim Students' Association (MSA). By the 1970s, the MSA would boast branches on college campuses throughout the United States.[32] Around 1975, the MSA established the North American Islamic Trust (NAIT) as its financial arm (which subsequently included AMANA Mutual Fund). By this time, moreover, the MSA had come to preside over several subsidiary organizations, including American Trust Publications, International Graphics Press, Islamic Book Service, The Islamic Teaching Center, American Muslim Scientists and Engineers (AMSE), American Muslim Social Scientists (AMSS), and the Islamic Medical Association (IMA).[33] In 1981, the MSA "gave birth" to what would become the parent organization of all of these, the Islamic Society of North America (ISNA). ISNA would add the Muslim Youth of North America (MYNA) as well as the Fiqh Council of North America, among other subsidiaries.[34]

ISNA would also be joined in its activities by a number of competing immigrant organizations, such as the Islamic Circle of North America (ICNA) and the Islamic Association of North America (IANA).[35] These were all national organizations that were dominated by Arabs and or Indo-Pakistanis, with visions that reflected their leadership's geographical and ideological roots in the Muslim world. Through annual conventions, monthly and quarterly magazines, building and establishing mosques and Islamic centers, and holding national and regional conferences, these organizations would provide a forum for the crystallization of immigrant Muslim thought, as the number of immigrant Muslims swelled to a critical mass and their native instincts, obsessions, and presuppositions found mutual support and a collective resonance. Moreover, given the scope, intensity, and level of their organizational activity, immigrant Muslims would acquire the ability to influence even Blackamerican Muslims who lay beyond their physical reach. Indeed, by the mid- to late 1980s, the rapid and staggering expansion of immigrant Muslim activity tended to dwarf, where it did not co-opt, that of Blackamerican Muslims.

Cumulatively, this would all evolve into a corporate will to re-create American Islam in the image of an idealized form of "back-home" Islam, more perfect, in fact, in America than it had been in any part of the Muslim world. This would be greatly facilitated, of course, by the aforementioned authority deficit in Blackamerican Islam and the long-standing association between Islam and the cultures and peoples of the Muslim world, an association that now translated into a proxy for bona fide religious knowledge. Armed with this authority and the influence garnered by their organizational activity, immigrant Muslims quickly introduced theological, juridical, and revivalist discourses that effectively banished native Blackamerican instincts and understandings to the periphery. As signatures of piety, the simple civic-minded rectitude of the folk proved no match for the ability to parrot revivalist, juridical, or theological doctrines or to invoke this or that Qur'ānic verse or Prophetic hadith—especially in Arabic! Indeed, among Blackamerican Muslims, the symbolism of growing a beard or donning Middle Eastern clothing (as markers of a commitment to a more authentic Islam) came close to burying the old folk piety and the pursuit of racial justice in the graveyard of "American *jāhilīya*," or pre-Islamic ignorance.

Meanwhile, "the West," as the primary preoccupation of culturally displaced immigrants, emerged as the new "counter-category," replacing white supremacy as the nemesis of American Islam. From this point on, almost everything from the Blackamerican Muslim's "tainted" Western past was rendered Islamically suspect. Almost all of the religious symbols and authoritative personalities in Blackamerican Islam would be replaced by substitutes from the Muslim world. Even a name like "Malcolm," which had to this point connoted Islam—or at least "Black Muslim"—now all but lost its Islamic connotation and resonance. For if it had stood as a symbol against white supremacy, it was now neither sufficiently identified with the traditions of the Muslim world nor emotive enough in its anti-Western resonance, "the West," not white supremacy, and perhaps not even Unbelief, now standing out in the popular American Muslim mind as the binary opposite of Islam.

All of this was accompanied by a palpable shift in the focus of the Blackamerican Muslim intellectual, social, and political agenda. Specifically American issues, such as police brutality, exploitation of blacks in the media and entertainment industry, the drug–prison complex, joblessness, education, urban violence and single parentage, Affirmative Action, or the wholescale criminalization of aspects of Blackamerican culture, were all suppressed by a single-minded focus on the problems of the Muslim world—Palestine, Kashmir, Egypt, Saudi Arabia, Afghanistan. Even where the overtly political problems of these countries were not the focal point, the intellectual fomentation of the region was, from the programs and translated writings of the *Ikhwān al-Muslimūn* (Muslim Brotherhood), to those of the *Jamāʿat-i-Islāmī* (Islamic Fellowship) to those of the *Salafī* movement.[36] With the exception of the tensions between the Old Guard, Imām Wārithuddīn Muhammad and the classical Nation of Islam (which have remained conspicuously civil), virtually all of the ideological rifts within the Blackamerican Muslim community have emerged as extensions of overseas divisions. Meanwhile, Blackamerican Christian writers of the period were producing titles like *Black Theology*,[37] *God of the Oppressed*,[38] *Prophesy Deliverance!: An Afro-American Revolutionary Christianity*,[39] *Race, Religion and the Continuing American Dilemma*.[40] All of this underscored the contrast between the ability of Blackamerican Christian thinkers to address Blackamerican concerns *as Christians* and the newly entrenched inability of Blackamerican Muslims to speak effectively to these concerns as Muslims.[41]

In all of this, however, perhaps the most lamentable development was the seemingly reversed effect that Islam was exerting on the pathologies and dysfunctionalities of the urban ghetto. Beyond the explicitly religious vices, for example, illicit sex or alcohol consumption, Islam was fast losing its significance as a fortifier of indigenous constructions of such values as manly pride, fiscal responsibility, or civic consciousness. Whereas under the "Islam" of the Honorable Elijah Muhammad, education, work, and community-uplift were synonymous with Black Muslim, Sunni Islam was increasingly being invoked as a reason *not* to work (for the infidel), *not* to be educated (in the infidel's institutions), and *not* to be involved in the (infidel) community. At least as far as the Old Guard was concerned, one could now almost assume that the stricter a Blackamerican Sunni Muslim adhered to Islam, the less educated, less gainfully employed and less civic-minded he or she was likely to be. In short, on the new, immigrant-influenced understanding of Islam, Sunnism was in many ways becoming a cause rather than a solution to the problem of Blackamerican Muslim dysfunctionality in America.

The Blackamerican Contribution

To be sure, Blackamerican Muslims were themselves complicit in this process of self-alienation. And there were at least five reasons for this, above and beyond the aforementioned authority deficit. First, Immigrant Islam's emphatically critical disposition vis-a-vis the West seemed from a distance to echo Black Religion's protest sentiment and its attitude toward white supremacy. The immigrant tendency to equate "Western" with "Unbelieving (*kāfir*)" both paralleled and vindicated the Blackamerican use of "white" as a synonym for "Unbeliever." This shared predisposition would lead Blackamerican Muslims to the expectation that their liberation and well-being would be included on the agenda of Immigrant Islam. For, if Palestine and Kashmir were bona fide Islamic concerns, why not police misconduct or Affirmative Action? In a similar fashion, Blackamerican Muslims saw in the immigrant critique of the dominant culture in America a more Islamically authentic basis upon which to construct an Muslim-American identity. This would apply more to the Old Guard than it did to the followers of Imām Muhammad. But even among the latter it would contribute to a mentality that increasingly equated the truly Islamic with the non-American. Glimpes of this can be seen in the change from bow-ties to skull caps, in the discarding of the long, white, women's MGT (Muslim Girl Trainer) uniforms and in such name changes as that from Wallace D. Mohammed to Imām W. Deen Muhammad to Imām Wārithuddin Muhammad.

Second, the overtly racist rhetoric of the Nation of Islam threatened to tarnish all Blackamerican Muslims, if not Islam itself, with the charge of racism. Throughout the preimmigrant era, non-Muslim America evinced an astounding inability to distinguish between a black Muslim, that is, a Sunni Muslim who is black, and a Black Muslim, that is, a member of the Nation of Islam. At the same time, most of America was unwilling or unable to recognize the difference between antiwhite racism and the pursuit of racial justice, taking refuge in a rhetoric of color blindness that accused those who spoke about race of exacerbating the problem. Because Blackamerican Sunnis wanted to be able to remain committed to the cause of racial justice without being associated with racism, they developed a desire to distance themselves from all racist overtones and associations. The ostensibly universalist, nonracialist rhetoric of Immigrant Islam (reinforced by the hugely diverse range of colors within that community) pointed to the latter as the perfect mechanism by which to avoid the stigma of racialism, continue the commitment to racial justice, and remain clearly identified with Islam.

Third, white American control over the creation of meaning and the possibilities of language in America has always translated into a certain openness, if not preference, among Blackamericans for extra-American intellectual homelands. Remaining intellectually bound to America has always meant to risk suffocating in the limited space allotted to Blackamerican self-discovery and expression. Going outside America, meanwhile, has always been seen as an effective means of circumventing or at least complicating the assimilationist versus rejectionist dichotomy that inevitably invades land-locked efforts at Blackamerican identity-formation.[42] More specifically, the East has traditionally represented the hope and expectation of coming into a relationship with others that is not defined by a master–slave syndrome, as obtained, for example, with King and Gandhi. Blackamericans have thus always expected self-discovery and expression to be more productive enterprises on the other side of the Atlantic.

Fourth, the rewards that rapidly accrued to those who could claim even the most tenuous connection to the Muslim world and its religious authority were simply too great to resist. Blackamerican students who flocked to the Middle East only to flunk out of seminaries or to go no further than the language requirements for admission returned (often in full "regalia") to positions of honor and respect, if not actual leadership. Indeed, a year (or even less) abroad, in *any* Muslim country (Arabic speaking or not), could offset completely the would-be negative implications of having barely graduated from high school or having never held down a steady job. In short, the "new" criterion engendered by the identification with Immigrant Islam provided a way for many of the less-accomplished to bypass traditional American paths to economic and social status, allowing them to cloak failure and the rejection of time-honored standards of social, interpersonal, and economic responsibility in the guise of religious commitment. In the end, the success rate of Blackamericans who ventured abroad to acquire the Islamic religious sciences turned out to be disappointingly low. As such, even if by the late 1980s almost every major U.S. city was home to a contingent of Blackamerican Muslims studying abroad, scholars who were capable of getting the Islamic religious sciences to speak effectively to their realities as Blackamericans were the exceptions rather than the rule.

Finally, if the rewards of pursuing the new authority were too great for some (i.e., the Old Guard) to resist, the liabilities attaching to such an enterprise proved too risky for others. The traditional Islamic sciences had rarely been used to empower Blackamerican Muslims. Rather, they had been routinely deployed as instruments for bludgeoning them into conformity. As a result, especially among those who descended from the Nation of Islam, there developed a sense that any attempt to gain authority on the new criterion would render one a permanent follower of immigrant, Old Guard, or overseas masters. This fear of domination translated into to a palpable diffidence if not aversion towards the traditional Islamic sciences. Thus, while the followers of Imām Wārithuddīn Muhammad remain today among the most accomplished in terms of secular education, they have had little or no representation among those recognized as being versed in the traditional Islamic religious sciences.

In sum, the cumulative result of the early encounter between Blackamerican Muslims and Immigrant Islam was a truncated transition from the old authority to the new. The old authority of the simple folk piety and the protest against white supremacy was effectively abandoned (*de jure* if not *de facto*) in exchange for a half-acquired, ersatz authority ostensibly grounded in historical Islam. This new authority in Blackamerican hands was "soft" in that it had been acquired largely through association rather than true learning. It was "derivative" (as opposed to original) in that those who purported to have it seldom ventured beyond what they understood to be acceptable to their overseas and immigrant patrons. Finally, it was functionally "counterfeit" in that its utility was limited almost exclusively to the Blackamerican community, where it tended, again, to confirm the immigrant perspective and ignore native concerns and aspirations. Reminiscent of Blyden's African Christians, Blackamerican would-be possessors of this new authority quietly acquiesced to the idea that they had "nothing [new] to say which foreigners would care to hear."[43] They would be unable, as such, to turn the problems of the inner city into bona fide *Islamic* priorities. And, they would be unable to insulate the positive features of their black, American heritage from the hostile reflexes of an Immigrant Islam whose ideological posture towards "the West" was one of confrontation.

The importance of the Great Muslim Migrations of the 1970s and 1980s, as well as the dislocations they engendered, cannot be overstated. The counterexample of Minister Louis Farrakhan is most instructive in this regard. Minister Farrakhan refused to make the transition to historical Islam en route to a Third Resurrection. Instead, he decided to remain with his Second Resurrection in which capacity he continued to authenticate his movement on the basis of classical Black Religion. While, on the one hand Minister Farrakhan failed to gain unanimous admission into the sanctum of Sunni orthodoxy, on the other hand one could argue that his very distance from the new authority enabled him to preserve enough political capital among Blackamericans at large to be able to spearhead the historic 1995 Million Man March in Washington, D.C. Similarly, his refusal to recognize immigrant and overseas authority afforded him enough intellectual confidence and independence to mount a constructive and relevant critique of the American social and political order, to a large extent summarized in his *The National Agenda: Public Policy*

Issues, Analyses, and Programmatic Plan of Action 2000–2008,[44] which, however flawed, has not been replicated by any Blackamerican Sunni. Indeed, among Blackamericans recognized as having any affiliation with Islam in America, Minister Farrakhan remains the only figure who has any significant presence in American public discourse.

The Immigrant Contribution: History, His Story, and Post-Colonial Religion

Yet, Blackamerican complicity in the establishment of the aforementioned régime of religion-based domination neither exonerates immigrant Muslims nor diminishes their contribution. Even if most immigrants never actively pursued this development, they were clearly and consciously its beneficiaries who made little or no effort to overturn it. Like Blyden's foreign missionaries to Africa, they entertained a strong sense of ownership over Islam, which endowed them with an equally strong paternalistic spirit. Like earlier European Christian immigrants to America, they arrived deeply suspicious of American ways and convinced that their religion could be properly understood and conveyed only by those versed in their native language and culture.[45] This not only ensured limited diffusion of religious authority outside immigrant circles, it effectively rendered immigrant status a proxy for bona fide religious learning. As such, even where it could not be assumed that an Arab or Indo-Pakistani had mastered the Islamic religious sciences, the fact that he or she hailed from a Muslim country was nearly just as dispositive. In the end, this benignly tolerated—if not consciously preserved—association between ethnicity and religious knowledge was crucial in sustaining the immigrant monopoly over Islamic religious authority in America.

Yet, beneath this association between ethnicity and religious authority lay the reality that Immigrant Islam was no less informed by the vision and sentiments of what I shall call "Post-Colonial Religion" than Blackamerican Islam had been informed by Black Religion. Like Black Religion, Post-Colonial Religion is not revealed but a product of history. At its core lies not so much a body of texts or interpretive tradition as does a particular historical *experience* from which its followers desperately seek redemption. It is ultimately this quest for redemption that determines priorities and provides the prism through which the revealed sources are "interpreted." In this capacity, Post-Colonial Religion is psychologically linked to what Arnold Toynbee once referred to as the "Ghost of Empire," that inner voice that incessantly highlights the disparity between a fallen present and a powerful and glorious past. Post-Colonial Religion seeks first and foremost to reverse the sociocultural and psychological influences of the West, either by seizing political power as a means of redirecting society or through an ideological rejection of all perceived influences of the West. Where these options are deemed undesirable or unattainable, the influence of the West is essentially overcome by denying the alien provenance of would-be Western influences, affirming in the process the complete compatibility between Islam and the dominant culture in the West.[46] While these various strains of Post-Colonial Religion may appear on the surface to contradict each other, they are all ultimately united in constituting reactions to the West that are driven by the need for redemption.

Immigrant Muslims may have been adept at concealing or inept at recognizing the impact of Post-Colonial Religion on their understanding of Islam, but this did not render this orientation any less operative. Beyond this, however, the immigrant claim to greater authority in defining American Islam was not simply a claim to greater knowledge of the Qur'ān and Sunna. This was a claim, rather, that insinuated that: (1) *as Easterners* their understanding of Islam was superior because it was less contaminated (and ideally uncontaminated) by the germ of Western civilization; and (2) the interpretive perspectives and presuppositions engendered by the history of the Muslim world were more legitimate than those generated by the history of Blackamericans. In other words, the *history* of the modern Muslim world was assumed to be more important, to be more Islamically probative, and to have a greater claim to be the proper object of Muslim religious thought and effort. The reason for this—and this is the crux of the matter—was that only by reversing the losses inflicted *upon the Muslim world* could Muslims under the influence of Post-Colonial Religion find true redemption. From this psychological posture, the realities of other Muslim communities could not be treated directly but only analogously on the basis of conclusions reached in contemplation of the situation in the Muslim world.

And yet, the history of the modern Muslim world was far from either "pure" or unadulterated. It included, *inter alia*, brutal Western colonialism, staggering poverty and economic backwardness, widespread illiteracy, artificial national boundaries and thus artificial nationalities, intransigent social and class stratification, gross scientific and technological dependency, an ossified and embattled religious and intellectual tradition, and the unprecedented centralization of state apparatuses presided over by autocratic, dictatorial rulers and corrupt, inefficient bureaucracies. All of this was consummated by the ultimate "set-back (*naksah*)" in the establishment of the Jewish state of Israel. These bitter experiences gave rise to a number of situation-specific responses, the majority of which were as informed by need-born pragmatism and Third World notions of anti-imperialism and national liberation as they were by Islam. In fact, up until the middle of the twentieth century, the most influential Muslim responses were not at all connected to Islam but grounded in various Western imports, such as nationalism, communism, socialism, or secularism. Meanwhile, reforms in education and the steady influx of foreign cultural norms—especially among the educated and the elite—led to deep and abiding transformations in the collective psyche of the Muslim world. As a result, just as upwardly mobile blacks in America are often an exaggeration of their white counterparts, educated classes in the Muslim world evolved into some of the biggest defenders of the dominant culture in the West and the harshest critics of those aspects of Islam deemed offensive by that culture. All of this reflected, again, not a new reality but one that had been in the making for nearly two centuries, since the landing of Napolean in Egypt and of the British in India. From that time, even if Western influences could be modified or appropriated, they could neither be stopped nor fully reversed. Thus, as early as the 1930s, the Egyptian thinker Ṭaha Ḥusayn would openly affirm the European roots of the modern Egyptian self and insist that Arab culture, if it was to flourish, would have to become more Western.[47] By the 1960s, the Iranian intellectual, Jalāl Āl-e Ahmad (a Marxist revert to Islam) would declare the entire Muslim world to be in a state of "West-struckness."[48]

To be sure, the rise of Islamic Revivalism, beginning in the 1960s, would pose a serious challenge to this situation and constitute a major turning point in modern Muslim history. But while there can be no doubt that these movements were dedicated to Islam, there can also be no doubt that they inherited much of the accumulated intellectual and emotional baggage bequeathed by these secular ideologies and this early encounter with the modern West. Thus, for example, the monopoly over law making assumed by the modern nation–state, in contradistinction to classical Islam, is unanimously accepted by Muslim Revivalists of all stripes and subsumed unto to their concept of "the Islamic state." Similarly, masters of the classical Tradition evince a certain preference for the title "doctor" over the title "*shaykh.*" In short, far from being "pure," the modern Muslim world, like the Muslim movements it has produced, is an amalgamation of Islamic, Third World, and Western ideas and values. All of this, in varying degrees, would be subsumed into the culture and religious understanding of immigrant Muslims and invoked against the presumed naiveté of their Blackamerican co-religionists.

Class and Color: Toward and Away from American Whiteness

Religion, however, was not the only (and in many instances, not even the most important) factor in the immigrant–Blackamerican encounter. Class and color would also collude to endow these two groups with conflicting polarities, most particularly regarding their relationship to American whiteness. As intimated earlier, most Muslims who came to America after 1965 came from the educated classes in the Muslim world. This endowed them with a certain cultural perspective that was indexed into the dominant civilization of the West, primarily in its European manifestation. The ability the speak French or English, for example, was both a symbol of class and "culture" and the *sine qua non* of upward mobility. So ingrained was this orientation that even as anti-Western a figure as Sayyid Quṭb (the radical chief ideologue of the Muslim Brotherhood) would reveal signs of its influence. In one of his letters dating from the 1950s in which he reflects on his experiences in America, Quṭb rails against the Americans' delight in a most insufferable "noise" they referred to as jazz (which, according to him, had been "invented by blacks in order to satisfy their primitive inclinations").[49] He praises, on the other hand, opera, ballet, and classical music as "high art (*al-fann al-rāqī*)."[50] None of the latter are products of Muslim culture. Yet, they constitute for Quṭb the artistic standard to which modern civilization is to be held.

On the other hand, Quṭb reveals a dimension of the influence of the West on the modern Muslim world that immigrant Muslims tend to play down but that Quṭb, as a radical Islamist, loudly decries. I am speaking here of the extolling of whiteness. Writing again from the perspective of his experience in America, this time reflecting on the maladies of his home-land, Quṭb declares,

> the goal of education among us must be to rid ourselves of the influences of the white man, not only politically and economically, but socially and on the level of thought and feeling as well. . . . Unfortunately, what we do in fact is the exact opposite. Our ministry of education is occupied by men who are slaves to the white man, slaves who worship him as if he were God. Nay, while they commit blasphemy against God, they would never commit blasphemy against America or Europe, openly or in private. Our teachers' colleges, whose graduates will influence generations upon generations, are filled with pathetic human beings who look upon the white man with sanctification while they shape the feelings of those who will themselves become teachers only to extol and sanctify (the white man).[51]

This pre-existing predisposition towards whiteness would reinforce the parallel impetus found among virtually every immigrant group that has come to America, namely the will to join American whiteness. Indeed, so powerful has this enticement been that the initial exclusion of Jews, Slavs, Armenians, Syrians, Irishmen, and others would only result in a redoubling of efforts to gain admission rather than oppose white supremacy on substantive or moral grounds. Upon gaining that admission, these "nouveau whites" tended to follow the pattern of ardently promoting and defending the false universals of white supremacy, as if these were their own and had actually originated with them. To be sure, as lamentable as this may be from a moral standpoint, it is tactically understandable. As Richard Dyer notes in his book *White*,

> Because whiteness carries such rewards and privileges, the sense of a border that might be crossed and a hierarchy that might be climbed has produced a dynamic that has enthralled people who have had any chance of participating in it.[52]

This proclivity on the part of immigrant Muslims inevitably pushes them and Blackamericans in opposite directions, the former towards American whiteness, as an ideal, a model, and a marker of privilege, the latter away from it, as the repository of a set of false universals that ultimately penalize them for being black. It is noteworthy, however, that in their pursuit of privilege, immigrant Muslims managed to separate whiteness from Westernness. This legitimated, on the one hand, their positive phototaxis toward the former, while allowing them to remain negatively predisposed (at least rhetorically) to the latter. Initially blind to the implications of this move, Blackamerican Muslims would ultimately come to understand that one could neither be anti-Western nor "nouveau white" without on some level being negatively predisposed towards American blackness.

The Immigrant Impact Between Modern and Modernized Islam

The majority of immigrant Muslims did not come to America with the aim of establishing or spreading Islam. Their primary aim was to find a better material life. Typically, however, just as blackness (or Negritude) provided a basis of unity and identity for disparate crowds of displaced Africans, Islam increasingly came to represent (especially following the 1979 Islamic revolution in Iran and the rise of Muslim Revivalism) a quiet source of pride and a basis of identity to offset their sociocultural alienation in the New World. This "attraction" to Islam divided the immigrant community into three basic types: (1) "cultural/ethnic Muslims," who tend to be more educated and nonpracticing (in terms of prayer, etc.) but not atheist; they constitute perhaps the shrinking majority; (2) "folk Muslims," who include highly educated individuals who are both religious and practicing but not doctrinaire; these are the people who tend to dominate Muslim political organizations and executive boards of mosques and Islamic centers; and (3) doctrinaire Muslims, who are religious, practicing, and doctrinaire; they tend to dominate the religious (as opposed to the organizational) leadership of mosques.

Specifically religious authority (as opposed to social or other types of authority) resides primarily with the doctrinaire. As such, the general thrust of the move to religion is from a cultural/ethnic expression to a more doctrinaire one. This invariably privileges movements and ideologies from the Muslim world. Indeed, Immigrant Islam derives its authority precisely from its implicit claim of fidelity to these movements.

Modern Islam

In terms of reliance on movements and ideologies from the Muslim world, Immigrant Islam can be divided into two main divisions: Modern and Modernized. Modern Islam preceded Modernized Islam to America and its adherents far outnumber those of the latter. Modern Islam is represented by two main orientations: Islamism and Neofundamentalism.[53]

(1) *Islamism*: This is the approach commonly referred to as "Political Islam." Its distinctive feature is its emphatic preoccupation with moving beyond theological *cum* juridical casuistry and simple piety to issues of power and politics. Spawned in large part by tyrannical and dictatorial régimes in the Muslim world that use their power to thwart and persecute Muslim activists, Islamism sees the acquisition of political power as the *sine qua non* of successful societal reform. Reform is necessary, of course, because the societies of the Muslim world have veered from the Islamic ideal. As we shall see, contrary to the ubiquitous American stereotype, this ideal is located not in the distant medieval past but in Islamist ruminations over the meaning of Islam in the modern world. In America the most influential Islamists hail from or are influenced by the Muslim Brotherhood (*Ikhwān al-Muslimūn*), the Islamic Fellowship (*Jamāʿat-i-Islāmī*), and, albeit to a much lesser extent, the Liberation Party (*Ḥizb al-Taḥrīr*).

(2) *Neofundamentalism*:[54] This designation refers to those who tend to reject the more politicized agenda of the Islamists, on the one hand, and the "intellectualism" of the premodern classical Tradition, on the other. In contradistinction to the Islamists, their approach to reforming Muslim society is through purifying and reforming religious beliefs and practices through direct (and often scathing) analysis and critique. Their vigilance in monitoring belief and practice, alongside their commitment to modeling the proper way and

showing that they practice what they preach, has resulted in a set of "symbolic" doctrines and practices that set them off from "less scrupulous" Muslims. Their attitude toward other Muslims is far less conciliatory than that of the Islamists. And they show little interest in Muslim ecumenicism or unity. They are generally literalist in orientation, but not exclusively so. And they are extremely hostile towards any mystical tendencies, especially those associated with Sufism. In America, the most influential Neofundamentalists hail from or are influenced by the Salafī movement.[55]

Islamism and Neofundamentalism were both born in and are products of the modern world. As a consequence, both are characterized by two love–hate relationships. One is with the West, which they simultaneously imitate and castigate. The other is with the classical Tradition, which they simultaneously attack and seek to appropriate. It is essentially this love–hate relationship that the French scholar Olivier Roy has in mind when he writes of the proponents of Modern Islam,

> By rejecting a Westernization that is already in place, they express the myth of authenticity in a borrowed, inauthentic language. For they borrow from this modernity the refusal to return to the real tradition in the name of an imaginary Tradition.[56]

This issue of creating and substituting contrived for authentic Tradition is a very serious one. For it is precisely through this appeal to Tradition that Islamism and Neofundamentalism are able to bolster and sustain their authority among Blackamerican Muslims.

Yet, on close examination, these representations of Tradition show clear signs of selective amplification and suppression. Even the Salafīs, who are most insistent in restricting doctrine and practice to scripture and authentic precedent, fail to conceal completely the synthetic element in their constructions. While they emphatically invoke the model of the Pious Ancestors, they cannot conceal the fact that the latter were not unanimous in all they believed or practiced. For example, the Pious Ancestor, Ibn Khuzaymah (d. 311/924), records disagreement among the Companions Ibn ʿAbbās, Anas b. Mālik, Abū Dharr, and the Prophet's wife Āʾishah over whether the Prophet actually saw God during his lifetime.[57] Yet, no Salafī would accept this as an "excuse" for a contemporary Muslim to claim that the Prophet saw God. Similarly, in his *Book of Consensus*, Ibn al-Mundhir (d. 318/930) catalogued all the views on which the religious scholars up until his time had agreed. This book amounted, however, to only a single installment of barely 130 pages of proper text.[58] Meanwhile, his contemporary, the famous jurist and exegete, Ibn Jarīr al-Ṭabarī (d. 310/923) wrote a book cataloguing all the *disagreements* among the religious scholars, and this work fell into several hefty volumes, originally some 3,000 pages in length![59] Clearly, if the Pious Ancestors entertained this much disagreement among themselves, the neat composites invoked by the Salafīs must be more the product of their synthesis than it is a reflection of the way of the Pious Ancestors. As such, their call to *go back* to the Tradition of the Pious Ancestors must amount in many instances to little more than a call to *come over* to contemporary Salafī constructions. Indeed, it may be far more contemporary Salafī constructions of Tradition than Tradition itself that hates the present and sees itself as the arch-rival of modernity.

Modern Islam also borrows from the modern West the latter's universalism, according to which only that which is universally true can be true at all, and that which is true (or useful) must also be "Islamic." Among Salafīs, this is manifested in the surfeited and overinclusive use of the concept of "unsanctioned innovation (*bidʿa*)," as the proscriber of all that was not embraced and allegedly handed down by the Pious Ancestors. Among Islamists, it appears in the increased use of the neologism "Islamic," by which we get such hybrids as "Islamic culture," "Islamic architecture," or even "Islamic traffic"![60] Both of these tendencies go beyond the simple preference for institutions that are based on scripture and or authentic Tradition, a preference shared by all committed Muslims. These tendencies are, rather, mechanisms for converting the choices and preferences (including imported choices and preferences!) of the contemporary Muslim world into normative if not binding religious institutions for Muslims everywhere. At bottom, both of these conversion mechanisms mask a deep and abiding obsession with issues of identity, according to which the compromising or shedding of an Eastern identity (or the taking on or retaining of a Western one) is equated with a loss or compromise of religion.

Related to this universalism and the use of the categories *bidʿa* and "Islamic" is Modern Islam's diffidence *cum* hostility towards culture. The problem with culture is that it is all too human, mired, as it were, in the specificities of human history. Islam, on the other hand, inasmuch as it is true, is wholly transcendent and directly revealed from God *in all its aspects and institutions.* On this understanding, Islam must be both unchanging and invariable across time and space. Thus, we find Islamists pressing the neologism "Islamic" into overtime, in order to be able to accommodate all manners of foreign, secular culture. Art, literature, or intellectual endeavors deemed necessary or desirable become "Islamic art," "Islamic literature," or "Islamic sociology." Neofundamentalists, on the other hand, reject, at least in theory, not only the alien products of the unbelieving West but also what they consider to be the cultural accretions of premodern Muslim civilization. For them, only those cultural expressions that can be identified with the Tradition of the Prophet and the Pious Ancestors of the first three centuries or so (e.g., archery, Arabic poetry) can be sanctioned as truly legitimate, and these ideally in their premodern forms.

In the end, Modern Islam is left with an extremely cramped aesthetic, on one side of which lie the "accretions" of premodern Muslim civilization, on the other side of which lies the hegemonic and youth-corrupting pop culture of the West. In its attempt to insulate itself from all of this, Modern Islam takes refuge in the position that the only model of behavior for a Muslim—at all times—is the devotional one. On this understanding, the entire space between the home and the mosque—the space for leisure activity, recreation, cultural production, and social interaction—is viewed and experienced as a threat. The result is a social order that consists of almost nothing but "don'ts."[61] For Blackamerican Muslims, the effects of this "culture phobia" have been triply catastrophic. First, artistic expression has always functioned as a substitute for freedom for Blackamericans, given their historical association of work with subjugation and bondage: "God made de world, and de white folks made work."[62] Second, suppression of Blackamerican creative energy severely jeopardizes the possibilities for the development of a cultural expression of American Islam that is a product of and is at home *in the West*. Given the decline and insularity of the cultures of the Muslim world, not to mention their prudishness, which is often mistaken for piety, these cultures are of limited portability and stand little chance of gaining mass appeal in the West. Finally, for Blackamerican Muslims to cease, even in the name of Islam, to be contributors to the broader Blackamerican culture is both to weaken their relationship with the Blackamerican community and to deny them a role in the production and shaping of America's most seductive export: pop culture. In this context, the absence of Muslims from the Blackamerican cultural scene shows itself to have serious implications both domestically *and* globally.[63]

Underscoring all of the above is Modern Islam's sustained diffidence toward the tradition of exegesis and jurisprudence established by the classical jurists. On the one hand, Islamists routinely point (correctly) to traditional scholars' accommodationism and traditional jurisprudence's neglect of matters of vital importance to the modern Islamic state, for example, taxation, the national economy, the political process, the scope and structure of government, etc. Classical jurisprudence, according to them, not only fails to address these issues but effectively impedes the ability of modern Muslims to do so, being steeped as it is in a formal logic and a social reality far removed from modern experience. On the other hand, at least in an American context, the classical

Tradition and the religious clerics are the pride of the immigrant Muslim. In fact, they are the reason his religion can be faithfully conveyed only by those who are at home in his native language and culture.

And yet, even as it nurses this deep ambivalence towards the classical Tradition, Modern Islam strives mightily to appropriate the latter. It is untrue, as some claim,[64] that Islamists and Neofundamentalists completely reject classical Islamic law (*fiqh*) and jurisprudence (*uṣūl al-fiqh*). What is true, however, is that both Islamists and Neofundamentalists are driven by a results-oriented thinking by which the validity of the classical theory is judged and made subservient to their Post-Colonial "vision of the truly Islamic." At bottom, this "vision," rather than any independent theory of jurisprudence or scriptural hermeneutic, determines the possibilities of Islam. And the absence of an independent theory of interpretation makes it impossible for "outsiders" to validate their views independently. Rather, only those who share the Islamist and Neofundamentalist "vision of the truly Islamic," which is far more historically than scripturally determined, can earn their recognition. This, more than anything else, reduces Blackamerican Muslims to a state of precarious dependency. For, even if they were to master the *putative* sources of Islam, they would be destined to remain the protegés of others when it came to the *real* sources of acceptable doctrine.

Given all of the above, it is clear that Modern Islam, in its present state, is incapable of transferring religious authority outside itself. Only its carriers can have any real control over its substance or direction. As such, Modern Islam can neither promote nor accommodate the indigenization of Islam in America. For indigenization in any context is a thoroughly indigenous enterprise. But, the only way that indigenous Muslims could acquire the requisite authority under Modern Islam would be to accept the latter's historically (pre)determined "vision of the truly Islamic." And this would mean accepting the polarity and status of American cultures and legacies assigned to it by Modern Islam. In this capacity, Modern Islam can only function as an instrument of religion-based domination for Blackamerican Muslims.

Modernized Islam

As for Modernized Islam, it may be described as the classical Tradition of Muslim law, jurisprudence, and theology ostensibly calibrated to the realities of modern times. In contradistinction to Modern Islam, Modernized Islam is a true genetic descendent of the classical schools of thought, the so-called *madhhabs*.[65] Among the tools and characteristics it inherited from the latter are a highly sophisticated tradition of jurisprudence and hermeneutics and a thorough commitment to intrareligious pluralism. It was this jurisprudential and interpretive tradition that chaperoned the early spread of Islam into non-Muslim lands. By separating essentials from coincidentals, the early carriers of Islam were able to accommodate the "harmless customs and prejudices" of the various non-Muslim peoples. At the same time, classical Islam's commitment to intrareligious pluralism prevented the commitment to "unity" from degenerating into a campaign to impose uniformity. Having established an independent theory of interpretation (the so-called *uṣūl al-fiqh*) upon which it conferred the authority to validate any view that could show integrity thereto, all views so validated were admitted, *ceteris paribus*, into the sanctum of "orthodoxy." And, because this classical theory was equally accessible to all Muslims, there was rarely a period in premodern Islam during which religious authority did not transfer in a timely fashion.

Classical Islam also avoided the trap of universalism into which Modern Islam has fallen by committing itself primarily to a *legal* rather than a *theological/philosophical* discourse. Legal discourses deal in concretes and are guided by the question "What should be done given a specific context and a specific set of facts?" Theological/philosophical discourses deal in abstract universals and are guided by the question "What is the universal and permanent truth of the matter?" Legal discourses can accommodate change and difference across space and time. Thus, jurists in Yemen or Timbuktu could openly recognize that what they sanctioned as legitimate might be legitimately proscribed by jurists in Cairo or Nishapur. Theological/philosophical discourses, meanwhile, can only accommodate change and difference by asserting the categorical incorrectness of the previous or competing view. Either quantum or Einsteinian physics, the philosophy of Derrida or that of Foucault, Process Theology or Traditional Christian Theology can be correct. All cannot be simultaneously correct.

Perhaps these differences between Modern and Modernized Islam can be best demonstrated through a concrete example. The following is a question posed by an immigrant Muslim living in the United States to a Modernized traditional scholar in the Muslim world. The question includes the petitioner's original thinking, which reflects a "vision of the truly Islamic" commonly invoked by Immigrant Islam. More importantly, it shows the manner in which this "vision" is passed off as the full range of legitimate options for American Muslims desirous of a properly constituted Islamic life. The response, on the other hand, exemplifies the approach of Modernized Islam, albeit in one of its more enlightened manifestations:

> We are among the Arab Muslims who have lived in North America for a number of years. God the Exalted has blessed us to be involved in Islamic work dealing with Muslims of all nationalities, colors and classes. Among us are Arabs; and among us are Indians and Pakistanis; among us are Malaysians and Africans; and among us are Americans, both black and white. From time to time, we are confronted with questions for which there is no precedent in our Arab and Muslim lands. Many of these questions are asked by our American brothers and sisters. And some of these are connected with the issue of sexual relations between men and women, including things that are common to this environment and have become a part of this people's lives and are deeply ingrained in their customs. Among these are such questions as (the permissibility of) stripping completely naked when having sex, or (the permissibility of) a man looking at his wife's private parts or a wife looking at her husband's. There are other questions of this nature which we are too embarrassed to mention publicly, including questions about various means of arousing a man or a woman sexually, it apparently being the case that widespread explicitness, nudity and promiscuity has brought a certain frigidity upon this people who now need arousers or aphrodisiacs that we have no need for in our Arab and Muslim lands. Now, it had been our habit to respond to these questions by flatly proscribing and forbidding (all of these things), based on what had settled in our minds in the way of statements and traditions which we heard largely from popular preachers as opposed to religious scholars (back in our Arab and Muslim lands). But some of the brothers mentioned that they had heard from you during some of your visits to America in which you responded to similar questions at conferences and private meetings a view that contradicts our response. Thus, we would like to confirm this with you directly and to know your opinion regarding these matters, backed up with proofs from the Qur'ān and Sunna.[66]

This petition bears all the markings of Modern Islam in America. The tradition of "Arab and Muslim lands" is conceived of as the normative code for Muslims everywhere. The purported sexual habits and customs of the Americans, on the other hand, are the result of the corruptive influences of Hollywood and the fashion industry (signatures of the West). As such, they are accorded no presumption of legitimacy whatever. Meanwhile, no proof and no method of validation is provided to the original American petitioners.

Rather, if they are to conduct themselves as good Muslims, they must simply reject their own tradition and accept, on faith, what is presented in its stead as Islamic. For its part, the classical Tradition plays no role in the initial response. It is only appealed to subsequently in order to validate that response and protect the religious authority of the immigrant would-be teachers. At the same time, these teachers are unwilling to accept from the Modernized cleric what they expect their American disciples to accept from them, namely answers unaccompanied by proof. In the end, one can only wonder if the cleric's response was actually communicated to the American Muslims.

In his response, the Modernized cleric begins by referring the questioners to a previous writing he had published, affirming that Islam does not view sex as some sort of "handiwork of Satan." He points out that the classical books of exegesis, hadith, law, and literature are full of references to sex, and none of the religious scholars ever took offense to this. He goes on to affirm that, as Islam is a religion for all races, classes, places, and times, the habits, tastes, and customs of no one people, "such as the Arabs or the Easterners," can dictate its rulings. Otherwise, one would "make difficult what the religious law has made easy and forbid people from partaking of that which the religious law allows." Moreover, the books and statements of popular preachers should never be taken as sources for religious rulings. For these invariably contain statements that are baseless and tend towards embellishment, exaggeration, and instruction through emotional and psychological intimidation. Finally, when consulting the writings of the traditional schools of law, one should not simply rush to the most stringent view. Rather, and this is especially true when dealing with the newly converted, one should seek the most accommodating view, since, as far as substance is concerned, this view is not necessarily any less valid than the more stringent view.

Turning more directly to the specifics of the question, the cleric agrees that a Western society like America may embrace sexual habits and customs—perhaps as a result of overexposure, as suggested by the questioner—which Muslims of the East frown upon or hold in contempt. This, however, does not provide a legitimate basis for declaring these to be forbidden. Rather, to do the latter, one must have sound proof from the Qur'ān or authentic Sunna. Otherwise, according to the agreed-upon principle of classical jurisprudence, the presumed status of all actions is "permissible until proven otherwise." Regarding the question at hand, he notes, "There are no sound, explicit texts (of the Qur'ān or Sunna) that would indicate that this manner of interaction among spouses is forbidden." This, he concludes, is the opinion that he had always expressed during his visits to mosques and conferences in America.[67]

For our purposes, two important points emerge from this pronouncement.

First, it demonstrates Modernized Islam's putative ability to accommodate non-Muslim cultural and civilizational habits and institutions. Second, the mechanism by which this is achieved is theoretically independent and open to all. *Any* Muslim with requisite knowledge of the Qurʾān, Sunna, and classical jurisprudence could produce religiously authoritative opinions. As such, Blackamerican Muslims who demonstrate such knowledge could produce opinions that were just as authoritative as the one imported from this Modernized Middle Eastern traditional scholar.

Herein lies the great promise of Modernized Islam. In contradistinction to Modern Islam, Modernized Islam is portable in a manner that is capable of: (1) approaching, in a culturally neutral fashion, habits and customs that are new or alien to Muslim experience; and (2) transferring religious authority from carrier to target group.

Yet, even Modernized Islam, in its American manifestation, poses a number of very serious problems for Blackamerican Muslims. First, the entire edifice of Modernized Islam is grounded in a medieval social order that was highly stratified and dedicated to the principle that religious knowledge was not accessible to everyone but was the preserve of a chosen elite. This was a society in which both literacy and access to books were severely limited, in contradistinction to modern (especially Western) societies, where mandatory education and easy access to books (and now the Internet) endows even the masses with a certain autodidactic spirit and the belief that religious knowledge is open to all. Modernized scholars in the West also tend towards a certain romanticism that portrays the classical Tradition as an unattainable ideal for most mortals. American-born scholars who have studied this tradition are often even more romantic and confirm the view that only those who were born into it, particularly Arabs, can ever master it to the point of justifiably claiming any authority. These scholars rarely speak or act with independence but tend to see and present themselves as pupils of their overseas teachers. Rather than contribute to the efficacy and empowerment of American Muslims and enhance their ability to indigenize Islam, Modernized American scholars often speak and act in ways that undermine their countrymen's confidence and reduce them to accepting the ascendancy of their overseas and immigrant brethren.

Second, Modernized Islam tends to be overly academic and removed from the problems and sentiments of the folk. In contradistinction to Modern Islam—and this is one of the latter's major draws—it is manifestly short on what Reinhold Niebuhr referred to as the "right dogmas, symbols, and emotionally powerful oversimplifications."[68] Even more so than its Modern counterpart, Modernized Islam tends to view the legacy of white supremacy and racial terror as the special property of Blackamericans rather than as part of the social, political, and psychological history of America as a whole. This enables it to identify with a sanitized version of the dominant culture and to convert its own mechanisms for accommodating non-Muslim ways into a tool of domestication and accommodationism. On this conversion, appeasing and deflecting the criticisms of the dominant group become far more urgent than addressing the concerns of the Muslim folk. And rather than confront America's social, economic, or political injustices, not to mention her racial domination, Modernized Islam tends to dance around these through juridical agnosia and an almost childish commitment to a hyperbolized pluralism, according to which there are rarely any *right* answers (that spawn commitment and action) only *acceptable* ones (that merely require recognition). This, to borrow the observation of one critic (in another context) translates into the perfect ideology for the bourgeois mind; for "[s]uch pluralism makes a genial confusion in which one tries to enjoy the pleasures of difference without ever committing oneself to any particular vision of resistance, liberation and hope."[69]

Finally, by virtue of its situatedness in the modern Muslim world—still the cradle of Traditional Muslim learning—Modernized Islam has not always been able to avoid the influences of Modern Islam. As such, it too has been known to succumb to Post-Colonial Religion's "vision of the truly Islamic," on the basis of which it proffers juridical opinions that it falsely presents as being both universally binding and the result of an objective application of classical theory. Given the continued ideological dependency of Modernized American Muslims on the Muslim world, this influence detracts significantly from the "independence" of Modernized Islam's interpretive methodology. This is why Blackamerican Muslims are often fearful of Modernized Islam and its traditional schools of law. For appealing to the schools of law is often the means through which certain immigrant and overseas prejudices and preferences are disguised and placed beyond critique.[70]

Blackamerican and Immigrant Islam: The Quest for a Shared Historical Consciousness

When Blackamerican Muslims first encountered Immigrant Islam, a major factor facilitating the latter's acceptance was its critical posture towards the West and the latter's legacy of domination. Blackamerican Muslims read into this critique their own indictment of the dominant hegemony in America. What they would discover, however, is that not only was their opposition to white supremacy not the same as immigrant resentment of Western domination, but that opposition to white supremacy could not command the same recognition as a bona fide Islamic value. Nor could the crises of urban America. Nor would it be possible, as long as immigrants monopolized religious authority, to shield Blackamerican culture from Immigrant Islam's hostile predisposition toward the West.

At bottom, all of this reverts to the seemingly unbridgeable chasm separating the historical perspectives of Blackamerican and immigrant Muslims. The ideological, practical, and interpretive presuppositions that inform their respective readings of Islam reflect the different histories out of which each emerged. For either group to set up its historical experience as the exclusive prism through which to determine the priorities and substance of American Islam would be to invoke a false universal. And yet, neither community can be expected to "un-live" or fully transcend its history. This is the heart of the problem facing Islam in America. And the challenge confronting Blackamerican and immigrant Muslims is essentially whether they can find common *historical* ground. For it is ultimately history, or more properly historical perspective, that separates the two communities.

It is also historical perspective, however, that holds the key to bridging this chasm. Were both immigrants and Blackamericans to accept their Western experience as a primary element in shaping their respective identities, rather than as a post-facto pollutant added to an otherwise unadulterated mix, both would be able to see each other as participants in a common history. In other words, mutual recognition of their respective legacies and experiences as "objects of the West" could bring immigrants and Blackamericans to a shared historical perspective. While this would not obliterate the other elements in their respective identities, it would greatly reduce, if not eliminate, the utility of appealing to the latter as an ultimate or greater authority in the context of contemplating *American* Islam. For, on a mutual recognition of a common history as "objects of the West," Modern Islam would have to abandon its claim to an historical perspective that is closed to everyone outside the Muslim world. And Modernized Islam would have to quit pretending that social injustice, cultural dislocation, and racial terror are negligible glitches that affect only a tiny (largely culpable) minority of marginalized Blackamericans.

At present, however, both groups remain locked in a racial and ethnic essentialism that impedes their ability to embrace their Western heritages. As Paul Gilroy suggests in *The Black Atlantic: Modernity and Double-Consciousness,* this is one of the results of the limited choices left by the racist, nationalist, and ethnically absolutist discourses of the dominant group in the West. Through their monopoly over the definition of such categories as "Western," "American," or (as in Gilroy's case) "European," the dominant group among white Westerners has cast black and other non-white Westerners as quasi-aliens, consumers, beneficiaries, or wards of Western cultures rather than contributors to or representatives thereof. In the eyes of the dominant group, Western culture and civilization are superior. And superiority is emphatically a white preserve.

In this context, blacks (and other nonwhite peoples) have found it difficult to find a space in which to think of themselves as authentic members of Western civilization, who, even as "objects," contributed in important ways to the latter's constitution. Authenticity tends, rather, to be located in some absolute otherness which is grounded in a fixed and permanent essence that was fully instantiated long before any contact with the modern West occurred. Blackamericans, for example, without whose presence contemporary American discourses on pluralism, equal rights, or democracy would be inconceivable, are rarely thought of as contributors to and thus owners and makers of American democracy. This myopic essentialism is ultimately what Gilroy insightfully alludes to when he writes,

> modern black political culture has always been more interested in the relationship of identity to roots and rootedness than in seeing identity as a process of movement and mediation that is more appropriately approached via the homonym routes.[71]

This tendency to privilege essence over process is by no means limited to black Westerners. Levantine, Egyptian, and North African Arabs who know for a fact that their ancestors "became" Arabs after having been defined by some other, older identity still hold to myths of a quintessential Arab essence and genetic Arab roots. Pakistanis, who just over fifty years ago were Indians, remain wont to acknowledge identity formation as a constituent of history. Even "white people," who used to see themselves as an unwieldy discombobulation of mutually hostile Slavic, Anglo-Saxon, Celtic, Teutonic, and Frankish hoardes now look upon whiteness as a sempiternal, transcendent essence. Indeed, the tendency toward fixed, monadic identities seems to have become part of the modern self. While perhaps originating with Enlightenment Europe, it has now passed to the latter's erstwhile subjects (or more properly, objects) at whose hands it functions to hold the modern hierarchy of peoples in place. Blackness, as the binary opposite of whiteness, settles at the bottom, with all the lighter shades desperately struggling "upward" toward redemption in the white ideal.

In the Muslim world, this white ideal is almost never acknowledged as such. On the contrary, it is routinely appropriated and inducted into the panoply of civilized (and authentic) Arab or Indo-Pakistani culture. This is always an awkward project that is never quite complete. And no one is more aware of this than white Europeans and Americans—especially Muslims—who have lived or traveled in the Muslim world, especially among the educated and the elite. Also aware, however, are the poor and semi-educated masses who are neither educationally nor culturally prepared to indulge these attributions. Reminiscent of the "low type coons" of the Great (Black) Migration, they remain only partially available to assimilation into this modern ideal. If the educated and elite are empowered by an attitude toward "the East" that is grounded in their own Westernization, the masses are empowered by an image of "the West" that is a product of a conscious opposition to such Westernization. This, incidentally, is one of the secrets behind the "success" of Modern Islam. There is, indeed, a striking parallel between the rejectionist posture of Modern Islam and the protest spirit of Black Religion. Where the two part, however, is in the former's failure to identify *white supremacy* (as opposed to "the West") as both an evil and a cause of its shattered sense of self. Ironically, part of the reason for this is that Modern Islam, and to a lesser extent even Modernized Islam, aspires to its own form of supremacy. Their opposition to Western domination is grounded, alas, not in morality but in interest. They are opposed not to domination per se but to domination of (ethnic) Muslims by non-Muslims, or even by other Muslims of the wrong ethnicity.

It is here, in this "will to dominate," that the Post-Colonial Religion of Immigrant Islam departs most fundamentally from the religious orientation of Blackamericans. Black Religion is grounded, first and foremost, in a "will to liberate," a dogged determination to be free of the dictates of the false universals imposed by white supremacy. The dehumanized Post-Colonial Muslim, on the other hand, tends to objectify his target and view him as a thing to be conquered, dismantled, and controlled. In contradistinction to his premodern predecessors, he transforms the category "*kāfir*" (i.e., "non-Muslim") into a reference to an almost subhuman species who is *inherently* and utterly different from Muslims, not only religiously but culturally, ethnically, and civilizationally as well.[72] From this perspective, Islam remains both the haven and the real property of the ethnic Muslim. Others may be "allowed" to enter. But there can be no mistake about who is guest and who is host.

If historical process, however, that is, routes rather than roots, is really the stuff of which human identities are made, the immigrant Muslim (like Muslims in the Muslim world) should be able to see himself as a product of the "process of modernity," a process that enthroned not all but a particular persuasion of "white" Westerners as the standard-bearers and definers of human value and achievement. From this perspective, the Post-Colonial Muslim might be able to see that *he and the Negro are products of the same historical process.* Both reflect the unlit side of the Enlightenment, the darker dimensions of the triumph of "Western" man, the scarred and mutilated underbelly of modernity, with all its hypocrisy, racial terror, and moral myopia: "We hold these truths to be self-evident," in the most brutal and inhumane period of American slavery; "*Liberté, equalité, fraternité*," on the eve of the most unequal, unbrotherly, and dehumanizing period of European colonial savagery. On this understanding, the immigrant and Blackamerican Muslim could join forces as part of the *corrective conscience of the West*, a new Western consciousness committed to liberating both itself and humanity from the debilitating self-alienation and idolatry imposed by the false universals of white supremacy. On this approach, rather than being divided and pushed in opposite directions by American whiteness, immigrant and Blackamerican Muslims could be united in a common cause to undermine its ill-gotten authority and ensure that domination (from the Latin *dominari*, to rule, to be lord, master of) remains emphatically and uncompromisingly the preserve of God alone.[73]

To date, however, it is precisely this historical consciousness that the immigrant Muslim appears to be least prepared to embrace. Instead, he labors under a relentless urge to identify with the conquerer rather than with the conquered. He is unable to see any positive meaning or value in a consciousness of the oppressed. Rather, to his mind, such a move could only endorse the superiority of the oppressor and his right to oppress. Thus his greatest ambition remains not in toppling or even challenging white supremacy but in joining or replacing it. For only then can he quit the company of the dominated and join—or rejoin—the ranks of the dominant.

To be sure, the events and aftermath of September 11, 2001, have complicated this process for immigrant Muslims. Given their new status as a "suspect class," it might not be unreasonable to hazard that their chances of penetrating the southernmost border of American whiteness are now, and for the foreseeable future, severely limited if not nil. But hope is a funny thing. And perhaps the only question is whether religious conviction or secular pragmatism dressed in religious garb will determine their course of action.

Yet, the Blackamerican Muslim must also be careful, for he, too, is subject to being seduced by a false sense of self-righteousness bred of a confusion between existential pragmatism and a sincere commitment to religion. Moreover, given the ideological roots and routes of Blackamerican Islam, Blackamerican Muslims must be careful not to commit the injurious mistake of confusing opposition to white supremacy with opposition to white people. Not all white people are white supremacists. In fact, some of the most courageous, articulate, and devastating critiques of white supremacy have come from the pens of whites. Moreover, as bell hooks reminds us, one does not have to be white to be a white supremacist. Some of the greatest proponents of white supremacy have been and remain black or nonwhite.[74]

But even beyond this, if opposition to white supremacy is to avoid degenerating into a self-serving power play, it must include white people among the *victims* of this false régime. Otherwise, it can only be perceived as an attempt to substitute one régime of domination for another. Under white supremacy, poor whites (from whose realities black and nonwhite intellectuals are just as removed as are white intellectuals and elites from those of blacks and other nonwhites) are systematically duped by a counterfeit currency of whiteness that fails to fill their bellies, educate their children, protect them from corporate greed, or even quell their feelings of nothingness and alienation from the modern world. Locked into a régime of normalness that is supposed to be theirs (since they are "white") but is not really theirs (because they are poor), poor whites are powerless to revolt against their "own way of life." Instead, despite the pathetic conditions in which they live, poor whites in contemporary America remain among the least revolutionary peoples on earth![75]

As for the educated and elite, white supremacy continues to seduce them into an almost childish confidence in their own infallibility. Supported by an endless concatenation of self-serving scientific and philosophical theories, myths and half-truths, they appear oblivious to the fact that their intellectual and instinctive idiosyncracies are no less culturally and socially determined than anyone else's, that they are no less attached to tradition than anyone else, that overdevelopment is no less a flaw than underdevelopment, and that the dislocations in modern social and interpersonal relations cannot be explained away through myths of social perfectibility and progress. In this age of Prozac and potential nuclear holocaust, when there is a need for voices other than their own to which they can listen and from which they can learn, white intellectuals and elites remain trapped and betrayed by their own feat of world domination. Like the invisibly clad ruler in "The Emperor's New Clothes," they are denied the advantage of consciousnesses that are not mere reproductions of their own from whose objective observations, genius, and insights they could benefit. Having created the modern world in their own image, they know instinctively that the latter can only reflect back to them the projections of their own minds. They are thus unable to trust or respect much of the world and in the end are consigned to their own devices, no matter how treacherous these may prove to be. It is a lonely existence. For it is ultimately an existence in which they can neither truly know themselves nor be known by others.

For upwards of a quarter century, from the beginning of the Third Resurrection, Blackamerican Sunni Muslims have struggled, at times more consciously than others, with an Immigrant Islam that monopolized religious authority and thus the interpretation of the meaning of Islam in America. Initially complicit in this process, Blackamerican Muslims have come to recognize the probative value of their own culture and history. As more and more of them become proficient in the religious sciences of the classical Tradition, the clash-of-civilizations mentality of Modern Islam will give way to an approach that is much more recognizably appreciative of American history and virtues. Contrary to the dominant trend among Modernized Muslims, however, this will be a critical American perspective, one that recognizes that intellectualized rhetoric is no match for quotidian brutality and that, in the language of Martin Luther King Jr., the fears, hopes, and ambitions of the masses are just as worthy of consideration as are those of the classes. In short, this will be a Blackamerican Islam that has modified the agenda of Black Religion. But it will not completely abandon it.

This raises the question, of course, of the future of Blackamerican–immigrant relations. As I hope to have shown, there are no insurmountable obstacles to immigrant–indigenous unity. Continued conflict between the two communities will only come of a conscious decision on the part of either to ignore or reject their own or the other's participation in a common history. Even on such a recognition, however, immense effort will be required to sustain a shared historical consciousness. And in the absence of the latter, the two communities are likely to continue to meander along their separate paths, co-existing in a pro forma mutual recognition, resigning themselves all the while to the impossibility of bridging their respective pasts, presents and futures.

3

Black Orientalism

If the stigma of blackness and the trauma of admitting to being creations of the modern West impede immigrant preparedness to assimilate an historical consciousness that ties them to Blackamericans, Blackamerican Muslims are also confronted with incentives, beyond simple frustration, to disassociate from their immigrant coreligionists. For at least a century, there has existed in Blackamerica a cultural/political orthodoxy dedicated to policing the boundaries between blacks and "pseudoblacks." Pseudoblacks have traditionally been identified as those who are of questionable cultural authenticity and or political loyalty to the black community. This cultural/political orthodoxy has always been indexed into the sentiments and mores of the folk. And paying homage to it has always functioned as the *sine qua non* of success for any serious movement among Blackamericans, including those, such as that of the Honorable Elijah Muhammad, that sought ultimately to alter the substance of Blackamerican culture. All of the early Blackamerican Islamizers and even the early Old Guard understood and respected this fact. Immigrant Islam arrived, however, oblivious to, where not contemptuous of, it. Much of this myopia passed to Blackamerican Muslims who came under its sway. The result has been the emergence within the greater Blackamerican community of a phenomenon I shall refer to as "Black Orientalism."

In its primary manifestation, Black Orientalism seeks to cast the Arab/Muslim world as a precursor and then imitator of the West in the latter's history of anti-blackness. In a secondary manifestation, the Muslim world is rendered not only the source of anti-black racism but of the most toxic reactions to this, reactions that continue to infect the otherwise civil approach of non-Muslim Blackamericans long after the propriety and usefulness of black radicalism in America has passed. In both cases, the implication is that through their association with immigrant Muslims and historical Islam, Blackamerican Muslims have contracted the disease of cultural/racial apostasy, alongside a set of sociopolitical attitudes that jeopardize the Blackamerican cause overall. On these attributions, Black Orientalism sets out to question, if not impugn, the status of Islam in the Blackamerican community and, by implication, the propriety of Blackamerican conversion to Islam.

The rise and logic of Black Orientalism must be seen against the backdrop of several converging facts. First, every Blackamerican convert to Islam defected either from the Black Church or some other secular movement among Blackamericans. In this context, Islam's gains were perceived, virtually from the beginning, as someone else's loss. At the same time, the charge of Christianity being the white man's religion only aggravated this feeling and perception of loss. Second, the early Islamizers' critique and reform of traditional Blackamerican culture announced the arrival of a new contender for cultural authority in Blackamerica. So did the cultural and linguistic innovations introduced by the rise of black Sunnism.[1] Third, the dislocations engendered by Immigrant Islam resulted in a certain cognitive dissonance among Blackamerican Sunnis, according to which fossilized doctrines and practices from the Muslim world were imagined to be viable tools with which to confront the challenges of urban America. The resulting dysfunctionality, along with the appearance of being intellectually and culturally overrun by immigrants, saw the power and prestige of Islam in the black community dissipate and give way to a sense of betrayal and disappointment and a feeling that Islam and Muslims were irrelevant where not detrimental to the black cause. In this multilayered light, the emergence of Black Orientalism must be seen not simply as a desire on the part of Blackamerican non-Muslims, particularly Christians, to regain lost ground. It must also be seen as confirming the fact that the perspective and approach of Immigrant Islam and its Blackamerican clients are liabilities that threaten the status and future of Islam in Blackamerica.

Having said this much, Immigrant Islam cannot be made responsible for the actual substance of Black Orientalism. Substantively speaking, Black Orientalism is a thoroughly Blackamerican enterprise,[2] an overtly ideological endeavor with far from objective methods or innocent aims. In this chapter, my objective will be to describe and critique three typologies of Black Orientalism: (1) Nationalist Black Orientalism; (2) Academic Black Orientalism; and (3) Religious Black Orientalism. I shall begin with a word about the genesis of the concept of Orientalism and how it relates to my construction of Black Orientalism. I will follow this with an important note on what Black Orientalism is and what it is not. From here I will enter my discussion proper of the three aforementioned modalities of Black Orientalism. In all of this, it should be noted that my aim is not to exhaust all instances and modalities of Black Orientalism. Similarly, my critique of the *substance* of Black Orientalism should not be mistaken for an attempt to deny or minimize the Muslim contribution, Blackamerican and immigrant, to the *causes* of its emergence.

Between Orientalism and Black Orientalism

The term, "orientalism," was popularized by the late Edward Said, a professor of English at Columbia University. In 1978, Said, a Palestinian of Christian background, published a book entitled *Orientalism*. This work, which would soon become a classic, was devoted to exposing and describing the manner in which the self-perception, prejudices, interests, and power of Europe and later America colluded to create both a geographical object called the Orient and a scholarly tradition of speaking and writing about it. This was not the Orient of Japan or China; this was the "Near" and "Middle East." And while Jews, Christians, and others contributed to the history and cultures of this region, Islam and Muslims were the primary if not exclusive targets. As the incubator and projector of Western fears, desires, repressions, and prejudices, occidental discourses on the Orient normalized a whole series of self-serving and condescending stereotypes about Arab and Muslim "Orientals." These, in turn, justified the propriety and inevitability of Western domination and privilege. This self-serving, power-driven, psychological predisposition, deeply rooted and often consciously indulged, was what Said aimed to capture by the designation "Orientalism."

Said was keen to note that Orientalism was not a purely political affair, something that only Western governments and armies did to Oriental despots and their cowering subjects. Western intellectuals and academicians played a major role in the enterprise. Even when British, French, or American scholars approached the Orient with no conscious foreign policy commitments, they could neither transcend nor disengage themselves from the social, historical, and institutional forces that shaped their mental schemas. The Western scholar, wrote Said, "c[a]me up against the Orient as a European or American first, as an individual second."[3] As an individual, he or she might look *across* the Atlantic or Mediterranean to the Orient; but as a Westerner, he or she could only look *down* from his or her self-appointed perch of superior civilization, a perspective destined to shape the Orient into a reflection of the most deeply ingrained Western fears and obsessions.

If white Westerners approached the Orient as Europeans and Americans, one would only expect Blackamerican thinkers to approach it as Blackamericans. The meaning and implications of this would depend, of course, on where Blackamericans happened to be in their own existential struggle. Prior to the shift from Black Religion to historical Islam, the Arab and Muslim world are almost invariably included as constituents of an idealized Third World, a regiment of Franz Fanon's *Wretched of the Earth* grinding out the universal ground offensive against white supremacy and Western imperialism. In fact, at the height of the black consciousness/Black Power era, the masters of Blackamerican sociopolitical satire were none other than The Last Poets who within a span of five years, went from being partly to completely Muslim.[4] After this shift, however, and the establishment of critical masses of immigrant Muslims in America, one begins to see a growing number of Blackamerican scholars who deny the Arab and Muslim world this status and portray it instead as a precursor, partner, or imitator of the West in its denigration, subjugation, and oppression of black people.[5]

Unlike Said's "white Orientalism," this attempt to recast the Muslim world was unrelated to any desire to control or dominate it. Like Said's Orientalism, however, its *bēte noire* was unmistakably Islam. Black Orientalism was and is essentially a reaction to the newly developed relationship between Islam, Blackamericans, and the Muslim world. Its ultimate aim is to challenge, if not undermine, the propriety of the esteem enjoyed by Islam in the Blackamerican community by projecting onto the Muslim world a set of imaginings, self-perceptions, resentments, and stereotypes that are far more the product of the black experience in America than they are of any direct relationship with or knowledge of Islam, especially in the Muslim world. By highlighting the purported historical race prejudice of the Muslim world, as well as, in some instances, the alleged responses to this prejudice, the aim is to impugn the propriety of the relationship between Islam and Blackamericans by ultimately calling into question Blackamerican Muslims' status as authentic, loyal Blackamericans.

Black Orientalism and What It Is Not

None of the above should be understood to imply, however, that any and all criticism of the stereotypes, prejudices, and practices of Muslim Orientals constitutes Black Orientalism. Valid criticism, however, is distinct from ideologically driven projections. The former is based on direct experience, verifiable facts, and substantively fair and consistent interpretations; the latter is based on imagination, prejudice, and ideology. When Blackamericans condemn the bloodsucking activities of Arab (Muslim!) liquor-store magnates in the greater Detroit or Chicago areas, this is no more an exercise in anti-Muslim Black Orientalism than earlier critiques of Jewish slumlords were of anti-Semitism. And if the old antimiscegenation laws prove how deeply ingrained anti-black racism was among white Americans, de facto antimiscegenation among Muslim Orientals cannot be written off as a benign "cultural preference." In short, if the association between Islam, Blackamericans, and the Muslim world should not be a cause for wild and unwarranted projections, neither should it be a cause for turning a blind eye to offenses and indiscretions that are known and or experienced firsthand.

Nor must Blackamerican criticism of Muslim Orientals be limited to contemporary facts or experience. Inasmuch as the premodern legacy remains the repository of the greatest authority for contemporary Muslims and continues to inform their thought and sensibilities, it remains a fair and reasonable target of critique. When we turn to this legacy, we find that Muslim legal, historical, exegetical, and belle-lettristic literature are replete with anti-black sentiments. Exposing and holding these up for criticism or analysis constitutes neither Black Orientalism nor anti-Muslim bias. On the contrary, such criticism and analysis is critical to the establishment of a standard that can be applied fairly and consistently across the board.

Consider, for example, the following. In his famous *al-Muqaddimah* (*The Prolegomenon*), Ibn Khaldūn (d. 808/1406), the celebrated and true father of sociology, says of blacks in the southernmost portion of Africa that "they are not to be numbered among humans."[6] The early Meccan jurist, Ṭā'ūs (d. 106/724), reportedly indulged the habit of refusing to attend weddings between a black and white because he deemed this to be "unnatural," in accordance with his understanding of Qur'ān 4: 119, which speaks of the Satanic impulse to "alter God's creation (*taghyīr khalq Allāh*)."[7] Numerous early Mālikī jurists (reportedly on the authority of Mālik) held that while under normal circumstances a valid marriage contract required that the woman be represented by a male relative (*walī*), there were instances in which this requirement could be relaxed, such as where the woman hailed from lowly origins, was ugly, or was black. This, they argued, was because blackness was an affliction that automatically reduced a woman's social standing.[8] In a similar vein, the twelfth/eighteenth century Mālikī jurist, al-Dardīr, categorically affirmed the Unbelief (*kufr*) of any Muslim who claimed that the Prophet Muhammad was black![9] On a slightly lighter (but no less suggestive) note, when the black poet, al-Ḥayqaṭān, showed up at the annual Eid celebration all decked out in white, the Arab poet Jarīr (d. 111/729) mocked him in improvised verse,

> It is as if, when he appears before the people,
> He were a donkey's penis wrapped in paper.[10]

Nothing would excuse the casual dismissal or platitudinous explaining away of such statements issuing from white Americans or Europeans. Nor should their author's status as Muslim Orientals earn them any such exemption.

Critical references to statements and actions by Muslim Orientals only approach Black Orientalism when they proceed on the uncritical assumption that their meaning—direct or illocutionary—*are* and *must be* the same as it would be had they issued from the ruling class of white Americans, that such statements reflect not an isolated or limited bias or predilection but an all-encompassing constellation of power relations that are driven by considerations of race (or color). Race and color, in other words, are assumed to function as consistent and permanent determinants of human relations and possibilities. In short, Black Orientalism implies not only that Muslim society produced expressions of race or color prejudice but that such prejudice *defined* these societies and circumscribed the lives and possibilities of black people within them.

Among the strongest factors giving currency to the assumption that black life was circumscribed in Muslim society is the erroneous notion that blacks in Islam were a slave class as they were in America. Not only does this add credence to the notion that black life was circumscribed, it also confers upon all statements and actions that are or appear to be racially biased the appearance of being part of an ongoing effort by the ruling class to confirm the propriety of its position of domination over its subjugated wards. In point of fact, however—and every historian of Islam knows it—most slaves in Muslim society were probably not black but of Turkish origin, and there is no evidence to the effect that most blacks were slaves.[11] But even if we assume that blacks were a slave class in Muslim society, there is a major distinction, as Ira Berlin points out, between "societies with slaves," such as Roman society or African society, and "slave societies," like America, where color and slavery, incidentally, were coterminous. According to Berlin,

> In *societies with slaves*, no one presumed the master–slave relationship to be the social exemplar. In *slave societies*, by contrast, slavery

> stood at the center of economic production, and the master–slave relationship provided the model for all social relations: husband and wife, parent and child, employer and employee, teacher and student. From the most intimate connections between men and women to the most public ones between ruler and ruled, all relationships mimicked those of slavery. . . . "Nothing escaped, nothing and no one." Whereas slaveholders were just one portion of a propertied elite in societies with slaves, they were the ruling class in slave societies; nearly everyone—free and slave—aspired to enter the slaveholding class.[12]

The presumption that blacks under Islam were a slave class in a slave society is a major premise of Black Orientalists and a primary means by which they are able to impose one and only one interpretation upon every racially tinged statement or action by an Arab or nonblack Muslim. But if views such as that attributed to Mālik regarding blackness as an affliction are to serve as proof that Arab Muslims were all Jim Crow segregationists, what is to be made of Martin Luther King Jr.'s statements about dark-skinned women,[13] or Frederick Douglass's reference to the "ape-like appearance of some of the genuine Negroes,"[14] or Alexander Crummel's reference to West Africans as "virile barbarians,"[15] or, for that matter, comedian Chris Rock's declaration, "I hate niggers!"? Clearly, Muslims south of the Sahara, who overwhelmingly adopted the Mālikī school of law, went against the view attributed to Mālik and upheld the requirement for a male relative to validate a marriage. Why should the prejudicial view attributed to Mālik or some Mālikīs be put forth or accepted as the final, definitive word?

Or, take the statement of Ibn Khaldūn. Is this necessarily a genetic antecedent to such scientific racialist theories as those of Jensen, Shockley, and the authors of *The Bell Curve*?[16] And in our attempt to make such a determination, how justified are we in ignoring Ibn Khaldūn's explicit statements to the effect that "race" is an imagined social construct,[17] the notion of black intellectual inferiority is flatly bogus,[18] the Old Testament story about Noah cursing his son Ham mentions nothing about blackness (only that Ham's descendents be cursed with enslavement),[19] and that it is climate, not blood, that affects such endowments as intelligence or civilization? According to Ibn Khaldūn's theory, the further removed a people were from the moderate climate of the Mediterranean, the less intelligence and civilizing potential they would have. Thus, the same savage status he imputes to Africans furthest removed to the south is imputed to white "Slavs (*Saqālibah*)," who are furthest removed to the north.[20]

Race, in other words, was simply not Ibn Khaldūn's thing. And one must ask why the history of race relations in America must serve as the only prism through which his statements can be understood.

It is true, and no amount of apologetics will change it, that the examples cited (and one could cite more)[21] clearly indicate that Arab and other nonblack Muslims were afflicted with race and color prejudice. The insinuation, however, that such attitudes issued from the same place, psychologically, and translated into the same social and political reality as that erected by white Americans is grounded far more in ideology than in fact. In the year 659/1260 (some seven centuries before the Civil Rights movement) a black man appeared in Cairo claiming to be a member of the ʿAbbāsid House, following the destruction of Baghdad by the Mongols. The Mamlūk Sultan (himself a former slave of Turkish origin) ordered the Chief Justice to make an official inquiry into this claim and, amid great fanfare, his genealogy was confirmed and, taking the name "al-Mustanṣir," this black man was inaugurated *amīr al-muʾminīn*!, that is, temporal successor to the Prophet Muhammad and leader of the worldwide community of Muslims.[22] To date, not only America but no major Western democracy has been headed by a black man.

Not only does the record reveal numerous instances where blacks were held in high esteem or occupied powerful positions in Muslim society, but there are even expressions that connote black superiority over whiteness. In fact, early in their history the Arabs—or more properly the Arabians—actually identified themselves as black, against the generally lighter-skinned Persians, Greeks, and others, whom they generally referred to as "red."[23] But even later, when this is no longer the case, we encounter expressions such as the following by the sixth–seventh/twelfth–thirteenth-century Arab poet, al-Bahāʾ Zuhayr:

> Do not revile blacks because of their features
> For they are my portion of this world
> As for whites, I am repulsed by them
> I have no appetite for the color of old age.[24]

Similar is the declaration of the third/ninth-century poet, Abū al-Ḥasan al-Rūmī, this time speaking of black women:

> Part of what renders blackness superior to whiteness—
> And truth has many levels and depths—
> Is that darkness is never blamed for being black
> While extreme whiteness may be rebuked for being white.[25]

Clearly, if the real, as opposed to imagined or ideologically driven, significance of race and color prejudice in Arab/Muslim society is to be apprehended, facts such as these must be duly considered and objectively assessed. Black Orientalism, however, proceeds on a deliberate and consciously sustained ignorance and or suppression of such facts. This is in order to be able to impute to race prejudice in the Muslim world the same significance it has in America. On this logic, however, cultural narcisism on the one hand, and deliberate, race-based monopoly and abuse of power on the other, become so indistinguishable that a cultural idiosyncrasy such as Rapper Sir Mix-A-Lot's contempt for the gaunt figures and flat buttocks idealized by *Cosmopolitan* magazine[26] takes on the same significance as Jesse Helms's and the Republican party's opposition to Affirmative Action.

Like any society, Muslim society (modern and premodern) included its share of good and evil. And like every people, Muslims (especially immigrants) like to think of their heritage as being essentially good and only accidentally evil. This may even deliver them into some rather facile and embarrassing apologies. But if the Muslim predilection for explaining away every unlovely fact finds little justification, Black Orientalism's attempt to turn every indiscretion into proof that Muslims were the precursors or imitators of "Whites Only" racism must be condemned as being equally biased and unjustified.

But beyond this seemingly intentional myopia, Black Orientalism engages in an even greater indiscretion that itself borders on cultural/political heresy. From David Walker to Nat Turner, from Henry McNeil Turner to Malcolm X and even Martin Luther King Jr., the perennial nemesis of Blackamericans was identified as white supremacy and its debilitating false universal.[27] Against this trend, Black Orientalism imagines Islam to be an equal if not a greater threat. One is tempted here to suggest that a significant contributor to the development of Black Orientalism is a tacitly accepted post–Civil Rights–era *modus vivendi*. As the Indian intellectual Ashis Nandy writes of Indian anti-Muslim bias, "the anti-Muslim stance of much of Hindu nationalism can be construed as partly a displaced hostility against the colonial power which could not be expressed directly because of the new legitimacy created within Hinduism for this [colonial] power."[28] Similarly, it may be that part of the price of sustaining the gains of the Civil Rights era is accepting the obligation to devise a critical discourse by which the black predicament can be addressed without expressing too much ingratitude or giving too great an offense to the powers that define the parameters of acceptable critique. In the end, however, it may be that such an approach, as the Sudanese say, "looks at the elephant but only curses its shadow."

The Three Typologies

The foregoing describes the general mindset and goals of Black Orientalism. In more specific terms, there are, as mentioned, at least three types or manifestations of the phenomenon: the Nationalist, the Academic, and the Religious. All three participate in the general aim of impugning the relationship between Blackamericans and historical Islam. Each speaks, however, to a different, albeit overlapping, audience with related but distinct points of emphasis.

Nationalist Black Orientalism: Molefi Asante

In the 1980s, Professor Molefi Kete Asante started a fire with the publication of his provocative work, *Afrocentricity*. This book constituted the "manifesto" of the "new" Afrocentric movement.[29] It was quickly followed in 1987 by *The Afrocentric Idea* and in 1990 by *Kemet, Afrocentricity and Knowledge*. The purpose of these works was to lay out the basic aims, ideological underpinnings, and practical methodology for an approach to historical, cultural, and sociological studies that looked out at the world, especially the African world, from the perspective of Africa and Africans, rather than from the dominant Eurocentric perspective that passed itself off as objective and universal. Asante severely criticized other approaches, including those of Africans and African-Americans, that he felt had been infected and overrun by biases and uncritical assumptions swallowed whole in the European and American academy. Chief among these was the negative assessment of the achievements of Africa and its contributions to world civilization. Afrocentrism was thus a clarion call to Africans and African-Americans to throw off the yolk of these negative stereotypes and to return to their true African selves. It was also an appeal to non-Africans to consider the African rather than the reigning European perspective as a more effective tool for rehumanizing the world.

Before proceeding to my analysis of Asante's Black Orientalism, I must clarify the following. I have neither the desire nor the competence to challenge Professor Asante's or the Afrocentrics' claims regarding the African character of classical Egypt. Nor do I identify with such critics as Mary Lefkowitz, who refers to the writings of black Afrocentrics as anti-Semitic and "hate literature," passing no such judgment on white or Jewish Afrocentrics such as Martin Bernal or Melville Herskovitz. My critique is limited strictly to Professor Asante's characterizations of Arabs, Islam, and the Muslim world as a means of impugning the propriety of the relationship between Islam and Blackamericans.

Two features of Asante's Afrocentrism deliver him to the shores of Black Orientalism. The first is the notion of the authentic African self. Throughout his campaign, Asante appeals to the notion that there is a quintessential African self that lies at the core of every black person. Given the tribal, cultural, religious, and linguistic diversity of Africa, not to mention the "diaspora," Asante is never quite able to settle on exactly what this is. In fact, over the course of his discussion, he appears to contradict himself, now endorsing the "Emotion is black, . . . reason is Greek" notion of the Négritude movement of Césaire Aimé and Leopold Senghor, now invoking the more disciplined rationalism of Chiekh Anta Diop (a Muslim, incidentally), who disagreed with Aimé and Senghor. At any rate, whatever this African essence might be, Asante assures us that it is incompatible with Islam. In his words,

> Adoption of Islam is as contradictory to the Diasporan Afrocentricity as Christianity has been. . . . While the Nation of Islam under the leadership of Elijah Muhammad was a transitional nationalist movement, the present emphasis of Islam in America is more cultural and religious. This is a serious and perhaps tragic mistake; because apart from its historical contradictions, there exists [*sic*] monumental contradictions in its application.[30]

The second relevant feature of Asante's Afrocentrism is his attempt to vindicate Africa and black people from the charge of cultural and intellectual inferiority and of having made no contributions to world civilization. This is the reason why Egypt, as the presumed cradle of human civilization, figures so prominently into the Afrocentric thesis. But, if Africa, including Egypt, was home to a thriving civilization that contributed so much to the ancient world, how is one to explain the continent's present decline? Following the lead of such writers as Chancellor Williams, Asante locates the culprit in the Arab Muslim "invaders" of Africa whom he casts as the destroyers of the once glorious African civilization before the onslaught of the Europeans. Indeed, he seems to intimate, had it not been for Arab Muslims, the Europeans might have encountered a thriving, powerful civilization in Africa which they would not have been able to dominate.

Asante combines these charges in the early pages of *Afrocentricity* and asserts that the Arabs have structured Islam in such a way that non-Arabs (read Blackamericans) are forced to soar into an air not native to their wing and to accept the inherent superiority of Arab idiosyncrasies and presuppositions. Of the factors that have "contributed to the overpowering submissiveness of Africans and other non-Arabs," he notes the following: (1) language, that is, the primacy of Arabic among Muslims; (2) *Ḥajj* or pilgrimage to Mecca; (3) the *qiblah*, or direction towards which Muslims must turn when offering ritual prayers; (4) the doctrine of Muhammad being the last prophet; and (5) customs, that is, esteemed by Muslims but apparently informed by specifically Arab culture, for example, dress.[31] Again, in assessing Asante's Black Orientalism, it is important to note that the determining factor is not whether his list is factually correct but whether the *meaning* attributed to it is grounded in objective analysis or ideological projection.

Let us begin with the issue of language. In response to the thesis that Arabic spread among Muslim populations because of its "prestige and usefulness," Asante writes: "While this is partially true, it is more correct to say that the language succeeded because of force and punishment."[32] No historical proof is offered, either from European, African, or Arabic sources. Rather, Asante appears to rely on the tendency of his readers to fall back on their American experience as the master-analogue in explaining all historical reality. The Arabs, in other words, *had* to have forced Arabic upon their vanquished populations, because the loss of African languages among America's slave population proves that white Americans did so in the case of their vanquished wards.

But if the ability to "force and punish" were the primary means by which language spread, one would have expected Turkish, for example, to wipe out Arabic in all those areas of the Middle East over which the Ottomans ruled for almost half a millennium. And if prestige and usefulness were really so marginal as incentives, how does one explain the existence in places as far removed from the Arabs as China, Russia, or Surinam of Muslim populations who continue to commit themselves to learning the language and pride themselves on their ability to do so? Most importantly, even if we concede the contention that Arabic spread by "force and punishment," would the ultimate effect and meaning of this be the same as what blacks experienced in the New World?

Here we come to a critical oversight that virtually compels Professor Asante to ideological projection. Asante equates Arabness with whiteness and then proceeds to argue as if the two function identically. On this understanding, Arab supremacy would have the same effect on blacks as white supremacy had, essentially relegating the latter to a negative category which their skin color permanently prevented them from escaping. In point of fact, however, following the failed attempt of the early Umayyads to perpetuate a system that reduced all non-Arabians to second-class citizenship, once a people adopted the Arabic language and certain cultural traits, they became full-fledged Arabs, equal in their Arabness to the original conquerors. This is what occurred with the Egyptians, the Syrians, the Sudanese, the North Africans, and others. This obtained whether the adoption occurred through force, choice, or osmosis. In this capacity, Arabized peoples often ended up superceding the "original" Arabs in intellectual, artistic, and other pursuits, including the acquisition of power, as occurred, for example, with Abū Nawās in Arab poetry, al-Ghazalī in Muslim theology, Abū Ḥanīfa in Islamic law, or the famous Barmakid family of politicians. By contrast, when the New World Africans were disabused of their language, religion, and culture in exchange for English and Protestantism, this rendered them neither English nor American. According to the naturalization law passed by the U.S. Congress in 1790, Americanness was defined by whiteness, and whiteness was a boundary that black people simply could not cross.[33] It is thus misleading to imply, as Professor Asante does, that the experience of subject populations, even under a régime of Arab supremacy, would be the same as the experience of New World blacks under a régime of white supremacy. I have often been asked by Arabs who hear me speak Arabic if I am an Arab. I have never been asked by a white person who heard me speak English if I was white. If Arabization, forced or voluntary, expressed a commitment to the principle of *E pluribus unum* (From the many, one), American whiteness emphatically excluded blacks on the principle of *E pluribus duo* (From the many, two).[34]

As for the issue of submissiveness, which is what the rest of Asante's list implies, one should note that white American Muslims change their names, perform the pilgrimage, turn to Mecca in prayer, modify their customs, and often replace their dress, based either on their understanding of their duty as Muslims or a preference for traditions deemed to be more identifiably Muslim. But Asante does not speak of white American submissiveness to the culture and religion of the Arabs. And the reason for this is that, in his experience, white people simply do not have culture and religion *imposed* upon them, certainly not by people or color. Being forced into the role of passive recipient is an exclusively black reality. And it is the force of this projection out of the Blackamerican experience that both leads Asanté to his submissiveness thesis and sustains its currency among his Blackamerican readership. This tendency to set up a very special and uniquely negative relationship between the Arabs and blacks based on internationalizations and projections grounded in the American experience caught the astute attention of Sylviane Diouf, who perceptively notes,

> For some, to see Islam's influence on and importance to Africans in both Africa and the New World acknowledged is almost a belittling

> of what they think are authentic African cultures and Africans. Islamic influence is wrongly perceived as Arabization and a reflection of the supposed weakness of traditional cultures in the face of foreign entities. Interestingly, Chinese, Indonesian, and Albanian Muslims are not seen as being Arabized; only sub-Saharans are viewed as acculturated, which seems to indicate that some advocates of African cultures have internalized the anti-African prejudices they are fighting in other settings.[35]

In identifying those to whom Blackamericans are supposed to be submissive, Professor Asante conspicuously restricts himself to the Arabs. Turks, Persians, Berbers, Kurds, Indo-Pakistanis, and subsaharan Africans are apparently immune to the habit of attempting to dominate others. This is a subtle departure from the view of his predecessor, Chancellor Williams, who spoke explicitly of Arab *and Berber* slave-masters in Africa.[36] Williams, however, was writing in the late 1960s and early 1970s, before the arrival in America of a critical mass of immigrant Muslims and before Islam became identified in the media and the popular imagination with the Arabs. Prior to that time, it was the Turks who were identified as the personification of Islam. In his critique, however, Asante all but ignores non-Arabs and proceeds on the stereotypical presumption that Turks, Berbers, Persians, Kurds, Indonesians, and others do things for all sorts of reasons, while Arabs only and always act on the basis of Islam. By restricting his criticism to the Arabs in this fashion, Asante is thus able to implicate Islam.

Again, however, there is a critical oversight at work here. Arabness—as a racial identity—is presumed ultimately to trump Islam. As such, it was not Islam that one had to join in order to transcend stigma and avert domination but Arabness. Of course, Christians and Jews who happened to be Arabs would beg to differ with this assumption. For in their experience, it was not race but religion, followed by tribalism, that constituted the primary fault lines in society. From their perspective, it was membership in the *Muslim* community, followed by mastery of the Islamic religious sciences, that constituted perhaps an all-too-expedient means to social status and domination, regardless of "race." As a Jewish convert to Islam once commented to me, Muslims wore the turban (i.e., as the symbol of religious learning) like white Americans wear their whiteness. On this basis, the early Shiites would recognize Alī al-Riḍā (d. 203/818) and his son Muḥammad al-Jawwād (d. 220/835) as the infallible Imāms of the entire Shiite community, while they were both believed to have been of Nubian mothers and were "very dark skinned."[37] Meanwhile, Sunni Arab writers could proclaim the sub-saharan African scholar, Aḥmad Bābā (d. 1036/

1627) to be the *mujaddid* of the eleventh/seventeenth century, the *mujaddid*, according to Muslim tradition, being a quasi-messianic figure who appears only every one hundred years to revive the religion for all Muslims.[38]

As for the charge that the Arabs were the destroyers of the grand civilizations of Africa, here, as mentioned earlier, Professor Asante is indebted to Chancellor Williams. Williams, however, was explicit about his motivations, namely to respond to the "subtle message from even the most 'liberal' white authors (and their Negro disciples): You belong to a race of nobodies. You have no worthwhile history to point to with pride."[39] Again, the starting point for Williams is the Blackamerican experience, which ultimately delivers him into historical anachronisms that actually deny him the benefit of certain facts that might otherwise bolster his case. For example, at one point he affirms, "Blacks are in Arabia for precisely the same reason Blacks are in the United States, South America and the Caribbean Islands—through capture and enslavement."[40] Now, every student of Muslim history knows that the Ethiopians *invaded* Arabia in the sixth century C.E., a fact alluded to by the Qur'ān itself (105: 1–5). But because the black experience in America contradicts such a role for blacks, Williams completely overlooks an example that could place black people in the company of those whose achievements constitute the benchmark for his comparisons.

More directly, however, if the Arab invasions are responsible for the destruction of African civilization, why did such black eyewitnesses as Edward Blyden, Martin Delaney, and others fail to report this? And if the Arab invasions led to the destruction of African civilization, why did it not lead to the destruction of all those other civilizations over whose lands the Arabs seized control? Why would the "Arab invaders" destroy every piece of civilization they could put their hands on in sub-Saharan Africa but leave the statue of the Buddha standing in Afghanistan, the ruins of Persepolis standing in Persia, and the Sphinx, Abu Simbel, and countless pagan gods and temples standing in Egypt? Clearly the analogue here is, once again, the black experience in America. The Arabs *had* to destroy the culture and civilization of the Africans *in Africa* because the white Americans destroyed the culture and civilization of the Africans *in America*.

Finally, a word about Egypt. Years ago my youngest son and I visited the ancient ruins at upper Egypt. I remember coming upon an image of a face etched into one of the pillars of some of the ruins stacked at Abu Simbel. What struck me about this face was that it bore a nose that was wide and round, like mine, my oldest son's and those of many Blackamericans I know. While the rest of the tour group stood, mouths agape, nodding in awe at these massive wonders, I remember being visited by a combination of anger, sorrow, and disgust. For while I, too, marveled at the majesty of these relics, I could not escape the recognition that all of this had come of brutal slave labor, many if not most of the laborers bearing noses like the one I saw on that pillar.

Now, Professor Asante and the Afrocentrics point precisely to the results of this brutal process of slave labor as proof of the cultural genius and civilization of blacks in antiquity. But if the Arabs (and others) stand condemned as the slavemasters of Africans, why are the ancient Egyptian slavemasters of Africans extolled as great contributors to world civilization? Plainly stated, Professor Asante appears to invoke a double standard when it comes to the issue of slavery. Slavery is benign, perhaps necessary, and may even be ignored when it contributes to the status and reputation of blacks. It is evil, unnecessary, and must be condemned, however, whenever it fails to do so. Practically speaking, this translates into the Black Orientalist tendency to employ two sets of lenses through which to interpret and project images onto the world: one for those identified as "blacks," another for those identified as "Arabs."

This shorthand critique of Professor Asante should not be misread, either as a wholescale condemnation of Afrocentrism or as a wholescale dismissal of his criticisms of Blackamerican Muslims. There are, indeed, many aspects of Asante's presentation with which I emphatically agree. His courageous, straightforward position on homosexuality, for example, reflects an enviable refusal to bow to the liberal pressures of the academy.[41] And his assertion that Blackamerican Muslims often "out Arab the Arabs" is just plain old truth.[42] But Professor Asante appears to be unwilling or unable to see the history of blacks in America as a *sui generis* experience for which there simply is no neat parallel in Islam. Speaking in this regard, even the Orientalist Bernard Lewis would affirm that "at no time did the Islamic world ever practice the kind of racial exclusivism . . . which has existed until very recently in the United States."[43] Professor Asante's apparent willingness, however, to flout the evidence in an attempt to graft this singular experience onto the face of Islam delivers him into the throws of Black Orientalism.

Academic Black Orientalism: Henry Louis Gates Jr.

In 1998 Harvard's Professor Henry Louis Gates Jr. released his documentary film, *Wonders of the African World*. This three-part series included a grand tour of Africa, beginning in Egypt and working down the east coast, cutting back to the west, and then piercing the interior, finally ending up at the southern extremity of postapartheid South Africa. This was a fascinating odyssey that unveiled the richness, depth, and beauty of black Africa and its history. It was marred, however, particularly in the segment from Egypt to Zanzibar, by a palpable and at times seemingly gratuitous measure of Black Orientalism.

Gates contextualizes his approach to Africa by referring up front to the many fables and old wives' tales he heard growing up in barber shops and other venues in the black community in West Virginia. These, in turn, had gone a long way in shaping his image, valuation, and expectation of the motherland. In a sense, *Wonders* was an attempt to establish the truth or falsity of the many images and understandings that Gates (and many other Blackamericans) had imbibed as a child. As such, far from even pretending to be a value-free exposé, *Wonders* was part of a mission. Africa had existed in the minds and hearts of Blackamericans long before it existed as an ontological reality for them. And in this capacity, it had played an important role, sometimes positive, sometimes negative—depending on who was defining it—in shaping the Blackamerican self-image. This would also contribute, however, to the image of various "Others." And these images, as we shall see, would often be based on the role these Others could be assigned in promoting or violating the image that Blackamericans had (or wanted to have) of Africa.

Gates begins in Egypt, noting that "Egypt has become a place of pilgrimage for African-Americans trying to rediscover their identity." Standing in front of the Great Pyramid at Giza, he asks a group of Blackamerican tourists why they have come to Egypt. One of them responds that he is, "trying to make a connection to a historical past that we've been misled about for so long." In order to preempt any possible confusion, Gates asks rhetorically who the "we" refers to. When the gentleman responds, "African Americans," Gates continues with a note of confidence. "When we were growing up in school, though, all of the Pharoahs looked like white guys; I mean, they could have been from Milwaukee, or some place." This whitening of the Pharoahs was part of the race-based mythology that *Wonders* set out to expose. In this context, however, indigenous Arab Egyptians would appear almost intrusive in their very presence in their own country.

This is the broader backdrop against which we begin as the camera narrows to focus more specifically on the black Pharoahs of Nubia. The Nubians, Gates had learned growing up, were a legendary kingdom of black people who once ruled the entire Nile valley. While the Nubian empire had long passed, the place and people still existed, straddled between the south of Egypt and the north of Sudan.

It is here, in his depiction of Nubia and the Nubians, that Gates begins his descent into Black Orientalism proper. Given the limitations of space, two manifestations of the phenomenon will have to serve. The first appears in his casting of the Arabs as the wanton destroyers of Nubian civilization, presumably on their contempt for the latter *as blacks*. The second appears in his depiction of all of the Muslim communities along the coast of east Africa as nursing deep, intractable complexes about their blackness. Again, in neither case is the issue the "facts" on the ground. The issue is, rather, the tendency to impose upon these "facts" a set of meanings that are more properly the domain of the Blackamerican experience *in America*.

At Nubia, Gates is "guided" to the home and village of a Nubian woman named Fawzīyah Sulaymān. This is preceeded by his editorial lamentations about how Egyptian president Gamal Abd al-Nasser's building of the High Dam destroyed Nubian civilization by submerging it under water, with the exception, that is, of the ruins (Abu Simbel, etc.) that were moved to their present location. Fawzīyah is supposed to confirm, from a native's perspective, just how devastated the Nubian community was. But when, through his Westernized Nubian translator, Gates asks Fawzīyah how she and her family were affected, she completely contradicts what we have been prepared to hear and insists that the benefits outweighed the cost. At this point, confusion breaks out, and after a lot of Arabic (none of which indicates to my ear what follows), Gates re-enters and tells us that he is confused, that Fawzīyah was *supposed* to tell us that she and her family were against the dam. He adds that the reason she changed her story is that there are policemen outside whose presence has programmed her to say that she was in favor of the dam when in point of fact, "it was . . . devastating, to her and her family, and to her neighbors, all of whom were forcibly removed and dumped in this makeshift village."

On the one hand, Gates assures us that Fawzīyah—who coincidentally happens to be a woman with very dark skin and distinctly West African features, in contrast with most of the other Nubians we see—has been "programmed" by the Egyptian police, all Arab. But he himself affirms that she was *supposed* to say that she was against the dam. One need not conclude from this that Gates or his Nubian translator had themselves "programmed" Fawzīyah. But he obviously had a certain response in mind and set out to find a Nubian who would voice it. Surely, however, there must have been Nubians who, without any programming from anyone, *supported* the building of the dam. Why is Fawzīyah's alleged opposition to the dam supposed to represent the communal resentment of the entire Nubian people? Fixated on the dream of beholding the remnants of ancient Nubia, Gates completely dismisses the value of development (though he incessantly reminds us throughout *Wonders* of the annoying deficiencies in African accommodations). But is it fair or even reasonable to hold the Nubians themselves to the same index of priorities?

Reflecting on development in Egypt a few decades after the building of the dam, R. Stephen Humphreys, an American historian of the Middle East, would observe the following:

> As under Nasser's Arab Socialism, the new regime can boast substantial achievements—most strikingly, an immense though incomplete overhaul of Cairo's once disintegrating infrastructure. (One takes infrastructure for granted once one has it, but its no trivial matter. During my first stay in Cairo in 1966, the water ran two hours a day—but never the same two hours—there were no telephone lines and they seldom worked, and electricity was spotty. In such circumstances, an orderly everyday routine was almost impossible to achieve.)[44]

Gates admits that the Aswan dam brought water and electricity to the entire country. He also admits that all the historic monuments were preserved (which means that what remained under water were largely rustic hamlets—unless we assume that the Nubians preserved the vernacular dwellings of the black Pharoahs fully intact!). But none of this is enough to exonerate the *Arab* Egyptian government nor to establish a reason other than anti-Nubianism (read, anti-blackness) as the motivation behind its action.[45] It may be that the Egyptian government under Gamal Abd al-Nasser was racist to the core. But *Wonders* falls woefully short of proving this. In fact, all *Wonders* proves is that the standard to which Black Orientalists will hold Arab governments in Africa is not whether the latter serve the practical needs of their people but whether they promote the ideological and psychological needs and interests of Blackamericans.

But if the Arab government of Egypt acted callously toward the Nubians because of the latters' blackness, the same could not be said of the *black* government of the Sudan. Here, however, we come upon another apparent enemy of African blackness: Muslim fundamentalism. In the segment on the Kajbar dam, which disrupted the lives and heritage of Nubians in Sudan, Gates implies that it was the black government's fundamentalism that drove its policy. None of the government officials are consulted (though it is well known that the Western-educated Islamist leader of the Sudan, Ḥasan Turābī, rarely turns down an interview with a Westerner). Instead, we hear from either "progressive" Nubians who confirm Gates's proposition or from "programmed" (Muslim) Nubians whose favorable comments about the Kajbar dam Gates himself has to editorially rectify. In the end, we are left with the distinct impression that Islam, either by proxy of the Arabs or of the black Sudanese fundamentalists, is a perduring threat to the interests and the image of black Nubians.

Against this backdrop, the fact that most Nubians appear to be Muslims gives the subtle impression that these black Africans either suffer from false consciousness or are victims of the kind of "force and punishment" referred to by Professor Asante.

From Nubia, Gates moves to a segment entitled "The Swahili Coast." Here we come upon the second manifestation of his Black Orientalism. In a word, Gates—like the Afrocentrics—embraces the concept and definition of blackness as institutionalized in the history, customs, and legal tradition of the Unites States and then seeks to impose this on East African Muslims. Any East African Muslim who does not identify with this definition of blackness is in turn cast as a self-hating Negro. No allowance and no agency at all is granted the East Africans themselves—at least not the East African *Muslims*—to indulge their own definitions of blackness.[46] Instead, Gates repeatedly reminds his interlocutors of what they would be considered in the United States. His attempt is to force East African Swahili Muslims into the ideological framework of a Blackamerican academic. When the Swahilis resist, the resulting tension produces a subtle but unmistakable message: African *Muslims* have a deep and abiding aversion toward blackness.

Gates interviews several Swahili men, all of whom minimalize their black African heritage and stress their alleged Arab or Persian ancestry. This is distressing to Gates, who sees in it parallels to the presumed self-loathing of Blackamericans who privilege, for example, their Native American heritage over their African one. In frustration, Gates proclaims that the Swahili Muslims will identify themselves as "anything but pure Negro." And this for a people who, according to him, "look about as Persian as Mike Tyson." For Gates, the Swahili Muslim claim to be Arab or Persian, "is a bit like me claiming to be white because my great-great-grandfather was an Irishman named Brady." Again, all of this is grounded in the false universal that equates American blackness with global blackness. Accordingly, Swahili Muslims are obligated to consider themselves black *in East Africa* because they would have to consider themselves black *in America*. In all of this, the distinctive tendency among Blackamericans to stress their African heritage over all other aspects of their genetic makeup is elevated to a universal imperative.[47] Its ideological dimension is completely ignored, and the possibility that others may choose differently is banned from consideration.

Having said this much, I am not at all convinced that the Swahili Muslims Gates interviews are not afflicted with certain complexes about their blackness, not to mention an even deeper aversion to considering themselves a species of Blackamericans. I am absolutely certain, however, that the will to maximize prestige and minimize disadvantage is not unique to East African Muslims. Americans of Lithuanian, Slavic, Italian, Irish, and other backgrounds routinely identify themselves as "Anglos" rather than risk a more ethnic identification that might jeopardize their whiteness. And American Jews are now white, now Hebrew, depending on whether they are speaking in a specifically sociopolitical or religious context. The question of why it might be preferable to be white or Anglo as opposed to Hebrew or Lithuanian may exercise university professors. But for everyday competitors in the social market of privilege and impediment, this is largely an academic question.

Here, however, we come to a major difference between Swahili and Blackamerican reality. In America, there has never existed an "alchemy of blackness" according to which groups could move in and out of this negative category, as Jews and others have done and continue to do with American whiteness.[48] In America, the prevailing rule has been "Once you go black, you can never go back." This is apparently the reality that Gates wants to impose on the East African Swahilis, and one almost wonders at times if they are not actually resented for being able to avail themselves of a more alchemic construction of blackness. To be sure, white supremacy is a debilitating evil. And the apparent Swahili aversion to their black Africanness is a painful thing to watch. But, given the natural aversion to stigma, I wonder what many Blackamericans—including those of known Irish ancestry—would do if blackness in America were a more alchemic category. I wonder if in such a context stressing other aspects of one's hybrid genealogy would be viewed as an affliction exclusive to Uncle Tom Negroes or self-hating Africans.

Whatever the answer may be, I find it hard to believe that in a world dominated by white supremacy the only Africans who have a problem with blackness are those who happen to be Muslims. And it is here that Professor Gates's Black Orientalism comes front and center. Only the *Muslims* of Lamu, Mombassa, and Zanzibar are confronted about their blackness. And only the Muslims are presented as evincing those disturbing complexes of apparent self-loathing. Blackness is *never* problematicized when speaking to African Jews or Christians. The black Christians in the Zanzibarian Church, for example, apparently not far from where the Swahili Muslims were interviewed, are not asked about their blackness. And in later segments, Ethiopian Jews and Christians are not asked about theirs. We never get a sense of how Ethiopian Jews reconcile their Hebrewness with their Africanness. Nor is the Ethiopian Jewish charge of Israeli racism given any attention. We are never granted any insight into how Ethiopian Christians relate to all those apparently "white" images in their icons. Nor do we get a sense of whether the Ethiopians' fine hair and pointed features place them, in their own minds, above their wooly-haired, full-featured West African brethren. Instead, in all of these instances, the *apparent* blackness of Jews and Christians is allowed to speak for itself, and Professor Gates leaves us to assume that African Jews and African Christians have a *Blackamerican* attitude toward their blackness. In the end, the message is, again, as clear as it is subtle: Not only do Muslims in Africa have a deep aversion to blackness, *only* Muslims in Africa are afflicted with this disease. This double standard, along with its implicit message, is repeated throughout *Wonders*.

In the end, *Wonders* turns out to be a wonderful reminder of the wages of projecting one's own perspectives and experiences onto the lives of others. It reminded me, in fact, of the folly of my initial reaction during a visit to Spain to the hooded KKK-looking characters in the Spanish *semana santa* (Catholic Holy Week). In fact, in its particular focus on Egypt, Wonders called to mind a painful lesson I learned as a student a couple of decades ago. On a blistering hot day, I was waiting in line at a cafeteria at the American University in Cairo for one of those "luke cool" sodas that lay at the bottom of a canteen where it received a steady drip of water from a large block of ice straddled across the top on two pieces of wood. (There were no refrigerated canteens in those days.) As I stood there fanning myself with hot air, a young white woman (a Westerner) came in and unceremoniously promenaded to the front of the line. The waiter, one of those all-too-vulnerable working-class Egyptians, promptly picked up a soda, removed the cap, and handed it to her. Young, fairly new to Egypt, and none too prepared to stand for this "racist crap"—especially not in Africa!—I stepped out of line and yelled toward the waiter, "What the heck is this? Who is she? (*Allah! Ay dah? Hiya dih tib'a min?*)" The waiter looked back at me with an expression laden with disgust and pity. "This is a woman (*Hiyya sitt*)," he said, in a tone that seemed also to ask, "What's wrong with you?" I turned to look around me and discovered to my horror that the line consisted of all males. At that instant, I knew that I had made a fool of myself and that a phenomenon I had witnessed several times on the streets of Cairo reflected not isolated instances but a social convention: Anytime there was an all-male line (at least in those days), it was a woman's place to step immediately to the front. To be sure, this incident could have been edited and reported as a classic case of white supremacy abroad. And perhaps a Black Orientalist would have done just that. Such a presentation, however, would have been based on a combination of ignorance and bias along with a certain momentum that is known to inform Blackamerican presentations whenever the imagined audience is predominately black.

Religious Black Orientalism: Richard Brent Turner

Professor Richard Brent Turner is the author of *Islam in the African American Experience*, which appeared in 1997. Among the major themes repeated *ad nauseum* throughout this work is that racism and racial separatism are African *Muslim* problems before they become Christian- or Muslim-American ones. In fact, Turner is explicit in asserting that Islam—particularly West African Islam—contributed directly to the development of these obsessions among Blackamerican Muslims. The book is intended, as such, to serve as a corrective to the widespread image of Islam as a racially harmonious religion. To this end, Turner warns, in his introduction:

> Some of the book's ideas may surprise the reader. The book takes the study of Islam as a world religion out of the realm of mythic racial harmony and positions it in a historical context of racial, ethnic, and political divisions that influenced the history of slavery in America. It offers evidence that racial separatism among Muslims in America in the twentieth century was not completely the result of black nationalism and was not a new phenomenon in Islam, but was, in fact a normative pattern for black people in Islam that was established in Africa before the Atlantic slave trade.[49]

Turner is careful to note that racial separatism was not "completely the result of black nationalism." It was born, in other words, of black nationalism plus something else. That something else is quickly identified, however, as the "normative pattern for black people in Islam." Elsewhere Turner goes on to affirm that black nationalism and Islam are actually not as distinct as the above depiction may have suggested. Rather, Islam turns out to be the actual *source* of black nationalism, transmitted to Blackamericans via the medium of Edward Blyden. The upshot of all of this is that racial separatism among Blackamericans is a product of black nationalism plus Islam; black nationalism, however, is itself a product of Islam. Thus, racial separatism is ultimately a product of Islam plus Islam.

> It is impossible to understand fully the transition between the old Islam of the original African Muslim slaves and the "new African-American Islam" of the early twentieth century without giving some attention to nineteenth-century Pan-Africanism. Pan-Africanism formed the ideological bridge between these two phases of Islam in the United States. Moreover, the Pan-Africanist ideas of Edward Wilmot Blyden (1832–1912) are the key to understanding how and why

> the black nationalist identity of twentieth-century black American Islam became so linked to a racial separatist West African community model that was endemic to global Islam in the nineteenth century. Blyden, who is sometimes called the "father of Pan-Africanism," used the example of Islam in West Africa as the paradigm for racial separatism and identity in his Pan-Africanist ideology and ultimately argued that Islam was preferable to Christianity as a global religion for blacks. These ideas were destined to have a profound impact on black nationalist and Islamic movements in America in the twentieth century.[50]

Lodged into the creases of Turner's thesis appears to be a perduring frustration with the fact that Christianity has been tarred with the charge of antiblack racism while Islam has not only been exonerated but cast as the friend of black people. It is ultimately his intention to refute this irksome proposition that compels him to warn readers that the book may surprise them. Turner never questions the fact that racism and racial separatism have been perpetrated in the name of Christianity. Instead, he restricts his efforts to showing that this is equally if not more so the case with Islam. If Christianity is to be charged with being the white man's religion and thus not suitable for any self-respecting black, Turner wishes to intimate that this must apply *a fortiori* to Islam. This is all helped along by his convenient identification of the Arabs as "white."[51]

Unlike such religious polemicists as G. Usry, C. Keener, or F.K.C. Price, Turner's ambitions go beyond merely disabusing Blackamericans of the notion that Christianity is the white man's religion. Turner is appealing, rather, to a wider, more sophisticated audience consisting of both blacks and whites. Included in his message is the assurance that the acrimony, radicalism and reverse racism emanating from certain quarters of the black community are native neither to Christianity nor America. These are, rather, aberrations that have been introduced into the black community via the medium of Islam. Under this lighting, Islam comes to be seen not only as a challenge to Blackamerican Christianity but as a threat to Blackamerican integrationism and improvements in race relations in the post-Civil Rights era. Indeed, it seems at times that a certain desire to keep the divisive debate over black–white relations outside the Church drives Turner to cast the Muslims as the originators of racial separatism. This tactic of pointing to Islam as a threat to American race relations is one of the unique characteristics of his brand of Black Orientalism.

Like other forms of Black Orientalism, Turner's depictions are grounded in projections that seek to further a particular cause *in America*. Blacks, whites, and Christianity in America may have had their problems in the past. But, thanks to the achievements of the Civil Rights era, these can now be easily reconciled, if only Islam would let them. This explains the sustained attempt to insulate "Christian America" from any serious consideration in terms of her contributions to the emergence of racial separatism among Blackamericans. It also explains numerous imaginings and irrelevancies, some of which border on the psychedelic. At one point, for example, Turner claims that Islam's "racial, ethnic, and political divisions . . . influenced the history of slavery in America"! Elsewhere he befuddles his reader with such assertions as "the racial separatism of West African Islam resulted from the signification of black Muslim identities by rich and powerful black rulers who attempted to reconcile their new religion with African traditional religious and cultural praxis."[52]

Among the most striking (and confusing) features of Professor Turner's argument is his repeated reference to the racial separatism of West African Islam without ever telling us in a clear and consistent manner who the races in question are or what the actual basis of the alleged separatism is. Now it is black African rulers separating Africans from Arabs and Berbers; now Arabs "enslaving Africans in record numbers"; now African Muslims declaring themselves independent of non-Muslim Africans as they prosecute the jihads against the latter. Perhaps the most charitable construction to be put on all of this would be to distill it down to the claim that Islam itself implied racial segregation and that *all* of these instances are simply manifestations of a tendency that was endemic to Islam as a religion. Even on this construction, however, Professor Turner's thesis remains problematic.

The whole point in citing the alleged racial separatism of West African Islam was to establish a Muslim precedent for the separatist programs of the Blackamerican Islamizers. We may dispense, of course, with any consideration of Blackamerican Sunnis, since the latter never embraced racial separatism as an ideal. (Intermarriage, for example, has always been practiced among Blackamerican Sunnis.) As for the early Islamizers, even if we concede (for the sake of argument) that West African or global Islam was racially segregationist, the separatist platforms of Noble Drew Ali and the Honorable Elijah Muhammad reveal themselves to be fundamentally different from the overseas practices described by Turner. Noble Drew Ali and the Honorable Elijah Muhammad both insisted that Islam was the black man's religion. For them, the very call to "Islam" was a call to separate from whites, because whites, *by nature*, were not and likely would not be Muslims, whereas Blackamericans, if they were true to their nature, would invariably be Muslims. Unlike Turner, these men did not cast the Arabs as whites but as people of color. And as E. E. Curtis IV has suggested, the early Islamizers embraced a "cultural nationalism" that drew all blacks into a common, nativist culture that excluded whites.[53] By contrast, in none of his depictions of West African or global Islam has Turner provided any evidence, or even suggested, that Islam was portrayed as the African's (or Arabs' or Berbers') religion or that entry into Islam required or even suggested that one separate from Arabs, Berbers, or other Africans, because the latter *could not* be Muslims. It is strange that the most obvious basis of any Old World separatism—tribalism—plays no role at all in Turner's depictions. This was necessary, however, in order to eliminate all possible alternatives to race as a primary motive. In short, Turner is taking the distinctly American preoccupation with *race* and projecting it onto West African and global Islam. To admit tribalism in this context, as perhaps the *dominant* hegemony in Africa, would be to undermine this effort.

But if the separatist programs of the early Islamizers diverge fundamentally from the alleged separatism of West African and global Islam, they correspond almost to the letter with the biological racism of nineteenth-century America, the segregationism of the post-Reconstruction and Jim Crow eras, the eugenics theories produced by the immigration debates in the first third of the twentieth-century, and the overall tenor of American society en route to its intractable *E pluribus duo*. Early twentieth-century America was a watershed in the production of racial segregationist theories, from D. W. Griffith's *Birth of a Nation* (1915) and Madison Grant's *Passing of the Great Race* (1916) to Lothrop Stoddard's *The Rising Tide of Color against White World Supremacy* (1920) and Thurman Rice's *Racial Hygiene* (1929). Indeed, the 1920s produced the Report of the Eugenics Committee of the United States Committee on Selective Immigration, which concluded, *inter alia*, that North and West Europeans were of "higher intelligence and hence provided the best material for American citizenship."[54]

All of these developments contributed to the confirmation of white supremacy as the dominant American hegemony, in the context of which blacks were looked upon as social, cultural, and political pollutants. The ubiquitous "Whites/Coloreds" signs of the Jim Crow South attest to this sentiment. And so horrifying was the specter of miscegenation that laws had to be passed to preempt or punish it. (No such signs and no such laws ever existed, incidentally, in the lands of Islam.) In 1921, soon-to-be-president Calvin Coolidge would remark in a contribution to *Good Housekeeping* magazine, "Biological laws tell us that certain divergent people will not mix or blend. The Nordics [whites] propagate themselves successfully. With the other races, the outcome shows deterioration on both sides."[55] In all of this, incidentally, whiteness connoted significantly more than just color. It signified, in addition, a distinct level of freedom, civilization, and an almost genetic connection to Christianity.[56] As one commentator put it, nonwhites had "not at all the faces of the fair-haired race from which our Savior is supposed to have sprung."[57]

Noble Drew Ali established the Moorish Science Temple in 1913. The Honorable Elijah Muhammad took over leadership of the Nation of Islam in 1934. Why should men who grew up in such a racially charged environment, drinking from separate water fountains and sitting in segregated pews, have to look outside America for instruction on racial separatism? And given the slavish imitations of Christianity reflected in their theologies, why should Islam alone be implicated as a source of their separatist doctrines? Noble Drew Ali's *Holy Koran* included direct quotations from Levi Dowling's *The Aquarian Gospel of Jesus the Christ.*[58] Elijah Muhammad's mythology of the big-headed scientist Yaqub and his creation of a degenerate white race is a page straight out of the eugenics manuals of his period. The source of his assertion that God is a man—a black man!—does not even require investigation. Why should Professor Turner be able to project theories of racial separatism onto Jenne, Songhay, or Timbuktu, when he presents no evidence that there is anything even close to this in the literature of West African or global Islam?[59] And why should he be able to ignore white American Christians when the parallels to their doctrines are so precise and so striking?

In point of fact, however, the Nation of Islam was actually *more* separatist than Professor Turner leads one to believe. And perhaps the reason for this oversight is that this added dimension of the group's separatism shows it, again, to diverge fundamentally from the alleged *racial* separatism of West African and global Islam. In addition to its campaign for specifically racial separatism, the Nation of Islam launched a stinging attack on those "cross-wearin', chittlin' eatin', yes sa bossin' Negroes," whose *cultural* (and religious) proclivities were cast as an aid and a comfort to the enemy. This was part of a campaign to redefine the proper modality of American blackness. And blacks who failed or refused to recognize this new orthodoxy were condemned as religio-*cultural* heretics. Clearly, this was unrelated to the kind of racial separatism that Turner attributed to West African and global Islam. Indeed, there is no evidence, or even suggestion, that black, Arab, or Berber Muslims separated from each other on the basis of mutual charges of cultural heresy.

But Professor Turner has little use for such twentieth century parallels and precedents that might point to possible white American, Christian influence on the Blackamerican Islamizers. Instead, he focuses on the nineteenth century and restricts himself to black precedents, specifically Edward Wilmot Blyden. This is neither accidental nor insignificant. It is critical, rather, to Turner's ultimate aim of implicating Islam.

Besides Blyden, several black intellectuals and religious leaders sojourned to Africa in the nineteeth and early twentieth centuries. The list includes Alexander Crummel, Martin Delaney, Henry McNeil Turner, Theodore Holly, Lucious Holsey, and others. All of these men were powerful advocates of black separatism and or emigration to Africa.[60] In fact, in his description of Blackamerican responses to American racism, Gayraud Wilmore describes the approach of A.M.E. Bishop Henry McNeil Turner as being among the most extravagant forms.[61] Clearly, such precedents should suggest themselves as possible avenues of influence upon the Blackamerican *Islāmīyīn*. For Turner's puposes, however, all these men lacked an important qualification that Blyden undeniably had: a publicly acknowledged appreciation for Islam. Turner knows that the early Islamizers freely availed themselves of the ideas and doctrines of Christians. But if Christians could be identified as a possible source of their racial separatism, this would severely weaken the case against Islam.

But even beyond these glaring oversights, Turner's thesis includes an even more conspicuous lacuna. This is his glossing over the redoubtable David Walker, who was at least as well-known as Blyden, if not more so.[62] In 1829, before Blyden was even born, Walker published a famous treatise entitled *Appeal to the Coloured Citizens of the World, but in particular, and very expressly, to those of The United States of America*. Already in the title of this work we see an inchoate pan-Africanism, the tract being addressed to the colored citizens *of the world*.[63] Beyond this, however, the substance of *Appeal* shows parallels to the separatist outlook of the early *Islāmīyīn* that suggest that it was more likely Walker than Blyden who inspired or at least influenced the Blackamerican Islamizers.

Walker preceded Elijah Muhammad in referring to white Americans, specifically white American Christians, as "devils."[64] In fact, he assigns the attribute of depravity not only to white Americans but to whites all over and throughout history, contrasting this to the inherently benevolent nature of blacks.

> The whites have always been an unjust, jealous, unmerciful, avaricious and blood-thirsty set of beings, always seeking after power and authority.—We view them all over the confederacy of Greece, where they were first known to be any thing, (in consequence of education) we see them there, cutting each other's throats—trying to subject each other to wretchedness and misery—to effect which, they used all kinds of deceitful, unfair, and unmerciful means. We view them next in Rome, where the spirit of tyranny and deceit raged still higher. We view them in Gaul, Spain and in Britain.—In fine, we view them all over the Europe, together with what was scattered about in Asia and Africa, as heathens, and we see them acting more

> like devils than accountable men. But some may ask, did not the blacks of Africa, and the mulattoes of Asia, go on in the same way as did the whites of Europe. I answer, no—they never were half so avaricious, deceitful and unmerciful as the whites, according to their knowledge.[65]

Little wonder it is that Walker harshly condemns interracial marriage.[66] And throughout the *Appeal*, he racializes "the Americans" and casts them as an entity wholly distinct from blacks, indeed, the latters' "natural enemies."[67] He warns of both American decline and of the destructions to be visited by God upon the republic, praising Haiti (after the revolts of Toussaint L'Ouverture) as "the glory of the blacks and the terror of tyrants."[68] Though a committed Christian, Walker excoriates white American Christianity for its hypocrisy in countenancing such inhumane treatment of blacks. In fact, like Blyden, he contrasts the conduct of Christianity with that of Islam:

> I believe if any candid person would take the trouble to go through the Southern and Western sections of this country, and could have the heart to see the cruelties inflicted by these *Christians* on us, he would say, that the Algerines, Turks and Arabs treat their dogs a thousand times better than we are treated by the *Christians*.[69]

No such antiwhite, militant, apocalyptic sentiments appear in Blyden. And, contrary to Turner's assertion, Blyden did not argue that Islam was a more viable option for blacks but only that Islam had succeeded in transferring religious authority to native Africans in a manner that Christianity had not. On the other hand, anyone familiar with the Honorable Elijah Muhammad's *Message to the Black Man* will recognize immediate parallels—in form *and* substance—with Walker. In sum, there is no reason, other than ideology—in this case Black Orientalism—to exclude Walker, a nineteenth-century Blackamerican *Christian*, as a possible source for the racial separatism of the Blackamerican Islamizers.

Of course, it is possible that Walker, too, was influenced by Islam. Turner himself notes that Walker met the African-American Muslim slave, Abd al-Rahman Ibrahima, and we have seen Walker's references to Muslims in *Appeal*. In fact, the opening pages of *Appeal* include words that he could have taken over from any Muslim: "God made man to serve Him *alone*, and that man should have no other Lord or Lords but Himself—that God Almighty is the *sole proprietor* or *master* of the WHOLE human family, and will not on any consideration admit of a colleague."[70] Thus, Walker *may* have been influenced by Islam. And, through him, Islam *may* have influenced the racial separatism of the Blackamerican *Islāmīyīn*. But Walker's connection to Islam was too indeterminate for Professor Turner to risk such an argument. Blyden, for his purposes, simply made a much easier sell.

Again, none of this is to deny the presence of racist sentiments among Muslims in the Muslim world, neither historically nor contemporaneously. Nor should this critique be extended to the point of casting aspersions on the many other insightful and informative aspects of Professor Turner's book. At the end of the day, however, as far as America is concerned, the claim that Christianity is the white man's religion has "made in America" stamped all over it. And it was made in deed by white Americans long before Blackamericans found the words to say it. Given this reality, it seems a bit fanciful, if not disingenuous, to imagine that, by affixing a similar charge to Islam, the historical association in America between whiteness and Christianity will somehow dissipate or disappear from the American collective psyche.

In 1790 the United States Congress passed a law that restricted American citizenship to "free white persons." In his book, *White By Law*, Ian Haney-Lopez reminds us "Though the requirements for naturalization changed frequently thereafter, this racial prerequisite to citizenship endured for over a century and a half, remaining in force until 1952."[71] This was the context in which the U.S. Supreme Court handed down the Dred Scott decision in 1857, in which Chief Justice Roger Taney argued that blacks were not citizens and that the Constitution never contemplated citizenship for blacks. In 1965, on repealing the 1924 National Origins Act, President Lyndon Johnson stated that his action "correct[ed] a cruel and enduring wrong in the conduct of the American nation."

This was the context into which immigrant Muslims would begin to pour into the United States. While the *legal* requirement of whiteness had been rescinded, its *social* significance continued to inform the instincts of everyone in America. Often acting on their own association between American whiteness and cognate signatures in their societies of origin (e.g., class, color, Western dominance, and supremacy), immigrant Muslims embraced this race-based arrangement, benefited directly and indirectly from it, and evinced little or no opposition to it. This, coupled with their newly established monopoly over Islamic religious authority, effectively obliterated a dimension of American Islam that had endured from its earliest beginnings: opposition to white supremacy and the promotion of a dignified existence for Blackamericans.

None of this, however, can support the Black Orientalist contention that Islam or the Muslim world provided the example on which "the enduring wrong conduct of the American nation" was modeled. Indeed, the Muslim world had itself been the victim of "enduring wrong conduct," going back precisely to the period that produced the American immigration law of 1790. Napolean landed in Egypt in 1798; the British began their defacto rule of (then Mogul) India in 1772. Immigrant Muslims may have evinced (and may continue to evince) a lack of moral energy in failing to oppose American white supremacy—and few who have benefited from the system have. But to point to Islam, Muslims, and the Muslim world as subjects rather than objects of this arrangement is truly to point to the elephant while only cursing its shadow.

Blackamerican Islam developed in the context of America's *E pluribus duo*, according to which blackness was devalued, as a social, cultural, and political pollutant. From the very beginning, opposition to white supremacy informed the understanding of virtually every Blackamerican Muslim movement in America, from the proto-Islamic to the Islamic, from Noble Drew Ali and the Honorable Elijah Muhammad through Malcolm X, Imām Wārithuddīn Muhammad and Imām Jamīl al-Amīn. It is difficult, in this light, to go along with the Black Orientalist insinuation that it is Islam that threatens the integrity of American blackness, that blackness would be somehow less devalued were it not for the presence of Muslims, or that Muslims rather than the sponsors of *E pluribus duo* are the greatest impediment to racial reconciliation in America.

It is true that from the time of the Third Resurrection and the shift in the basis of Islamic religious authority, Blackamerican Muslims have experienced great difficulty in addressing American reality on the basis of the super-tradition of Islam. Given the esteem in which Blackamericans had generally held Islam theretofore and the hopes and expectations that went along with this, this inability has bred a natural disappointment among non-Muslim Blackamericans. But the shortcomings of Blackamerican Muslims should not be abused and cast as some sort of willful betrayal or scripturally mandated neglect. It took upwards of a century and a half for Blackamerican Christians to find in Black Theology a way to "Christianize" the agenda of Black Religion so that they could pursue their aspirations for a dignified American existence not simply as blacks but as Christians. Blackamerican Muslims will have to pass through a similar evolution en route to finding ways to reconcile blackness, Americanness, and Islam. Moreover, as in the attempt of their Christian predecessors, they will have to execute this in a manner that neither reduces their religion to a cultural performance nor converts it into just another secular ideology in religious garb. Without question, this is *the* challenge facing Blackamerican Muslims in the Third Resurrection. This will be the subject of the next two chapters.

4

Between Blackamerica, Immigrant Islam, and the Dominant Culture

The rise of Black Orientalism reflects an incipient fissure in the relationship between Islam and Blackamericans. In earlier times, however, whatever criticism black leaders and thinkers may have had of Blackamerican Muslims, it never reached the point of actually altering the place of Islam in the collective psyche of Blackamericans, especially not the folk. But in the present atmosphere, given the diminished connection between Islam and Black Religion, on the one hand, and the nationwide rise of anti-Muslim mania, on the other, the danger is far more imminent. Any permanent estrangement between Islam and Blackamericans would be nothing short of disastrous for Muslims. For, the efforts of Black Orientalists notwithstanding, blacks remain the only Americans whose conversion to Islam connotes neither cultural nor ethnic apostasy. As such, it is almost uniquely through Blackamerican conversion that Islam enjoys whatever status it does as a bona fide American religion. In this context, without Blackamerican Muslims, Islam would be orphaned in the United States, with no indigenous roots to complicate attempts to relegate it to the status of an alien, hostile intrusion.

Even against this threat of American rootlessness, however, full integration into the American social and political order is not the problem-free panacea that many may take it to be. To begin with, such an enterprise would invariably entail an effort to reconcile (if not identify) Islam with the dominant culture. And to the extent that the masses of Blackamericans continue to view the dominant culture as a threat, such a move is bound to be interpreted as a confirmation of Blackamerican Muslim self-absorption and disloyalty. At the same time, given their own cultural and class-based affinities, many Blackamerican Muslims are themselves negatively disposed to the idea of "Americanization." Like many non-Muslim Blackamericans, they do not equate being rooted in the black community with embracing America. To them, Blackamerica is one thing; America is quite another.

Beyond these considerations of race, class, and culture, there is the Blackamerican Muslim understanding of Islam as a religion and a political ideology. Here the issue becomes the legitimacy, on purely religious grounds, of embracing America as a political entity. Given its status as a non-Muslim country, there is a fundamental and widespread belief among Blackamerican Muslims—reinforced, where not dictated, by certain tendencies in Immigrant Islam—that they are religiously banned from embracing, let alone pledging allegiance to, America. This position has generated several liabilities and dislocations. First, it has undermined Blackamerican Muslims' ability to invest in their American citizenship. Voting, lobbying, and holding political office have all been frowned upon, where not proscribed. Second, it strengthens the hand of those who would deny Blackamerican Muslims constitutional and other legal protections on grounds that Muslims themselves do not recognize the very constitution that guarantees such rights and liberties. Third, and in some ways most importantly, it threatens to exempt Blackamerican Muslims from the added layer of insulation that American blackness has conferred upon Blackamericans for the past several decades.

Since the rise of the Civil Rights movement, Blackamericans have functioned in effect as the "canary in the mine" of American politics. Jews, Irish, Slavs, Italians, and other "nouveau whites" all tend to measure their social and political security through the barometer of the *official* treatment of blacks. In this context, all of these groups have an indirect interest in protecting what is essentially their first line of defense.[1] American politicians, meanwhile, all have an instinctive awareness of the political cost of overt anti-blackness. Of course, given Blackamericans' otherwise naked vulnerability, this particular feature of contemporary American blackness is often overlooked, especially by immigrant Muslims. One need only consider, however, how the Justice Department and the Immigration and Naturalization Service would have responded had the Blackamerican "D.C. Sniper" John Muhammad been a Middle Easterner, or how the American public would have responded had attorney general John Ashcroft rounded up hundreds of *Blackamerican* Muslims and held them for months without charges, or whether Mississipi senator Trent Lott would have been forced out as Senate Majority Leader had he merely expressed the belief that America would have been better off had it not rescinded the National Origins Act.

As *Blackamericans,* American blackness confers upon Blackamerican Muslims a layer of insulation beyond that of the First Amendment. This is all the more relevant today, given Islam's association in both the popular and the official imagination with fiery-eyed, olive-skinned peoples who drive airplanes into tall buildings. This insulation is conferred, however, only as long as Blackamericans themselves are seen as embracing—and certainly not opposing—the American Constitutional order. If, on the basis of Islam or any other source, they cease to identify with that order, so, too, will American blackness cease to be a source of added insulation for Blackamerican Muslims.

To be sure, the backlash of September 11 has tempered the isolationist impulse among Muslims, especially immigrants. In fact, even before September 11, Blackamerican Muslim leaders such as Imām Wārithuddīn Muhammad were loudly proclaiming their belief in the complete compatibility between America and Islam. To date, however, neither group has succeeded in defining the precise terms of this acceptance nor in grounding its willingness to embrace America in authoritative, widely accepted renderings of Muslim scripture and or Tradition. As a result, neither the isolationist nor the integrationist position has achieved a decisive victory. Instead, a deep and abiding diffidence towards America continues to plague Muslim-Americans.

All of this is reminiscent of what W. E. B. Du Bois referred to as the "contradiction of double aims." According to Du Bois, the black craftsman, for example, had to struggle to escape white contempt for being a "mere" craftsman. At the same time, he had to struggle to perfect his craft in order to be able to turn his skills to the benefit of his people. This simultaneous struggle both *to be* and *not to be* produced a most debilitating form of what Du Bois famously referred to as "double-consciousness." Afflicted with this malady, the black craftsman was neither at home with being black nor with being a craftsman, because "he had but half a heart in either cause."[2] Similarly, in the absence of a true (as opposed to rhetorical) coming to terms with America, Blackamerican Muslims will continue to find themselves neither at home with being American nor with being Muslim in America, because, in truth, they have but half a heart in either cause.

In the present chapter I shall endeavor to respond to the challenge of coming to terms with this problem in a manner that reconciles the interest of embracing America with the need to preserve the traditional relationship between Islam and Blackamericans. I shall attempt to ground this response in the classical Tradition of Muslim jurisprudence calibrated to a particular understanding of the meaning of American blackness and of being American. To state the broad outline of my conclusion at the outset, it is not Islam but certain oversights and obsessions of Black and especially Post-Colonial Religion that impede the Blackamerican Muslim's ability to come to terms with America. At the same time, however, even an Islam that is unencumbered by such drawbacks must confront the challenge of how to reconcile itself with America without becoming domesticated to the point of forfeiting its higher calling and being seduced into adopting positions based solely on their popularity or proximity to power, wealth, or influence. It is here, in fact, that we come to see the importance of perhaps modifying but not breaking the relationship with the cosmic "No" of Black Religion.

American Precedents and Parallels

I should like to preface my response, however, by pointing out that on purely religious grounds Blackamerican Muslims are neither unprecedented nor unparalleled in facing the difficulties they face in seeking to come to terms with America. This is made necessary by some of the wild assertions and insinuations by nationally recognized Christian, Jewish, and secular figures to the effect that Islam alone among religions has issues with America. Such statements are clearly ideologically driven and ignore a consistent feature of the history of all religions in America.

In his magisterial work, *A Religious History of the American People*, Sydney Ahlstrom reveals that it is more the norm than the exception that religious communities encounter difficulty finding their place in this emphatically secular, pluralistic democracy. This difficulty is captured in what Ahlstrom refers to as "The American Problem." Speaking, for example, of the early Catholic community, he writes,

> Inevitably, the largest [group] was a traditional party that assumed Catholicism and the American way of life to be fundamentally at odds. Pope Pius IX with his detailed Syllabus of Errors (1864) had provided support for such a stand, and Leo XIII, surprisingly, would bolster this support in the 1890s. All that conservative Catholics hoped for, therefore, was a kind of mutually advantageous truce between two hostile cultures.[3]

Not only did this traditional party of Catholic Americans look askance upon the dominant culture in America, they found utterly alien the notion that a centralized ecclesiastical authority could receive proper recognition and function as it ought in a pluralistic, secular society in which churches existed as only one among many voluntary organizations.[4] The resulting fear and dislocation found resolution in a rather prudish maxim: "Unless forced by necessity to do otherwise, Catholics ought to prefer to associate with Catholics, a course which will be very conducive to the safeguarding of their faith."[5]

Such growing pains were neither the exclusive preserve of Catholic immigrants nor of Christian Americans of the nineteenth century. In his classic, *Christ and Culture,* H. Richard Niebuhr, a twentieth-century Protestant theologian, writes of a multiplicity of responses proffered by Protestant Americans seeking to come to terms with both the state and the dominant culture. Among these responses is that of those who reject not only America but all secular orders, on the grounds that the latter necessarily competes for a loyalty that Christians must reserve for Christ alone:

> Divinity, it seems, must not only hedge kings but also other symbols of political power, and monotheism deprives them of their sacred aura. The Christ who will not worship Satan to gain the world's kingdom is followed by Christians who will worship only Christ in unity with the Lord whom he serves. And this is intolerable to all defenders of society who are content that many gods should be worshipped if only Democracy or America or Germany or the Empire receives its due, religious homage. The antagonism of modern, tolerant culture to Christ is of course often disguised because it [modern culture] does not call its religious practices religious.[6]

This "Christ-Against-Culture" position, as Niebuhr calls it, was predicated on the belief that, "The conflict of the believer is not with nature but with culture, for it is in culture that sin chiefly resides. . . . [O]riginal sin is transmitted through society, and . . . if it were not for the vicious customs that surround a child from its birth and for its artificial training its soul would remain good."[7] Christians, in other words—at least on this view—can only preserve their Christianity by rejecting not only the secular state but the dominant culture in America as well.

More recently, a Blackamerican Protestant writer, Stephen L. Carter, has called attention to what he presents as an intractable problem confronting all religious communities in America. Carter points out that in considering the role of religion in society, Americans tend to begin with the state and ask how religion can be safely fit into the state's agenda.[8] Because they start out thinking about the needs of the state, Carter contends that Americans tend to reduce religion to an inferior status. Against this trend, however, Carter observes,

> Many citizens . . . believe that God wants us to put our faith in him and obedience to him ahead of everything else. Any argument that thinks about the state before it thinks about religion can scarcely be persuasive, or even plausible, to citizens for whom their connection to God is of first importance.[9]

For Carter, religious communities in America face at least two basic challenges. The first is the attempt by the state to "domesticate" religion, whereby it moves religion from a position in which it potentially threatens the state to a position in which it can only support the latter.[10] The second is the tendency on the part of the dominant culture both to marginalize religion and to make it harder for religious people to practice their faith and pass it on to posterity.[11] In this context, religion is confronted with the task of struggling to find and remain true to its higher calling and of avoiding becoming "so culturally comfortable that one can scarcely find differences between the vision of the good that is preached from the pulpit and the vision of the good that is believed by the culture."[12] For Carter, popularity is not at all the true measure of religion. Rather,

> Religion, at its best, is subversive. . . . Religion resists. It often resists, in particular, the values of the dominant culture. It resists because religious people sometimes feel called by God to stand for something different than what everybody else believes, no matter how radical the vision they are pressing might seem to others.[13]

All of these writers were or are mainstream scholars at premier American academic institutions. At bottom, their depictions point to the fact that whenever religion in America takes itself seriously it comes up against "The American Problem." Traditionally, this has entailed at least two interrelated challenges. First, how are religious communities to relate to the dominant culture? Second, how is religion to operate under a secular, democratic state? Ultimately, what the depictions of these scholars suggest is that in the context of American religious history, there is nothing particularly unique or "Islamic" about Blackamerican (or other) Muslims harboring initial misgivings about the legitimacy of embracing America on purely religious grounds.

There is, however, one important difference between the situation confronting Blackamerican Muslims and that confronting other religious communities in America. With the lone exception of the Black Church, no other community has had to pursue reconciliation with America through the *weltanschuaung* of a "protest people" who defined themselves in conscious opposition to the dominant culture. If German, Irish, and other European immigrants initially labored under what they perceived to be a conflict between American and Old World identities, this would soon be reconciled by their entry into American whiteness. Through the vehicle of American whiteness, these groups would be able to assimilate into the dominant culture and embrace it as "their own." Blackamericans, on the other hand, have had to contend with the daunting task of appropriating aspects of the dominant culture in the context of a consciously sustained dichotomy between the proper domains of black and white in America. If Blackamerican Muslims appear to encounter added difficulty in trying to find their place in America, this racial/cultural dichotomy, rather than, or in addition to, religion per se should be looked to as a most probable cause.

America: A Culture or a Political Arrangement?

For Blackamericans—Muslim and non-Muslim alike—the problem with America begins with the fact that they tend to conceive of and experience it primarily as a culture. Centuries-long denial of full participation in the political and legal order has bred a certain cynicism, if not obliviousness, towards America as a political ideal. Malcolm X went a long way in capturing this sentiment when he proclaimed, "No, I'm not an American. I'm one of the twenty-two million victims of Americanism. One of the . . . victims of democracy, nothing but disguised hypocrisy."[14] W. E. B. Du Bois further clarified this identity conflict when he asked, "Am I an American or am I a Negro? Can I be both? Or is it my duty to cease to be a Negro as soon as possible and be an American?"[15] Among the masses of Blackamericans, this conflict finds resolution in a heightened sense of *cultural* insularity and distinctiveness, promoting an almost desperate attachment to a unique and powerful cultural legacy that informs the only real sense of ownership they have in America. In this context, the dominant culture is experienced as a threat, and resistance to it is equated with cultural purity and authenticity. This is why, even today, after all the advances of Civil Rights and Affirmative Action, "cultural apostasy," that is, assimilationism, remains the most unforgivable sin among the masses of Blackamericans.

Speaking more specifically of Blackamerican Muslims, this tendency to experience and react to America as a culture is reinforced by the perspective of their immigrant co-religionists. Given the cultural nationalism dominating their countries of origin, immigrant Muslims tend to equate citizenship itself with culture. To be Egyptian, Syrian, or Pakistani has nothing to do with a pledge of allegiance or subscribing to a particular form of government. To belong to these nationalities is to be a member—an active member—of a particular *culture*. Egypt, Syria, and Pakistan are not political entities but cultural legacies encased in political structures. These cultures preceded these structures by centuries, and the latter are wholly nonessential to the constitution of these nationalities. Thus, for example, Egypt in the 1950s and 1960s was no less Egyptian under ʿAbd al-Nasser's Arab socialism than it is today as the nonsocialist Arab Republic of Egypt. And Palestinians who spend their entire lives in Jordan, Egypt, or Kuwait continue to identify themselves as Palestinians. This tendency to identify citizenship with culture deeply informs the immigrant perspective on America. Like their Blackamerican coreligionists, they tend to view and experience America as a *culture*, loyalty to which is equated with cultural treason or apostasy.

This tendency to experience America as a culture, alongside these deeply rooted sentiments on cultural identity and authenticity, severely impedes Muslim-Americans' ability to embrace and commit to the idea of America itself. As such, the first step towards a more positive predisposition towards America would be to explore alternative ways of looking at and experiencing America.

Liberal Versus Conservative America

In an important essay entitled "What Does It Mean to Be an 'American'?"[16] Michael Walzer reveals that there are two competing understandings or constructs of America: (1) the liberal–pluralist construct; and (2) the conservative–nativist one. The first sees America as a political *cum* economic arrangement that is culturally, religiously, and ethnically anonymous.[17] On this understanding, America connotes a manyness that is cultural *cum* religious while denoting a oneness that is political *cum* economic. To be an American, on this construction, all one has to do is "commit [one]self to the political ideology centered on the abstract ideals of liberty, equality, and republicanism [i.e., representative government]."[18] For the liberal–pluralist, the true meaning and value of America resides in the right and duty to live in peace with all other Americans, "by agreeing to respect social manyness."[19] As far as religion is concerned, America as a political arrangement is either unqualified by religion or qualified by so many religions as to render it free of any one of them.[20]

The conservative–nativist understanding, on the other hand, invests more heavily in the notion of America as a melting pot. Like liberal–pluralists, conservative–nativists see America as a political *cum* economic arrangement. But unlike pluralists, nativists perceive a certain danger in cultural/religious manyness. The latter, they fear, threatens the kind of political integrity and allegiance that is essential to the country's welfare. To nativists, not only is there a positive correlation between cultural oneness and political unity, there is also a clear advantage (if not necessity) in converting the cultural *pluribus* into a uniform national *unum*. This for nativists is the very meaning of *E pluribus unum* ("From many, one"), at least regarding those who qualify on the basis of whiteness. Undergirding this perspective is the belief that a very particular cultural genius brought forth the miracle of America and that this particular culture must be preserved, promoted, and reproduced. Those who hail from or identify with "other" traditions must be assimilated into this unique and seminal "American culture."

These two approaches to the meaning of America can be summarized in the different understandings of the hyphenated American. For conservative–nativists, the "American" in "Jewish-American" or "Asian-American" is the repository of both the greatest significance for the country and the greatest happiness for the hyphenated citizen. It is this side of the construct that denotes citizenship and rightly devotes its energy to coopting the other side. To be sure, as the British immigrant Randolph Bourne pointed out almost a century ago, far from being culturally neutral, nativists both identify "American culture" with their own processed version of the "Anglo-Saxon tradition,"[21] seeking to extend its hegemony over the left side of the hyphen. Their aim, in other words, is to "conserve" the primacy of what they purport to be the neo-Anglo Saxon element of the cumulative American legacy.

For liberal–pluralists, on the other hand, economic and political interests may be rightly sought from the right side of the hyphen, but the greater meaning and happiness for the individual resides to the left. This liberal model implies two things. First, ethnic and religious groups can intervene in political life only to *defend themselves* and advance their legitimate interests but *not* to impose their culture or religion on others. Second, the primary function of the right side of the hyphen is essentially to *protect the left side*. On this understanding, the true value of citizenship resides in both the ability to live (culturally and religiously) as one sees fit and in the knowledge that government will protect this ability as a full-fledged civil right. As such, individual citizens' primary commitment to the right side of the hyphen is essentially an effort to *protect their protection*.[22]

Clearly, these two approaches to the meaning of America bear far-reaching implications for Muslim-Americans. On the nativist approach, full commitment to and inclusion in America would entail a commitment to a neo-Anglo Saxon culture that sets itself up as the determiner and protector of all that is "truly American."[23] On the pluralist approach, however, commitment to America would not entail any commitment to any particular culture but rather to a political arrangement that protects their right to remain culturally *cum* religiously independent. This is essentially what conservative critic Samuel P. Huntington had in mind when he lamented (in an essay revealingly entitled "The Erosion of American Identity") that America is now taken by many minorities as the greatest protector of the right to remain themselves.[24]

Can Muslims Embrace America Even as a Political Arrangement?

For all the advantages of the liberal–pluralist perspective, there is one aspect of it that poses a major challenge to Muslim-Americans. I am speaking here not so much of what this model confers upon Muslims (though this, too, is an issue to which I shall return below) but rather of what it confers upon non-Muslims. The issue, to be more precise, is not whether Muslims can support a system that protects their right to be Muslims. The issue is, instead, whether they can support a system that protects the rights of gays, atheists, and witches to be gays, atheists, and witches. This is an enormous challenge for Muslim-Americans, indeed, to many a mortal flaw in the liberal–pluralist vision. To date, however, no serious attention has been devoted to this topic. Instead, the dominant trend has been to try to send it away by hurling pious rhetoric at it. This should justify my rather lengthy treatment of it here.

The Modern Muslim Political Mindset

We begin with the political model guiding the thinking and sensibilities of the modern Muslim world and passed, via the medium of Immigrant Islam, to Blackamerican (and other) Muslims in the United States. This model is neither what the Prophet Muhammad established in Arabia nor the system subsequently endorsed by the classical Tradition. These are often appealed to for purposes of authentication. But the real source from which the popular Muslim mind draws political inspiration is the concept of the Islamic State. This is a modern construct, inspired in large measure by the European concept of the nation-state. Indeed, at bottom, the Islamic State is a nation-state that is governed by Islamic law. In terms of political ideals, it stands as the ultimate goal of almost every Muslim activist. In many ways, its establishment has come to represent for Muslims what Francis Fukuyama has termed (in another context) the "The End of History."[25]

For our purposes, two features of this political mindset call for attention. First, the Islamic State, like its secular counterpart, views itself as being indivisible as a legal authority, assuming a monopoly over the enactment and implementation of law and the definition of the rights of all citizens. An important corollary to this is that, within its boundaries, all citizens must be brought under the jurisdiction of a "uniform law of the land," and there can be no appeal to any "higher" legal authority hovering above the state. Legal pluralism, in other words, is a move *away* from the ideals of the modern nation-state, secular and Islamic. It is true that modern Muslim jurists, following the example of their classical predecessors, recognize certain exemptions for religious minorities. The Constitution of the Islamic Republic of Iran, for example, grants Christians, Jews, and Zoroastrians the right to "act according to their own canon in matters of personal affairs and religious education."[26] In the popular Muslim understanding, however—which informs the general attitude of Muslim-Americans—recognition of such dispensations fades to almost nothing.

Second, the Islamic State is viewed primarily *not* as a "political arrangement" but as a religious ideal, the apotheosis of all that the Prophet taught and strived for. The Islamic State is not the result of any attempt to effect a compromise over competing political rights and interests. It is the result of Muslim ability to carry out their *religious duty* to impose their will on society at large, the only real value there could be in the institution of jihad[27] (an understanding, incidentally, far more indebted to early 'Abbasid history than it is to the actual experience of the Prophet Muhammad[28]). On this understanding, there is no legitimate political activity outside the pursuit of the kind of power that would enable Muslims to impose their will on society via the mechanism of an Islamic State. And either one is actively working for this or all of one's political activity is effectively directed against it.

This popular understanding, however, is neither the most plausible construction to be put on Muslim scripture or Tradition nor the understanding that best serves the interests of Blackamerican (or other American) Muslims. On the contrary, both the examples of the Prophet and Muslim Tradition allow for if not encourage a political culture according to which Muslims pursue political arrangements that directly serve their interests even as they indirectly serve the interests of those whose actions may contravene the rules and values of Islam. Indeed, far from constituting a theocratic commitment to societal homogenization, Islam is quite at home with negotiated political arrangements that accommodate religious and ideological pluralism.

The Prophetic Example

All of the standard biographies of the Prophet Muhammad record several events in his career in which he sought and or agreed to political arrangements that were specifically designed to afford him the ability to continue his mission as prophet, even as they left the other parties free to pursue their pagan, Jewish, or other non-Islamic ways. As is well known, the Prophet spent roughly thirteen of his twenty-three-year mission (610–632 C.E.) in his home town of Mecca, where the majority of his countrymen rejected and opposed him. In the final years before his migration to Medina, the situation in Mecca deteriorated to the point where the Prophet resorted to seeking the *political* protection of various tribes even if these tribes should refuse to accept his claim to prophethood. In the year 620, for example, he traveled to the neighboring city of Ṭā'if, where, upon the residents' refusal to embrace Islam, he asked if they would simply agree to provide him with physical protection.[29] The next few years included an activity referred to in Muslim biographical literature as the Prophet's "appealing to the tribes (*ʿarḍ nafsih ʿalā al-qabāʾil*)." Here again he showed himself to be willing to settle for no more than physical protection.[30] In all of this, from the Prophet's perspective, as long as a tribe was willing to offer him protection from physical harm, he would be able to continue his ministry. And as long as this was the case, he was willing to leave their moral and religious conversion to the power of persuasion. As he explained to one tribe whose protection he sought,

> I shall not pressure any one of you to do anything. Whoever is pleased with that to which I invite him [i.e., my religious message], so be it; whoever disagrees with it, I shall not pressure him. I simply want you to protect me from those who want to kill me, so that I may deliver the message of my Lord and so that God may settle the affair of me and those who follow me as He sees fit.[31]

Later, when the Prophet migrated to the northern city of Yathrib (later called Medina) he entered into another political arrangement that left the other parties free to pursue their pagan and non-Muslim ways. In fact, the so-called Constitution of Medina, which ratified this arrangement, recognized *all* of the parties to it, including Jews, as a single *ummah* (community, nation): "*inna yahūd banī ʿawf ummatun maʿa al-muʾminīn.*"[32] This was an agreement according to which all of the parties would recognize and support one another in the mutual interest of preserving the internal security of Medina and of protecting it from outside attack. This was not an attempt to gloss over or minimalize religious differences, for example, between Muslims and Jews. In fact, the Constitution stated explicitly: "To the Jews their religion and to the Muslims theirs."[33] It was simply to say that these religious differences did not preclude the possibility of mutual cooperation over other mutual interests. In short, Medina was a *political arrangement* according to which Muslim, pagan and Jewish beliefs and lifestyles were protected by virtue of their agreement to be "citizens" of the nascent "Prophetic State." Indeed, it was apparently in Medina that the Prophet proclaimed that had the nonbelievers invited him to an arrangement like the so-called *Ḥilf al-Fuḍūl* (*Alliance of the Virtuous*), which was a pact among a group of pre-Islamic Arab clans to defend the interests of the weak against all transgressors, he would have accepted such an invitation.[34]

Of course, it could be objected that all of the above comes from either the late Meccan or early Medinan phases of the Prophet's career, phases that were transitory and not representative of his full or final teaching. In other words, it might be argued that the Prophet's normative example comes not from this period but from the later Medinan period, where he acquired power and was able to impose his will on society to the end of establishing a social, economic, and political order in perfect harmony with Islam.

To the extent that this is true, however, that is, that the Prophet's normative teaching is to be culled from the late Medinan period, it actually confirms rather than detracts from my argument, namely, that even under the ideal political order where Muslims have the ability to impose their will, Islam recognizes the right of others to live in accordance with values that contradict its religious or moral vision. For example, in Qur'ān 5: 42, the Prophet is given the choice in his dealings with non-Muslims between judging among them or turning away from them: "So if they come to you (seeking judgment), either judge between them or turn away from them. And if you turn away from them, they will not harm you in the least. But if you judge between them, then render a judgment that is just. Verily God loves those who are just." The significance of this verse goes far beyond its content. For chapter 5 is from the very late Medinan period, believed, in fact, by many scholars to be among the last revelations the Prophet received. As such, it represents a very late if not final teaching of the Prophet and must be seen to reflect not a transitional holding pattern but an option granted the Prophet at the very end of his mission (and the very height of his power) to be exercised even under the most ideal political circumstances.

Muslim Tradition

Turning to the post-Prophetic era of the classical Tradition, here, too, we find that Muslim jurists' conception of a normatively functioning "Islamic State" did not preclude the countenance of non-Muslim beliefs and behaviors that violated Islam. This applied not only to "soft disagreements," for example, pork consumption, but to practices deemed by Muslims to be downright morally repugnant.

One example in this regard will have to serve. In his three-volume opus, *Aḥkām ahl al-dhimmah* (*Rulings Governing Non-Muslim Minorities*) the eighth/fourteenth century jurist Ibn Qayyim al-Jawzīya takes up the issue of whether the Muslim authorities may countenance what he explicitly refers to as repugnant marriages (*ankiḥa fāsida*) among non-Muslims. Ibn Qayyim was a member of the reputedly "puritanical" Ḥanbalī school and the star pupil of the celebrated Ibn Taymīya. His book, however, is not an explication of his personal views per se but an attempt to establish what could be defended as the going opinion of his school as a whole. Among the repugnant marriages taken up by Ibn Qayyim are those between a man and his mother, sister, or daughter. This was the institution of "self-marriage" practiced by Zoroastrians (*al-Majūs*), who were protected minorities under the Muslim state. Such marriages being repugnant under the law of Islam, the question arose as to whether they should be recognized or not.

Ibn Qayyim begins by addressing the issue of substantively objectionable minority practices in general. Such practices, he explains, are to be recognized under two conditions: (1) that the religious minorities who engage in them not present their case to a Muslim court; and (2) that these religious minorities believe the practice in question to be permissible according to their religion. If a religious minority either seeks the judgment of the Muslims or does not accept the marriage in question in its own religion, the Muslim authorities are not to recognize them. Otherwise, religious minorities are to be left to their own judgments. Here, however, the question of incestuous marriages among Zoroastrians is raised. Ibn Qayyim responds that some in his school held that the Muslim authorities were not to recognize such marriages, basing their position on a discretionary ruling of the second Caliph, Umar. He himself, however, insists that the most reliable opinion was that the Muslim state was to recognize such marriages. This, according to Ibn Qayyim, was based on the precedent of the Prophet, about whom he notes that there were no reports of his overturning marriages of Zoroastrians, despite his knowledge that they practiced this custom. In the final analysis, despite his own moral indignation, Ibn Qayyim insists that the going opinion in the Ḥanbalī school was that the Muslim authorities were to recognize such incestuous marriages.[35]

Clearly, Ibn Qayyim did not consider granting Zoroastrians (and other religious minorities) the right to maintain marriages that were condemned by Islam to be a violation of an optimally functioning "Islamic State," an attitude that would obviously extend to less morally significant matters. Indeed, as we saw in the case of the Prophet, premodern Muslim political culture simply did not see Islam as a politically and legally homogenizing force that sought to impose its legal and moral norms on the rest of society as a matter of religious duty. Of course, out of considerations of public policy, Muslim authorities might be obligated to stop non-Muslims from engaging in certain practices. Thus, for example, Ibn Qayyim notes that if non-Muslims publicly engage in illicit sex in ways that threaten public morals, the Muslim authorities were to intervene to stop them.[36] This, however, was a matter of public policy (on the basis of which the legitimate rights of Muslims too might be provisionally curtailed). On purely religious grounds, what religious minorities did in their own homes or neighborhoods was generally to be left to their discretion.

In sum, if the Prophet and the premodern tradition could view the "Islamic State" as a political arrangement that afforded religious minorities the right to pursue their own ways, even under circumstances where Muslims were capable of imposing their will, surely it should not violate Muslim political orthodoxy to recognize America—where Muslims do not have dominant political power—as a political arrangement that protects their basic rights, even as it affords non-Muslims the right to engage in behaviors that violate the moral and religious vision of Islam.

Islam and the U.S. Constitution

Having said this much, a major stumbling block complicating Muslim-Americans' full embrace of America, even as a political arrangement, remains, ironically, the U.S. Constitution. There are two issues here. First, many Muslim-Americans question the legitimacy of recognizing the authority of the Constitution on theological grounds. Second, Muslims question the propriety of embracing a Constitution that explicitly insists on a separation between religion and state.

As a preface to my own response to these challenges, I must point out that it is emphatically *not* my aim to vindicate the Constitution by conferring upon it the status of law (or even a source of law) that is binding on the Muslim moral/religious conscience on a par with *sharīʿah* (the Sacred Law of Islam). My aim is simply to gain for the Constitution recognition as an immovable *fact* of American life, which, like so many other facts, must be integrated into the Muslim-American's understanding of *sharīʿah* and inform his *sharīʿah*-based approach to American life.[37] In my approach, the U.S. Constitution is no more binding on the Muslim-American moral/religious conscience than was, say, tribalism or agrarianism on that of the early Muslim-Arabian community. But, as the Constitution is for Muslim-Americans as intractable a reality as were tribalism and agrarianism for the early community, the Constitution cannot be viewed as being any less relevant to constructions of normative Islam in America than were tribalism and agrarianism to earlier constructions in Arabia and elsewhere. Indeed, an American Islam that did not come to terms with American constitutionalism, *as a matter of fact*, would be as improbable, if not as grotesque, as a medieval Islam that ignored its agrarian or communitarian context.

The Authority of the Constitution

The U.S. Constitution guarantees American citizens numerous rights and freedoms. On a practical level, Muslim-Americans are as accepting of these as is anyone else. As a matter of religious conscience, however, they are often hesitant, if not hostile, toward acknowledging the validity of these provisions. This is because such an acknowledgement carries for them theological implications that call into question the indivisibility of divine sovereignty and authority, what Modern Muslim scholars like Abū al-Aʿlā al-Mawdūdī and Sayyid Quṭb refer to as *al-ḥākimīyah* or exclusive, ultimate rulership. According to this doctrine, part of the meaning of the Muslim Testimony to Faith (*shahādah*) is that God and God alone has the authority to confer rights and impose obligations. As such, any man-made law that does not derive its authority from God must be illegitimate, as a violation of God's rightful monopoly on authority. On this understanding, any Muslim who recognizes the validity of a man-made constitution is guilty of attributing ultimate authority to an entity other than God, a clear violation of Islamic monotheism (*tawḥīd*) and an open act of polytheism (*shirk*). To be sure, there is a certain forcefulness to this logic that renders it at times difficult to resist. Closer examination, however, suggests that while this argument *might* apply to Muslim governments that arrogate to themselves the right to rule independent of God, this is by no means the only or even most plausible construction to be put on the relationship between Muslim Americans and the U.S. Constitution.

To begin with, the U.S. Constitution was the result of an agreement among a group of *non-Muslims* about how to distribute political rights and power within a non-Muslim polity. Not being Muslims, it was only natural that this agreement not be based on Islamic scripture or law. To recognize this fact, and concomitantly the validity of such an arrangement, in no way entails any recognition of the right to flout God's law. Rather, this would be more akin to Muslim jurists' recognition of the validity of a couple's Christian or Jewish marriage after they had embraced Islam.[38] Obviously, this marriage did not take place in accordance with Islamic law; in fact, it may have even explicitly violated specific rules of Islam, for example, by not having witnesses present or by including a bride-price consisting of some Islamically banned commodity, such as wine or pork. Still, the marriage of this couple is almost universally recognized by Muslim jurists. And no jurist has ever hinted at this being based on any recognition of anybody's right to violate or flout God's law.

Similarly, one may take the issue of buying from and selling to non-Muslims. Clearly, this entails a recognition of the property rights of the latter, since such transactions assume a legal transfer of property. This obtains despite the fact that this right could not have accrued to these non-Muslims on the basis of their recognition of any divine authority, at least not in accordance with the creed of Islam. Yet, this alone is not sufficient to deny their rights over their property. Thus we see the Prophet Muhammad engaging in all sorts of transactions that recognized non-Muslim property rights. For example, when upon his triumphal entry into Mecca he asked the pagan Ṣafwān b. Umayyah if he could borrow some tools and weapons, Ṣafwān asked the Prophet if he would be simply borrowing these things or actually confiscating them under the pretext of borrowing. The Prophet responded that he merely wanted to borrow them, clearly recognizing Ṣafwān's right over them.[39] Of course, some Muslims might argue that what is really going on here is that Ṣafwān's property rights are being established by God's commanding the Prophet not to confiscate his property. But even if this were true (which I do not concede) this could hardly be expanded into a general rule negating the Qur'ān's recognition of all kinds of non-Muslim rights and obligations before the coming of the prophets. Indeed, in many instances the Qur'ān's reference to "the good (*al-maʿrūf*)" clearly points to what is commonly accepted among non-Muslim peoples before the coming of revelation.[40] Thus, for example, at Qur'ān 7: 85–87 and 11: 84–85, the prophet Shuʿayb clearly assumes that his people know that they are wrong in denying some of their countrymen certain rights even before his arrival with revelation. Similarly, God's negative description of Pharoah as having "transgressed the bounds" even before Moses was dispatched to him as a prophet clearly implies that Pharoah had a clear sense of what these bounds were.[41] In short, in many instances the Qur'ān does not establish but actually *confirms* pre-existing rights and standards of conduct among non-Muslim peoples. And this is done without the slightest suggestion that the prior existence of these rights and standards constitute an affront to God's monopoly as Law-Giver.

The Qur'ān and Sunnah are also full of exhortions to the Muslims to honor treaties and agreements brokered with non-Muslims. Again, however, this implies a tacit recognition of the legitimacy of non-Muslims as bargaining parties, despite the fact that they may not derive the right to do so from divine authority, at least not from a Muslim perspective. Yet, we find that even agreements to which non-Muslims attached stipulations that curtailed or infringed upon Muslim rights, as occurred, for example, in the Treaty of Ḥudaybīyah, were honored by the Prophet. In this particular treaty, the Prophet's tribe of Quraysh stipulated that Muslims who left Mecca to join the Prophet at Medina must be sent back to Mecca, but the Meccans were not required to return Muslims who left Medina to return to a still pagan Mecca. Clearly, however, the Prophet's honoring this treaty did not imply any acceptance on his part of the right of non-Muslims to challenge or violate God's monopoly as Law-Giver.

On these examples (and one could easily add more) it would appear to be a gross exaggeration to insist that Muslim recognition of the validity of the U.S. Constitution implies a violation on their part of God's rightful monopoly as Law-Giver. How can recognition of a decision among non-Muslims to confer certain advantages upon non-Muslims (and later Muslims) be said to amount to a violation of Islamic monotheism? Would all U.S. foreign aid to Muslim countries be banned under a similar logic (since such transfers assume prior property rights)? And would the acceptance by Muslims of all grants of U.S. citizenship be equally proscribed? America is not the only non-Muslim country where Muslims reside. Should Muslims in China, India, Surinam, or Nigeria be equally reticent about accepting citizenship and other rights and protections provided by their respective constitutions?

To my mind, a far more profitable approach would be not only to accept the provisions of the U.S. Constitution but to commit to preserving these by supporting and defending the Constitution itself. According to the Constitution, the U.S. government cannot force a Muslim to renounce his or her faith; it cannot deny him or her the right to pray, fast, or perform the pilgrimage; it cannot force him or her to eat pork, shave his beard, or remove her scarf (*ḥijāb*); it cannot deny Muslims the right to build mosques or schools or to vote or to hold public office; it cannot deny them the right to criticize and seek to change government officials and policies, including the person and the policies of the president. The U.S. government cannot even force a Muslim (qua Muslim) to pledge allegiance to the United States! Surely it must be worth asking if Muslims in America should conduct themselves as "nouveau free" who squander these and countless other rights and freedoms in the name of dogmatic minutiae, activist rhetoric, and uncritical readings of Islamic law and history, rather than turning these to the practical benefit of Islam and Muslim-Americans.

The First Amendment and the Separation Between Church and State

In terms of its actual substance, however, the U.S. Constitution does pose at least one apparent challenge to Muslim-Americans. This is its insistence on the separation between religion and the state. Many, if not most, Muslim-Americans understand this to mean that Islamic law (or Jewish or Christian law for that matter) is, as a permanent constitutional provision, disqualified from becoming the basis of law and or public policy. This, in their view, renders the Constitution unacceptable from their perspective as committed Muslims.

Here it should be noted, however, that the doctrine of separation between church and state does not mean that religion can play no role in public policy, or even that religious rules cannot be applied as law. Otherwise, one could not explain such laws as those banning polygamy or gay marriage. What the separation between church and state does mean, however, is that religious rules cannot be applied *simply because someone's religion says they should.* In other words, the separation invoked by the Constitution is between the *institutional* church and the state, not between religious beliefs and state officials and the laws and policies they adopt. In this context, law and public policy are conceived of as being both secular (i.e., this-worldly) and a public trust. As such, only those laws or policies that prove serviceable to the public here and now are, at least in theory, eligible for adoption by the state.

In this context, the real challenge for Muslim-Americans lies not in the Constitutional ban on admitting religious rules and values into the public domain (since, again, there really is no such ban). The real challenge lies in two other areas. First, Muslim-Americans must articulate the practical benefits of the rules of Islamic law in terms that gain them recognition by society at large. Second, assuming their success in meeting the first challenge, Muslim-Americans must resist the temptation to carry legal sanctions into areas where Islam never contemplated taking them. In other words, concern over the separation between religion and state must extend in both directions. Not only must the state be monitored for specifically antireligious bias, Muslims must also guard against seeking to translate every Islamic rule or value into a civil or criminal sanction that is backed by the state.

Regarding the articulation of the practical benefit of Islamic law to society, this is all predicated upon the basic recognition of the distinction between matters of public interest and civil transactions (*muʿāmalāt*), on the one hand, and matters of religious observance (*ʿibādāt*), on the other. In Muslim jurisprudence, matters of religious observances are those through whose implementation the primary benefit (*maṣlaḥah*) obtains in the Hereafter. These would include such things as prayer, fasting, pilgrimage, and the like. Because the primary benefit sought here is the glorification of God, these acts are not subject, *mutatis mutandis*, to social and historical considerations; nor can they be made the basis for any analogy. One cannot say, for example, that there are social or historical circumstances under which the whole purpose of prayer or fasting might be rendered redundant. Nor can one say that where God commands the performance of two units of prayer, the performance of four or seven would be better, in the same way that it would be better to pay a vendor four or seven dollars where God only requires the fulfillment of an agreed-upon two-dollar contract. On the other hand, the rules governing public interest and civil transactions are those through whose application humans derive some benefit in the here-and-now (above and beyond whatever other-worldly reward they might receive for complying with God's will). These include such rules as those governing sales, contracts, theft, drinking, marriage, divorce, etc. It is precisely because Muslim Tradition deems the worldly benefits contained in these rules to be accessible through human reason that Islamic law is extendable to cases not directly addressed by scripture.[42] It is also because of this, however, that jurists are able to debate the application, modification, and even suspension of such rules, depending on whether or not the purposes for which they were legislated are likely to be served. It was on this basis, for example, that the reputedly puritanical Ibn Taymīya once stopped his disciples from interrupting a group of newly converted Mongols who were drinking wine. Ibn Taymīya's explanation was that God had banned wine drinking because intoxication turned people away from prayer and the remembrance of God. But when these Mongols drank, he insisted, it incapacitated them and in so doing turned them away from looting, rape, and murder.[43]

It is only through this ability to penetrate and articulate the rules of Islamic law in ways that clearly define their benefit to American society that Muslim-Americans are likely to be able to influence the American social and legal order. Throughout this process, however, rather than essentializing Islamic law on the basis of the legal order in any particular Muslim country, American custom (*ʿurf*) must be recognized as a legally valid consideration in areas where Islamic law admits reliance on custom.[44] Once these compatibilities and benefits have been clearly laid out, there should be no constitutional impediments preventing a representative from bringing to the floor of the state or federal legislature proposals that are grounded in the vision and values of Islam.

It is precisely because of this, however, that Muslim-Americans must exercise extreme diligence in reminding themselves of a fundamental difference between the American and the Islamic legal systems. In American law, the legal process (i.e., the system for adjucating disputes in court) is coextensive with the system's body of legal rules. Every legal rule, in other words, is the basis for a civil or criminal action. While there are certain "sensitive areas" in which society insists that "law stays out," these are protected by simply insisting that these areas be exempted from both legal rules and legal contemplation. In other words, such sensitive issues as, for example, whether or not a mother breast-feeds her child are left to custom, religion, popular morality, malicious gossip, or other means. In the event, however, that Americans should decide that there be a legal rule governing this issue, this would mean, *ipso facto*, that civil or criminal liabilities would attach thereto.[45]

In Islamic law, on the other hand, "sensitive areas" are protected not by insisting that they be exempt from legal *rules* but by exempting them from legal *sanctions*. In other words, the scope of Islamic legal sanctions is significantly narrower than the scope of Islamic law. That is to say, Islamic law includes many legal rules that are essentially moral exhortations that carry no civil or criminal sanctions in the Here and Now and over which no court or coercive power has any jurisdiction.[46] Thus, for example, while abortion, even during the first trimester, is forbidden according to a minority of jurists, it is not held to be an offense for which there are criminal or even civil sanctions.[47] On this understanding, Muslim-Americans who oppose abortion should assiduously limit their activism to the moral sphere and avoid supporting positions that favor the imposition of criminal or civil sanctions in an area into which Islamic law itself never contemplated injecting these.[48] Indeed, this is an issue on which Islam's own version of the separation between religion and state should be assiduously observed.[49]

Between Immigrant Islam, the Dominant Culture, and Blackamerican Identity

The Problem

Having established the propriety and legitimate basis upon which Muslim-Americans can embrace America, Blackamerican Muslims are immediately confronted with a problem. On the one hand, if the left side of the hyphen in "Muslim-American" is defined through the prism of Immigrant Islam, this is likely to result in either the complete domestication of Islam or in a mildly duplicitous anti-Westernism that encourages Blackamerican Muslims to reject their Westernness while reserving the right to their immigrant coreligionists to invest in theirs. On the other hand, if Blackamerican Sunnism is to define the left side of the hyphen, its blind rejectionism and protest reflex are likely to deny Blackamerican Muslims access to norms and institutions without which they are doomed to hobbling along the bleakest margins of American society.

Let me be clear here about the stakes in all of this. Given their increased vulnerability in the aftermath of 9/11, there is a perduring temptation among many immigrant Muslims to seek acceptance by mainstream America in exchange for a domesticated Islam that can only support the state and the dominant culture and never challenge these. This invariably entails an attempt to identify Islam with the proclivities and sensibilities of the dominant group. On such a reconciliation, however, Blackamerican Muslims who feel penalized, threatened, or devalued by the dominant culture are effectively called upon, now in the name of Islam, to abandon protest and the legitimate aspects of Black Religion and acquiesce to the indignities implied by white supremacy. Meanwhile, having failed or refused to acknowledge how much Western civilization the Muslim world itself has internalized and passed on as part of an "Islamic" heritage, the other trend among immigrants is to persist in a rhetorical anti-Westernism that both feeds into and confirms self-defeating and dysfunctional definitions of American blackness. On this rhetoric, in the name of Islam, Blackamerican Muslims are called upon to reject sociocultural norms and institutions that religiously committed Arab, Indo-Pakistani, and other immigrant Muslims see no contradiction in freely accepting. The result is an "Islamic" anti-Westernism that leads Blackamerican Muslims to poverty, lack of education, and crime, while Arab, Indo-Pakistani and other immigrant Muslims continue to swell the ranks of America's doctors, lawyers, and entrepreneurs.

It should be understood, however, that the problem here is neither Immigrant Islam alone nor Blackamerican Sunnism alone. The problem is, rather, a certain synergism between these two that has welded together particular constructions of "black" and "Islamic" identities. This has resulted in a Blackamerican Muslim self-definition that, on the one hand, can only contribute negatively to the left side of the hyphen or, on the other hand, only suffocate under a hyphenated identity defined by immigrants. The only way out of this predicament is to develop alternatives to these particular constructions of "black" and "Islamic" identities.

Blackamerican Identity

Blackamericans are arguably the most American of all peoples. Unlike such nations as Britain, France, or Germany, America had to *decide* such basic things as the language it would speak, the name it would assume, and the official relationship among its races. Like America, Blackamericans have also had to *decide* how to construct out of the disparate and often conflicting pieces of their history a self-understanding that effectively serves their quotidian and cosmic needs and aspirations. The difficulty of this enterprise has been reflected in the phenomenon, almost unique to them, of repeatedly changing the name by which they identify themselves as a people: Negro, Colored, black, Bilalian, Afro-American, African-American, Blackamerican. Yet, the very fact of these changes points to a prerogative and a range of possibilities that few other groups in America can boast.

The quest for a constructive, dignified American identity has always been complicated for Blackamericans by their corporate predisposition as a "protest people" rooted in a cosmic "No." On the one hand, certainly since the frustrated back-to-Africa aspirations of the 1930s, Blackamericans have recognized America as home. At the same time, almost every gesture towards embracing those aspects of the dominant culture that would enable them to operate effectively at home has been subject to the veto power of a corporate reflex that proscribes the object under consideration—from academic performance to the use of standard English, from certain forms of sartorial neatness to "making it" in the white man's world. As noted earlier, this protest reflex has translated into a marked preference for extra-American intellectual and cultural repositories out of which to construct a Blackamerican identity.

This openness to extra-American cultural and intellectual repositories has been critical to the development of Blackamerican Muslim identity. Their protest reflex toward America has prompted them, indeed, to transfer their sense of cultural identity to the Muslim world, or, more properly, the Middle East and, albeit to a much lesser extent, Asia and Africa. Far from turning their backs on American blackness, however, this move was always conceived of as an act of confirming the latter. It was (and remains) part of the ongoing search for the proper response to the disquieting suggestion by H. Rap Brown (now Abdullāh Jamīl al-Amīn) that "racism systematically verifies itself when the slave can only break free by imitating the master: by contradicting his own reality."[50] Going outside America is still perceived by Blackamerican Muslims (and other Blackamericans) to be an effective and expedient means of breaking free of the master without imitating him and of constructing a Blackamerican identity that does not contradict their sense of authentic self.

Meanwhile, Blackamerican Muslims' relationship with Immigrant Islam has added a distinctly religious dimension to both this search and this protest sentiment. Aided by the interpretive goadings and assurances of their immigrant brethren, Blackamerican Muslims commonly construe Islam as implying that any imitation of the infidel West is tantamount to Unbelief. In this context, if Blackamerican "cultural orthodoxy" threatens to condemn and ostracize those deemed guilty of participating in "white" ways, "Islamic orthodoxy" now bans Blackamerican Muslim participation on pain of divine retribution. To bolster this position, a Prophetic hadith, ubiquitously cited in the 1970s and 1980s, is strategically pressed into service:[51] "Whoever imitates a people becomes one of them (*man tashabbaha bi qawmin fa huwa minhum*)."[52] On this construction, not only is participation in the dominant order a violation of true blackness, it is additionally a violation of Islam—or more properly "Islamic identity"—at least for Blackamerican Muslims.

"Islamic" Identity

While it is commonly assumed that the use of the adjective "Islamic" comes of a natural tendency to relativize nouns, there is actually much more to this neologism than initially meets the eye. It is true, as a simple matter of linguistic convention, that that which relates to America is commonly rendered "American," just as that which relates, say, to philosophy becomes "philosophical." It is also true, however, that relative adjectives have both the capacity to *describe* and *prescribe*. "American," in this regard, can be used both to denote what Americans do, as a matter of course, and what Americans should do, as a matter of duty. In this latter capacity, relative adjectives cease to be mere linguistic conventions and enter the realm of ideological tools. Through the ideological use of the term "American," one can actually sit in judgment over the actions of all who purport to belong to America. This, far more often than is admitted or perhaps even realized, is the use to which Immigrant Islam has put the term "Islamic."

To be sure, the real power of this term resides in its implied assertion that all that is not so designated must be "un-Islamic." For Blackamerican Muslims, this would mean the bulk of their Western heritage. Ironically, however, while the neologism "Islamic" had the effect of proscribing Western civilization for Blackamerican Muslims, it was precisely through its *acceptance* of aspects of Western civilization that the Muslim world had come to convert the term into a full-fledged religious and civilizational marker.

Prior to modern times, the term "Islamic" (*Islāmī* in Arabic) was almost never used to define the provenance, status, or substance of things. There was no such thing as "Islamic art" (*fann islāmī*), "Islamic economics" (*iqtiṣād islāmī*), or even "Islamic law" (*fiqh islāmī*). To be sure, there were anomolies, such as the famed al-Ghazālī's referring to Ibn Sīnā and al-Farābī as "Islamic philosophers" (*al-mutafalsifah al-islāmīyīn*). This, however, was clearly an anomaly and the exception that proved the rule. For the very men to whom al-Ghazālī refers as "Islamic" are precisely the men he condemned as infidels.[53] "Islamic," in other words, had no clear descriptive nor prescriptive power but was used as a throwaway for those who in one way or another associated themselves with Islam. The term was rarely used in the body of serious writings but appeared mostly in titles of books, and this for the manifest purpose of maintaining rhyme, in accordance with Arab convention (e.g., *Ijtimāʿ al-juyūsh al-islāmīyah ʿalā al-zanādiqah wa al-jahmīyah* or *Maqālāt al-islāmīyīn wa ikhtilāf al-muṣallīn*).

The encounter with the modern West, however, ultimately changed the status of "Islamic." Inasmuch as the rise of the West converted the achievements of Darwin, DesCartes, and Hegel from mere English, French, or German achievements into explicitly "Western" ones, it also engendered the need for a parallel convention for demarcating the non-Western "other." The Western provenance of the modern neologism "Islamic" is perhaps best revealed in its tendency to connote both geography and ethnicity. "Islamic," in other words, connotes not simply that which is related to or a product of Islam as a religion but that which relates to a particularly non-European people in a non-European part of the world. In this capacity, it carries both descriptive and prescriptive force.

To be fair, it must be pointed out that medieval Islam offers what appear at first blush to be precedents for this. For example, in his famous work on theological sects, the sixth/twelfth-century al-Shahrastānī includes certain Christian thinkers under the rubric of "philosophers of Islam."[54] While al-Shahrastānī does not use the term "Islamic," his reference is clearly to Christians who live under Islamic rule and may thus be included as part of Muslim civilization. It is precisely here, however, that the parallel to the modern convention among Muslims and non-Muslims breaks down. For no modern Muslim nor non-Muslim would include the likes of such Arab Christians as Michel Aflaq or Ṣanʿ Allāh Ibrāhīm among the "thinkers of Islam." Rather, in Western parlance, the modern "Islamic" began as an instrument to demarcate the boundary between the West and a particular set of "others." In Muslim hands, it would go on to evolve into a full-blown signifier of normative Islam and a tool for delineating the boundary between it and non-Islam. Its added utility, moreover, as a mechanism for elevating the achievements of Muslims to the level of a civilization rivaling that of Europe rendered it all the more irresistible and gained for it universal acceptance throughout the Muslim world.

Through this convention, Muslims in (and later from) the Muslim world would be able to convert their agreed-upon conventions and preferences into normative institutions for Muslims everywhere. Middle Eastern, and to a lesser extent Asian, food, clothing, and social etiquette became "Islamic" and thus the signature and standard for Muslims all over the world. From this point on, "texts," be they the Qur'ān, hadith, or the books of Tradition, cease to be the reference for what is normative for Muslims, and the *experience* of a particular time, place, and people emerges as the model with which all understandings and expressions of Islam must be reconciled if they are to be considered "Islamic."

On this criterion, the modern Muslim world would be transformed into a set of transcendent, one-size-fits-all solutions and precedents that were to be dutifully applied by pious Muslims everywhere. In this context, if the protest reflex in Blackamerican identity demanded the rejection of all that was construed to be a dictate of American whiteness, "Islamic" identity not only reinforced this by proscribing all that was Western, it concretized it by identifying the only acceptable alternatives available to a Muslim. On this understanding, any thought of mining America for elements from which to construct a positive Blackamerican Muslim persona was preempted by the *prima facie* presumption that such an enterprise would be un-Islamic.

The Solution

As mentioned, there are two aspects to solving the problem of constructing a positive Blackamerican Muslim persona and religio-cultural identity. The first is connected with the definition of American blackness. The second has to do with the manner in which Islam is understood and applied to American reality.

An Alternative Modality of American Blackness: Embracing America In Protest

Key to the success of any attempt to reconstruct Blackamerican identity is the recognition that American history has transformed Blackamericans into a protest people. While the attending cosmic "No" may complicate efforts to ingratiate Blackamericans with middle-class and genteel values that are essential to socioeconomic well-being, the solution can never be as simple as abandoning this protest sentiment. To do so would be to abandon the only insulation Blackamericans have against the dreaded threats of assimilationism, domination, and cultural apostasy. In this light, the perennial problem for Blackamericans—Muslim and non-Muslim alike—has been how to embrace ways and institutions that are identified with the dominant culture without violating one's sense of agency and authentic self.

This is what the early Blackamerican proto-Islamic movements understood so well. Their alternative modalities of American blackness were at once functionally pragmatic and virulently antiassimilationist. This presented Blackamericans not only with the opportunity to escape the negative definitions of blackness imposed by the dominant culture but also to embrace in good conscience aspects of the collective American heritage that prepared them for a dignified social, economic, and political existence. This was an alternative modality of American blackness that not only rejected the inherent superiority of whiteness but also highlighted and took aim against the most egregious pathologies and dysfunctionalities of the urban ghetto. Wanton hedonism, the glorification of ignorance, victimology, and the dereliction of traditional duties of manhood gave way to thrift, discipline, social etiquette, and education as essential features of any self-respecting "black man."

What is important, however, in all of this is that much of the *substance* of the Blackamerican Islamizers' alternative modality of American blackness was drawn from the most conservative repositories of American culture and history. Yet, this new way of being black enjoyed the advantage of being both perceived of and embraced as act of *protest*. This is a large part of what set the proto-Islamic Islamizers apart from the Black Church, whose subscription to some of the same cultural norms and practices drew the charge of Uncle-Tom assimilationism. A Black Muslim wearing a suit and a bow-tie and speaking "Ivy League" English simply did not connote the same meanings that were associated with a black Christian doing the same. And it is here, in this masterful feat of appropriation, that we come to understand and appreciate the genius and significance of the early Blackamerican Islamizers, especially the Honorable Elijah Muhammad: *In the name and spirit of protest* they were able to construct a Blackamerican "Muslim" persona that fully embraced middle-class and genteel American norms and values!

What the Honorable Elijah Muhammad and the early Islamizers seemed to have understood was that, in the words of Harold Cruse, "Two cultural negatives cannot possibly add up to a cultural positive in society at large."[55] If white America acted against Blackamericans by denying them a positive place in the culture, the negative effects of this could not be offset by a simple act of reciprocal rejectionism on the part of blacks. At the same time, as a protest-people, Blackamericans could not hope to solve this problem in good conscience by simply capitulating to the standards imposed by the dominant group. Elijah Muhammad recognized, however, a subtle but critical difference between the *substance* of middle-class and genteel culture and the claim of exclusive *ownership* over these by white Americans. His approach was thus to *embrace* large aspects of the substance of the dominant culture while *rejecting* white Americans' claim of exclusive ownership. As a result, he was able to create an alternative to the modality of American blackness that reveled in embracing only what white America rejected. In its place, the Honorable Elijah Muhammad created the BASp, the "Black Afro-Saxon 'protestant,' " complete with its own black version of Weber's Protestant work ethic and all.

Elijah Muhammad recognized that Blackamericans were a protest people. He also understood that any successful self-understanding of American blackness would have to be rooted in the cumulative legacy of America as a whole. His strategy was thus to develop a mechanism for embracing needed aspects of the dominant culture as an act of protest. His success at balancing these coequal interests is what distinguished his from almost every other religious and nonreligious group in Blackamerica in the twentieth century.

As mentioned, the Black Church embraced the same middle-class and genteel values. But it failed to do so in manner that connoted protest. Instead, with the exception of such firebrands as A.M.E. Bishop Henry McNeil Turner (whose statements and actions appear to be a bit too radical for its taste) the Black Church seems to have accepted the substance of middle-class culture without obviating its rejection of white America's claim of ownership over it. In fact, the Black Church appears to have realized little success in concealing the appearance that what rendered education and the like valuable was precisely the fact that it was esteemed as such by whites. This left it open to the charge of assimilationism and helped sustain the image of Christianity as the white man's religion. In the 1980s, the Afrocentrics emerged. They chose, this time in a spirit of protest, to reject much of the substance of middle-class and genteel culture. But they failed (in fact refused) to replace this with a viable *American* alternative. As for black academics and intellectuals, in addition to the distance that has traditionally separated them from the black masses, the academy has always exercised a taming effect on black protest, with the threat of either banishing protest-intellectuals to the periphery or drumming them out of a job.

More recently, Hip Hop (at least in its "pure" form) has emerged to replace Christianity, Afrocentrism, and Islam as the voice of black protest. Yet, it, too, has proved to be blind to the critical distinction between substance and ownership. On this oversight, it reproduces the perennial mistake of rejecting the substance of middle-class and genteel refinement and cedes ownership over these to white America. As a result, no viable, alternative composite of cultural values and institutions emerges. Instead, the masses of black youth are given over to customs and habits that thoroughly undermine the possibility for a dignified American existence. Meanwhile, protest—if we can still call it that—ends up as a commodity bought, sold, and manipulated by music companies and a narrow sliver of the top superstar Rappers.

The solution to the negative implications of existing régimes of black self-definition resides in "protest appropriation." This is the only means of devising an alternative modality of American blackness that can both provide for the legitimate needs and aspirations of Blackamericans in America *and* be embraced as fully authentic. Given all the talk of late about how racial and ethnic identities are social constructions, it should be easier today to recognize that American history has fashioned Blackamericans into a protest-people and that any positive vision for Blackamerica will have to begin with this fact. It may be, however, precisely this fact that falls from conscience as the first casualty of black upward mobility and intellectualism.

Islam over Islamic

As far as Blackamerican Muslims are concerned, since the Great Migration to Sunni Islam the process of "protest-appropriation" has been arrested. Rather than mining America for positive elements for the construction of a Black*american* Muslim persona, the focus of Muslim cultural authenticity has radically shifted to an imagined overseas utopia. Whereas Elijah Muhammad rejected white America's exclusive claim of ownership over the cumulative American heritage, Blackamerican Sunnis have shifted their protest back to the *substance* of that heritage as being "un-Islamic."

The result has been nothing short of disastrous. As James Baldwin once put it, "Negroes do not . . . exist in any other [country]."[56] As such, only a persona rooted in the knowledge, history, and experience of America could be effective in serving the needs and interests of Blackamericans.[57] As for the "virtual blackness" pieced together from disparate imaginings about the Muslim world, it could neither recognize nor accommodate the concrete realities of Blackamerican Muslims. On the contrary, it could only breed a certain sociocultural agnosticism, as a result of which Blackamerican Muslims ended up deflecting and pretending not to be affected by the problems and dysfunctionalities of the urban ghetto. And because this self-perception was vested with the authority and imprimatur of Islam, it actually concealed and placed beyond critique numerous fears, complexes, and inadequacies. It became common, for example, to hear Blackamerican Sunnis dismiss entrepreneurship as "Just *dunyā* (the fleeting life of this world)" or to dismiss education on the grounds that "The Prophet Muhammad didn't have a college degree!" In varying degrees, all of the Old Guard Sunnis displayed aspects of this mentality. And even Imām Wārithuddin Muhammad, still dogged by a perduring authority deficit, has had difficulty sustaining a positive expression of American blackness that is recognized as being sufficiently "Islamic."

Fortunately, America is not the first new society into which Islam found its way.[58] And when we look at the early approach to processing non-Muslim reality we find a fundamental distinction between non-Muslim and "un-Islamic." Sustaining this distinction was the work of what is technically known as Muslim jurisprudence (*uṣūl al-fiqh*), what I have been referring to as the classical Tradition. It is on the basis of this tradition that Blackamerican Muslims are likely to find their way out of the present crisis.

At the risk of oversimplification, there are two elements of the classical Tradition whose consideration would greatly modify the manner in which Blackamerican Muslims process American reality. The first relates to the range of possible religio-legal statuses that might be assigned to American ways and institutions. The second is connected to Islamic law's recognition of custom as a probative consideration in legal deliberations.

At its most elementary level, Muslim jurisprudence subsumes all human actions under one of five legal categories or statuses. These are: (1) obligatory (*wājib*); (2) forbidden (*ḥarām*); (3) recommended (*mandūb*); (4) discouraged (*makrūh*); and (5) neutral (*mubāḥ*). When failure to perform an act incurs punishment or censure in the Afterlife while its performance incurs reward or favor, the act is said to be "obligatory." An example of this would be the five daily prayers. When failure to eschew an act incurs punishment while eschewing it incurs divine reward, the act is said to be "forbidden." Adultery would be an example here. When failure to perform a commanded act is not deemed to incur punishment while its performance is deemed to incur reward, the act is said to be "recommended." Paying a severance gift to an erstwhile wife following divorce is deemed by many jurists to be recommended (though others, e.g., in the Shāfiʿī school, hold it to be obligatory). When God, or by extension His Prophet, prohibit an act whose nonperformance incurs reward but whose performance incurs no punishment, this act is said to be "discouraged." Washing more than the designated members during ritual ablutions is deemed by many jurists to be discouraged. Whenever neither the performance or non-performance of an act are deemed to entail reward or punishment, the act is said to be "neutral," for example, standing up or washing one's car.[59]

In modern times, it has become customary to speak of the rules of Islamic law in the binary terms of forbidden (*ḥarām*) and permissible (*ḥalāl*). This is actually something of an oversimplification that conceals the gradations of propriety and impropriety represented in the recommended (*mandūb*) and discouraged (*makrūh*) categories. Oftentimes, this results in matters that are actually only discouraged or recommended being appropriated to the forbidden or obligatory categories. This latter tendency is further complicated by the fact that among the alternate terms for "recommended" is the term "*sunna*," which is the same term used to denote the normative practice and teachings of the Prophet Muhammad. On this dual use of "*sunna*," one who abandons an act that is simply recommended stands to be accused of having abandoned the Prophet's *sunna*, a matter of no mean consequences.

For our purposes, the functional significance of this approach to assessing human actions is two-fold. First, not everything deemed good, bad, wholesome, or repugnant is necessarily rendered obligatory or forbidden. Second, the provenance of a practice, that is, where it originated, is virtually irrelevant in determining its legal status. The classical tradition simply did not recognize "foreign" or "alien" as legal categories. This is clearly demonstrated in the manner in which numerous institutions and practices of alien or unknown origin were treated. To take just one example, when hashish first entered Muslim society in the fifth/eleventh century, the ensuing legal discussion ultimately produced a consensus condemning its use. This was a gradual development, however, that included many nuances and variations along the way. In the end, despite the obvious sensitivities raised by such an issue, the foreign origins of hashish were totally excluded as a probative factor in determining its legal status.[60]

As for the issue of custom, classical jurists understood that scripture did not prescribe *everything* needed to establish and maintain a societal order grounded in the rule of law. Scripture might require, for example, the reliance upon only upright persons as witnesses in court. But different societies would rely upon different social indicators in seeking to identify such individuals. For example, in places like Iraq, a man who did not wear a respectable head-covering was generally deemed unacceptable as a witness, presumably because the apparent lack of self-respect reflected in his flouting this social norm suggested that he would have no compunctions about lying. In places like Muslim Spain, however, wearing a head-covering had no significance at all.[61]

Outside the area of "religious observances (*ʿibādāt*)," that is, prayer, fasting, and the like, jurists relied on custom in virtually every area of Islamic law. Because of this, monitoring changes in custom was a major concern, for if jurists in Spain relied uncritically on manuals written by jurists in Iraq, rulings that had been reached in contemplation of one set of circumstances might be wrongly applied to other cases. This is precisely the concern expressed in a question put to a seventh/thirteenth-century Egyptian jurist, Shihāb al-Dīn al-Qarāfī:

> What is the correct view concerning those rulings found in the school of al-Shāfiʿī, Mālik and the rest, which have been deduced on the basis of habits and customs prevailing at the time these scholars reached these conclusions? When these customs change and the

> practice comes to indicate the opposite of what it used to, are the rulings recorded in the manuals of the jurisconsults rendered thereby defunct, it becoming incumbent to issue new rulings based on the new custom? Or is it to be said, "We are mere followers (*muqallids*). It is thus not our place to issue new rulings, as we lack the qualifications to perform unmediated interpretation (*ijtihād*). We issue opinions, therefore, according to what we find in the books handed down on the authority of the independent interpreters"?[62]

> Al-Qarāfī's response was both clear and unequivocal.

> Holding to rulings that have been deduced on the basis of custom, even after this custom has changed, is a violation of Unanimous Consensus (*ijmāʿ*) and an open display of ignorance of the religion.[63]

This view was by no means exceptional among premodern jurists. Nor has it been abandoned in modern (or more properly, Modernized) Muslim jurisprudence. In a recent work, a Saudi scholar, ʿĀdil Qūtah, confirms the duty of every jurist to give due consideration to the specificities of time and place. Drawing on the views of several premodern and modern jurists, Qūtah affirms that it is naive and erroneous to imagine that jurists in one place or time could arrive at rulings that serve the legitimate needs and interests of Muslims in all places and times:

> It is obvious that any authoritative jurist of any school, nay, any independent jurist (*mujtahid*), period, can only devise rulings for his particular time and place. It is impossible for him to extract rulings for all times and places. Rather, the most that he can do is lay down general precepts, universal maxims and basic principles on the basis of which his followers and descendents can proceed (to extract rulings).[64]

The point in all of this is that in seeking to establish the extent to which Blackamerican Muslims may avail themselves of this or that particular cultural practice or social institution, Islam neither dictates nor warrants looking to the latter's Western, Eastern, "white," or "black" provenance. On the contrary, what Islam requires is simply that the choices made do not, *ceteris paribus*, contradict interests that the religious law seeks to promote. This would include, in my view, the construction of a modality of American blackness that is both rectifying and empowering in a specifically American context. And if the cumulative American cultural legacy constitutes the richest repository from which to draw in this regard, the only impediment to exploiting this would be where doing so violated the religious law *on substantive grounds*. Indeed, as the Modernized jurist ʿAbd al-Wahhāb Khallāf put it, "sound custom" is simply "that which the people generally recognize as good, which does not violate the sources of Islamic law by rendering what is forbidden permissible or what is permissible forbidden."[65] Of course, for historical, cultural, or other reasons, Blackamerican Muslims may find themselves inclined towards or repelled by this or that general American practice. This visceral preference should not be confused, however, with religious prohibition or obligation. And where there is no prohibition or obligation at Islamic law, such preferences should be indulged or eschewed only to the extent that they do not obliterate other legitimate interests.

Take, for example, the issue of working for non-Muslims. While some (classical) jurists hold this to be discouraged (*makrūh*),[66] Islamic law does not prohibit it (assuming that the work itself does not violate Islamic law).[67] For historical reasons, however, many Blackamerican Muslims may object to "working for the man." As there is certainly no religious *obligation* to work for non-Muslims, this sentiment could be fully indulged, assuming that it did not obliterate the basic obligation upon Muslim men to support themselves and their families. Where, however, there proved to be no other sources of sustainable income, no Muslim would be justified in wrapping personal bias, laziness, or misplaced pride in the guise of religious piety by raising to the level of an absolute prohibition the discouragement expressed by some jurists for working for non-Muslims.

Or take the issue of education. Among the masses of Blackamericans, education continues to be viewed as a *cultural* marker. Perhaps nowhere else does the claim of ownership implied by the dominant group go farther in nudging Blackamericans into a "self-identity" that perpetuates economic, political, and even social marginalization. Blackamerican Muslims, meanwhile, routinely reinforce this cultural boundary by grounding it in articulations of Islam. By means of such mechanisms as the aforementioned hadith, "Whoever imitates a people becomes one of them (*man tashabbaha bi qawmin fa huwa minhum*)," education is frowned upon as a vehicle and manifestation of assimilation into the ways of the white, unbelieving "Other." To be sure, this is misguided protest at its worse. For it can hardly be denied that the Prophet strongly encouraged if not required the pursuit of beneficial knowledge; and the classical Tradition confirms this value from beginning to end. Blackamerican Muslim biases against particular aspects of secular education are one thing; blanket judgments to the effect that secular education is religiously proscribed or valueless is another thing altogether.

If the sentiments of protest are to inform Blackamerican Muslim judgments, this cannot be allowed at the expense of bona fide interests in Islam.

Secular education must be assessed in terms of the real harm or benefit it confers upon the individual and or the community. On this criterion, the Ḥanbalī jurist Ibn Qudāma (d. 620/1219) proscribed the study of Greek rationalism on grounds that it corrupted the beliefs of the Muslims.[68] On the other hand, the legendary al-Ghazālī (d. 505/1111) insisted that there was a communal *obligation* (*farḍ kifāya*) to produce medical doctors without whose services the community could not thrive.[69] As for the issue of religio-cultural authenticity, certainly we must question the notion that as doctors or attorneys Blackamerican Muslims become somehow inauthentic (as blacks or as Muslims) while Arab or Pakistani doctors and attorneys retain both their ethnic and their religious authenticity.

In sum, to the extent that the classical Tradition replaces the modern "Islamic" as the basis for material judgments, Islam ceases to be an impediment to a Blackamerican Muslim construction of a modality of being both black *and* Muslim *in America* that enables them to live both fully and righteously. Key to the success of this enterprise, however, given Blackamericans' predisposition as a protest-people, will be maintaining the distinction between substance and ownership and the understanding that meaningful protest is not against the substance of wholesome and functionally useful features of "American culture" but against the implied claim of exclusive ownership over these by the dominant group. In this regard, it is reported that when the Prophet Muhammad migrated from Mecca to Medina, he found the Jews there fasting the day of *Āshūrā'* (the tenth day of the first month of the Arabian calendar). Upon inquiring about their reasons, he was told that the fast marked the commemoration of the Exodus of Moses and the Children of Israel from Egypt. To this the Prophet replied, "We have a greater right to this, then." He fasted and urged his followers to do the same.[70]

Embracing America Without Embracing the American False Universal

Having established the foregoing, I must rush to add that it would be no more prudent or principled for Blackamerican Muslims to engage in a blind acceptance of middle class and genteel America than it would be for them to contine in blind protest against it. In this regard, even Martin Luther King Jr. would express reservations, in the final weeks of his life, about the consequences of full Blackamerican inclusion. During a private moment with his friend, Harry Belafonte, he confessed that he believed that full integration was merely a matter of time. But, he added, "I've come on a realization that really deeply troubles me. . . . I've come to the realization that I think we may be integrating into a burning house."[71] At bottom, King's sentiment summarizes the other side of the perennial question confronting Blackamericans: If Blackamericans can no more fully reject America than they can fully embrace her, to where are they to turn for extra-American values and institutions with which to promote their own way of life?

The dominant trend among Blackamericans has been to ignore this question. Cornell West draws on the insights of the Russian writer Anton Chekov and calls himself a "Chekovian Christian"; and the efforts of the Afrocentrics to de-center America are well known. But these are exceptions to the general tendency to rely on the anticipated rewards of full-inclusion to crowd out questions of substance and provenance. This may work for a while. But, in the end, it is not likely to extinguish the nagging feeling that even if one is able to move from the back to the front of the bus, it remains nonetheless someone else's bus that can only deliver one to destinations predetermined by them.[72] No one is more instinctively attuned to this feeling than Blackamerican youth. And it is perhaps this more than anything else that explains their alienation from both the dominant culture and Blackamerican intellectual and political leadership.

In varying degrees, Blackamericans continue to labor under the false universal that enshrines the values and aspirations of the dominant culture as both normal and normative. In this context, Blackamerican identity, proclivities, and aspirations remain not original but additive. Upwardly mobile blacks commonly aspire to the achievements of white Americans *plus color*, despite (or perhaps because of) their experience as *objects* of a social, economic, political, and legal history over which the latter reigned as subjects. This experience, while cognate in many ways with the Third World colonial experience, is in other ways significantly different from the latter. For while the European colonial masters were setting up French, British, and German schools and civic organizations to "civilize" the best and brightest among their subjects, Blackamericans, all the way up to the second half of the twentieth century, were attending segregated schools, fighting in segregated armies, and living in emphatically segregated neighborhoods. While the African or Asian tendency to extol the achievements of "the West" came thus of a more "natural" assimilation of ideas over time, it was far more power and control that produced this tendency among Blackamericans. For many Blackamericans, especially conservatives, this exercise of power and control has constricted their universe of spontaneous meanings and translated into an indiscriminant devotion to replicating the ideals and achievements of the dominant culture, perhaps in kunte cloth. This short-circuits self-understanding and arrests the development of alternative means through which individual and collective well-being might be contemplated and pursued.

To take just one example, in his controversial New York Times best-seller, *Losing the Race*, the black conservative John McWhorter criticizes the black community for, among other things, failing to call their leaders and public figures to account. He mentions in this regard the sexual indiscretions of Adam Clayton Powell and, especially, Elijah Muhammad. For the record, sexual indiscretion was not the main point of this section of McWhorter's book (suggestively entitled "Black People Can Do No Wrong"). But his tone and attitude towards black "philanderers" painfully demonstrate his obliviousness to the possibility of going beyond the moral and institutional categories of the dominant culture, if not as a criterion for judging Blackamerican public figures then as a basis for contemplating alternative arrangements for coming to terms with their concupiscible tendencies.[73]

McWhorter's list of "philandering" black men could have been easily extended, from Martin Luther King Jr., Johnny Cochran, Muhammad Ali, Jesse Jackson, Bill Cosby, and, more recently, Kobe Bryant, to the local roving-eyed preacher and the "brother on the block." But if this is the case and monogamy is really as big a challenge to black men as such a list would seem to suggest, is there any reason not to consider polygamy as a viable option other than the fact that it is not accepted by the dominant culture? If only 39 percent of Blackamerican women are married while 67 percent of Blackamerican children are born out of wedlock,[74] is the black community really served by a régime of morality that so clearly goes against its sensibilities and interests? Of course, no moral system can command respect by simply catering to the undisciplined passions of its adherents. But neither can it be sustained through blind and blanket condemnations that fail to effect a balance between interest and principle. For his part, even in the purported interest of the Blackamerican community (the whole point of his book) McWhorter does not even *consider* polygamy as an option. Instead, he restricts himself to the categories of the dominant culture and its state-sponsored "norm," and then proceeds to bludgeon would-be dissenters into adjusting to this presumably universally valid régime. As Nancy Cott notes in her recent work on the history of marriage in America, for those who are members of the dominant group, enforcement of such a standard might feel a lot like freedom.[75] But for those outside this privileged community, such enforcement can only connote the antithesis of liberty.

Embracing America should not be equated with embracing the American state's or the dominant culture's false universals. To pretend that there is only one American history and social reality and thus only one normal or acceptable response to these is to reinforce the invisibility of American whiteness as a socially constructed mode of being whose "normalness" reclines fundamentally on the use (and at times abuse) of power. Especially for Blackamericans, this tendency must be resisted and opposed. Otherwise, like George Orwell's protagonist in the classic *1984*, Blackamericans will be forced to continue to pretend to be served by values, customs, and institutions that betray their most deeply-felt sensibilities and bring them neither solace nor improved individual or collective lives.[76]

And yet, it is only and precisely by virtue of their conspicuous participation in the American constitutional order that Blackamerican (and other) Muslims can qualify to enjoy the kinds of rights and protections that make protest and the creation of alternative modalities of Americanness even possible. In fact, it may be these very protections that afford Muslim-Americans the greatest ability to rise to their highest selves. For only these—and no other—American protections can sustain the possibility of their expressing the kind of religious commitment to which they feel scripturally bound, on the one hand, and which they hear conscientiously expressed by other American religious groups, on the other. To take just one example of such non-Muslim-American religious expression, Stephen Carter proclaims in his recent manifesto:

> I write not only as a Christian but as one who is far more devoted to the survival of my faith—and of religion generally—than to the survival of any state in particular, including the United States of America. I love this nation, with all its weaknesses and occasional horrors, and I cannot imagine living in another one. But my mind is not so clouded by the vapors of patriotism that I place my country before my God. If the country were to force me to a choice, and, increasingly, this nations tends to do that to many religious people, I would unhesitatingly, if not without some sadness for my country, choose my God.[77]

It may be a while, given present realities, before the dominant culture in America is prepared to hear such words from a Muslim. But America as a political arrangement makes it possible for Muslims to speak these words now. Indeed, in the final analysis, it may be that of all the Americans, Muslim-Americans have the greatest stake in a constitutional order that enables them to "protect their protection." And, given all that has been said, it may be, from the perspective of the law of Islam, more a duty than a right to uphold and fully support that order, as a matter of fact if not as a scriptural imperative.[78]

Were Malcolm X alive today, he would be able, in good conscience, as a practicing Sunni Muslim, to abandon his earlier rejectionism and proclaim without hesitation, "Yes, I am an American." This would neither threaten nor compromise his status as a champion of protest in the Blackamerican community. For such a proclamation could now be made in a spirit and as an act of protest. Nor would this jeopardize his status as a committed Sunni Muslim; for he could now argue and show that such a position was consistent with the best tradition of Sunni Islam. In fact, by this time Malcolm himself might be leading the way in the transfer of Islamic religious authority from immigrant to native-born hands. And in this capacity, he would have come full-circle from a marginalized *consumer* of "Islamic" ideas to being among the *producers* of the parameters of a properly constituted orthodox Islam in America, in effect from Malcolm X to "Ibn Taym-X." Being grounded in both American reality *and* the classical Tradition, Malcolm would be in a position not only to challenge the authority of articulations of the religion that are rooted in the vision and experiences of the modern Muslim world but to re-evaluate America as well, as a political arrangement to be embraced as part of an effort to "protect his protection" as a Muslim-American.

From such a position, that is, *within* the American constitutional order, the enterprises of resistance and protest would be able to reassert themselves as acts dedicated to reforming America and to holding her to her own ideals, rather than as attempts to destroy her or impose upon her an alien vision from without. Resistance, however, would have to emerge as a positive, efficacious effort that served a higher good. Indeed, Blackamerican Muslims would have to recognize that blind resistance is no less grounded in a false universal than is the order that it blindly resists. Their aim, as such, must be to move Blackamerican Muslims from a position in which they can only be defined and controlled by the state and the dominant culture to one where they are self-defined and exercise enough influence over social and political institutions to be able to protect their interests and self-determination. Given the power and resources of the dominant group, many may initially scoff at the suggestion that Blackamericans might exercise any influence over the dominant order. But we should remind ourselves that the attitudes of deferential or contemptuous treatment that form the basis of how people see themselves and interact with others in society are far more the result of how ideas and images are manipulated through cultural production and institutions than they are of pure economics or politics.[79] America's cultural genius has always resided in her *popular* culture. And few groups in America can claim the influence over America's popular culture that Blackamericans can claim.

Directed, positive resistance: This is what the two most successful groups in America over the past two decades, women and gays, have been so successful at effecting. Not only have they made enormous political, economic, and legal gains, they have radically altered the manner in which society views them as citizens, simultaneously promoting and defending their self-defined identity as women and gays. In these achievements (and whether we agree with the substance thereof is irrelevant) women and gays have exemplified the distinction between "indigenization," that is, carving out a space for oneself in society, and "assimilation," that is, accepting the place in society assigned to one by the dominant group. In the case of Blackamerican Muslims, this is a critical distinction, for, as both blacks and as Muslims, experience has suggested that the dominant culture does not have all the answers and that in many instances accepting the invitation to be included in the latter might be tantamount to accepting admission into a burning building.[80]

5

Blackamerican Islam Between Religion, Nationalism, and Spirituality

Few committed practitioners of revealed religion would argue with Stephen Carter that, at its best, "religion resists." The challenge to religion, however, is to make sure that resistance remains a means rather than an end in itself and that it is exercised in consideration of goals that lie beyond self-serving quotidian interests. Otherwise, there is little that separates religion from secular movements and utopias. And in this confusion lies the ultimate impoverishment and potential abuse of religion. For it is here that religion is subject to being reduced to a thinly veiled form of eudaimonism that substitutes the whims and wishes of men and women for the will and pleasure of God. In such a context, it matters little whether or not religion is *true* in any ultimate sense. All that matters is that it is *effective* in promoting this or that worldly interest.

Of all the religious orientations, Black Religion is perhaps the most susceptible to this liability. Afterall, Black Religion does not even pretend to originate in revelation from beyond the pale of human history. On the contrary, it is explicit in recognizing its emergence out of a concrete set of historical circumstances. As such, its very raison d'être is to address not the God-human relationship per se but the concrete sociopolitical realities that brought it into being and from which it continues to draw its relevance. Islam, on the other hand, of all the revealed religions, is among the most emphatic in its insistence on belief in an Afterlife. From its perspective, neither success nor failure in this earthly life is of ultimate meaning. Ultimate meaning resides, rather, in eschatological success and failure. These, moreover, are indexed into issues of personal piety, religious devotion, and disinterested service at the heart of which lies the God–human relationship.

If Islam is to retain concrete meaning in the everyday lives of Blackamerican Muslims, it will have to continue to show its ability to address the concrete circumstances that inform and circumscribe their lives. At the same time, if Islam is to remain true to its constitution as a religion and avoid degenerating into what W. E. B. Du Bois once described as "a complaint and a curse . . . a sneer rather than a faith,"[1] it will have to remain God-centered and committed to matters of personal piety and eschatological success, even where these evince no direct relevance to the worldly plight of Blackamericans. God-centeredness, moreover, is the key to Blackamerican Muslim spirituality, an aspect of religious life so far poorly developed in Blackamerican Islam.

At stake in all of this is not whether Blackamerican Muslims choose between piety and protest, activism and spirituality, or secular interest and eschatological success. The issue is, rather, whether these competing interests can be reconciled through an understanding of Islam that avoids both fideistic obscurantism and self-serving eudaemonism, while resonating with deeply-felt meaning in the concentric contexts of black and white America. Without doubt, this is *the* greatest challenge confronting Blackamerican Muslims as they enter the Third Resurrection. And it is this challenge that I shall seek to address in this final chapter.

I shall begin with an exploration of the religious (as opposed to the sociopolitical) incentives for Blackamerican protest and resistance, with specific reference to the challenge this poses to religion in general and to Blackamerican Islam in particular. From here I will attempt to vindicate religion-based protest on the basis of theological postulates grounded in the orthodox Sunni tradition. This will be followed by a discussion of Blackamerican Muslim spirituality and the various forms and contours it might assume. Finally, I will end with a discussion of Sufism and the ways in which it may and may not contribute to the development of personal piety, spirituality, and God-consciousness among Blackamerican Muslims.

The Protest Imperative: Blackamericans and the "Second Creation"

Every serious student of religion is familiar with the German scholar Rudolf Otto's concept of *mysterium tremendum. Mysterium tremendum* refers to that ineffable fear that accompanies the experience of encountering the Divine. This is not a natural fear, such as might obtain should one happen upon a lion. This is a supernatural, "cosmic" fear that is grounded in the recognition of a power so awful, inescapable, and beyond restriction that it nearly stupefies. Here one is brought face-to-face with one's contingency and creatureliness before an irresistible Creator whose very presence inspires an inscrutable sense of danger, indebtedness, and a will to appease. All of this is accompanied, moreover, by a "personal feeling of nothingness and abasement before the awe-inspiring object directly experienced."[2] To be sure, there are other emotional and psychological moments attending *mysterium tremendum*, for example, fascination, love, mercy, even pity.[3] But none of these are capable of fully breaking the association of the Divine with the elements of categorical otherness and inescapable power.

Mysterium tremendum, in Otto's analysis, lay at the center of all religion. From primitive times to the present, religion has been essentially a manifestation of and response to *mysterium tremendum*. For the most part, throughout human history, the real or putative object of *mysterium tremendum* has been God. A notable exception emerges, however, in the encounter of the Negro with the white man on the transatlantic slave ships and the plantations of North America. In a brilliant essay, "The Oppressive Element in Religion and the Religions of the Oppressed," Charles H. Long speaks of a false or "spurious *mysterium tremendum*" that befell Blackamericans in the New World. This was a *mysterium tremendum* in which the fear-inspiring, inescapable other whose presence engendered a sense of danger and a will to appease was not God but the white man and the critical categories of modernity he had created: race, civilization, culture, primitiveness, I.Q., and so on. According to Long,

> "The other" of religious experience, with its impenetrable majesty, was replaced by the quixotic manipulation of a fascinating trickster whose rationality was only a veneer for control.[4]

In a real sense, Blackamericans (like other orphans of modernity) were "created" by the forces of white supremacy and the theoretical disciplines of the Enlightenment. This "second creation" complicated the task of breaking through to the First Creation and the primordial meanings enmeshed in the God-created self. In many ways, Blackamerican religiosity and protest are manifestations of a desire to transcend this second creation and reconnect with the first. For Blackamericans are instinctively driven by the belief that the "second creator" can only be trumped by the First, and the First Creator can only be accessed by resisting, indeed rejecting, the second creator (*qua* creator). It is precisely here, however, that means are subject to getting confused with ends and the detour is susceptible to turning into the road. Blackamericans, in other words, are confronted with the perennial task of negotiating a hopelessly blurred and shifting boundary between religion on the one hand, including the struggle to reconnect with the First Creator, and "black nationalism" on the other, as the secular revolt against white supremacy and the "quixotic manipulations of the fascinating trickster."

This is essentially what Joseph R. Washington Jr. had in mind in his critique of Black Religion. According to Washington, "Black religion has never been primarily concerned with contributing to worship, liturgy, theology or the ecumenical movement in Protestantism. . . ."[5] Instead, "The root of this folk religion is racial unity for freedom and equality."[6] Thus, "the Negro . . . depend[s] upon civil rights, religious feeling, sentiment, and color as substitutes for faith."[7] And, "Negro protests have been rooted for the most part outside the Christian faith."[8] Even among those who feel that Washington may have gone too far in his characterizations, there is a recognition that Blackamerican Christianity is susceptible to degenerating into a "cultural performance,"[9] a spiritualized coping mechanism or holy counterculture in which not God but "the man" is the real focal point. The challenge, as such, for Blackamerican Christians has been to keep God at the center of religion without compromising the mission to expose and frustrate the manipulations of the fascinating trickster. It is the challenge of remaining focused on God not simply as the Great Intervener in the crucible of race relations but as the ultimate source of value and the true object and motivator of love, awe, obedience, religious contemplation, and worship.

This has been and remains no less a challenge for Blackamerican Muslims. The habitual use of the term "*kāfir*" (Unbeliever) as a cultural/racial delineator between black and white instead of being restricted to marking the boundary between those who accept and those who reject the religion of Muhammad is ample testimony to this effect. In fact, whereas Blackamerican Christianity has produced a towering edifice of Black Theology to obviate, or perhaps establish, the relationship between the worship of Jesus and the liberation of Blackamericans, Blackamerican Sunni Islam has witnessed no such effort to ensure that its consciousness remains religious and that the religion itself does not degenerate into a cultural performance. The Islamists of Modern Islam have contributed nothing in this regard. And the theological tradition of Modernized Islam, as well as that of the Neofundamentalists, consists, outside the basics, largely of abstractions grounded in the Aristotelian–Neoplatonic presuppositions of Late Antiquity or equally abstract reactions to these.[10] These theologies emphasize such doctrines as the noncreatedness of the Qur'ān, the beatific vision in the Hereafter, and the anthropomorphic versus the nonanthropomorphic interpretation of the divine attributes. Beyond the question of how readily the average Blackamerican Muslim can understand or identify with much of this tradition, in its present form it obviates little relevance as a source of liberation or a bridge to primordial meanings. Moreover, if this theology, as presently articulated, is to occupy the center of Muslim religious consciousness and serve as the criterion for determining who is and who is not a Muslim, it may not be obvious how relevant Islam itself is to the present and future of Blackamericans.

Beyond the issue of theology, there is the more subtle and complicated matter of the relationship between protest and resistance, on the one hand, and spirituality, personal piety, and moral rectitude, on the other. Here, however, we confront again the problem of a possible mismatch between an imported tradition and an indigenous heritage. The most commonly recognized régime of pietism and spirituality among Muslims is that of Sufism. Sufism includes, however, at least two distinct aspects: (1) a focus on matters of personal piety and moral refinement (*tahdhīb al-nafs, tahdhīb al-akhlāq, tazkīyat al-nafs*); and (2) a concern with mysticism, including the supernatural extraction of service from nature and achieving mystical union with the Divine (*fanā', ḥulūl, waḥdat al-wujūd*). In terms of substance, the personal piety side of Sufism is a veritable gold mine for Blackamericans, especially in its psychology of rectitude. Its institutional structure, however, tends towards a highly stratified authoritarianism, including a master–disciple relationship that borders at times on the cultic. Moreover, in its American manifestation, organized Sufism has most often taken the form of a quietistic critique of and alternative to what are cast as the more politicized or even radical expressions of Islam. As for the mystical dimension of Sufism, it tends to ground itself in either the Neoplatonic tradition of Late Antiquity or the superstitious traditions of sub-Saharan Africa, neither of which are easily reconciled with the deeply protestant, lay predisposition of the masses of Blackamerican Muslims, not to mention the protest sentiment of Black Religion.

If Blackamerican Sunni Islam is to subvert false *mysterium tremendum* and the "second creation" without degenerating into just another secular ideology or cultural performance, it will have to ground its protest mission in articulations of the religion that show such a mission to be consistent with the pursuit of divine pleasure. This will require certain adjustments and modifications to the theological and spiritualist traditions handed down from the Sunni past. And issues of personal piety and spiritual development will have to assume their proper place in the everyday lives of Blackamerican Muslims. Over the remainder of this chapter, I shall attempt to lay out a framework within which such a reconciliation might be effected. While I am confident that my views are entirely validatable from the perspective of Muslim scripture and Tradition, it is perhaps too early in the history of American Islam to expect anything approaching consensus. As such, my statements might be taken as more of a beginning than the end of a process that I hope will be long and fruitful.

A Theological Postulate: *Fitnah* and the Preservation of Divine Transcendence

Given what has been said about the masterful feat of appropriation effected by the early Blackamerican Islamizers, it is easy to assume that any purported opposition of Islam to white supremacy could not be original but only artificially grafted onto the religion from without. Such opposition, in other words, would be grounded not in the Qur'ān and the teachings of the Prophet Muhammad but in the appropriations of the Honorable Elijah Muhammad and the teachings of *Message to the Black Man*. This is part of the whole point of Black Orientalism. It is also part of what sustains the image of Blackamerican Islam as being more a black nationalist movement than a *bona fide* religious tradition.

The Qur'ān itself, however, at least on my reading, evinces an emphatic opposition to white supremacy, not as an institution aimed specifically at Blackamericans but as a system of normalized domination that idolizes a second creator and promotes a false *mysterium tremendum*. Rather than recognizing black humanity as a matter of divine fiat, white supremacy grants this recognition only on the satisfaction of its own self-serving criteria. On this arrangement, the Blackamerican achiever ends up contributing to his own domination by paying homage to, indeed validating, criteria that are "untrue to the natural direction of his powers" and thus force him to "soar into an atmosphere not native to his wing."[11] Privately, the seeming arbitrariness of this falsely universalized criterion inspires the belief that there is no such thing as Blackamerican genius. To become noteworthy as a Blackamerican is simply to excel at things that are held in high esteem by whites, such as quantum physics or playing Beethoven's Fifth, or even Rap or basketball, once the latter acquire value among whites. The primary and dominant impulse among Blackamericans is thus to look neither inward nor upward but rather outward to the dictates of white supremacy's criterion for esteem and humanity. In this context, black achievement is often privately self-alienating and publicly looked upon as an exception, in which capacity it contributes little to true self-realization and changes little about the way society at large assesses black worth and possibility in the world.

This system of normalized domination has the cumulative effect of confirming the second creation and functions as the moral equivalent of the Qur'ānic concept of "*fitnah*," which the Qur'ān characterizes as being worse than murder (*wa 'l-fitnatu ashaddu mina 'l-qatl*). Islam, in other words, is not artificially but genuinely opposed to white supremacy, inasmuch as white supremacy constitutes a form of *fitnah* and does the work of a second creator.

Fitnah *and White Supremacy*

In his book, *White*, Richard Dyer observes that,

> There is no more powerful a position than that of being 'just' human. The claim to power is the claim to speak for the commonality of humanity. Raced people can't do that—they can only speak for their race.[12]

According to Dyer, race as a tool of differentiation is rarely applied to white people, particularly by whites themselves. "[T]o say that one is interested in race has come to mean that one is interested in any racial imagery other than that of white people."[13] This habitual failure to see whiteness as a race, as an idiosyncrasy, a social construct, as it were, with the same immediacy with which we see blackness or Hispanicness, puts white people in the position of being "normal" or "just people," in contradistinction to everyone else, whose normalness is both negotiated and implicitly measured in relation to white people. Whiteness, in other words, reigns supreme precisely because it is *invisible*. As Dyer put it, "White people claim and achieve authority for what they say by not admitting, indeed not realising, that for much of the time they speak only for whiteness."[14] On this perception of the world, the fears, assumptions, proclivities, prejudices, and specific genius of whites take on the appearance of a transcendent, "natural" order whose validity and normativeness is obvious to all save the stupid, the uncivilized, or the morally depraved. In the end, the entire constellation of human worth, possibility and expectation is indexed into this perception of "normal."

Nonwhites, meanwhile, are, ironically, expected to conform to this "natural" order while at the same time being tacitly assumed to be incapable of mastering it. Even more importantly, the very functioning of this order as a criterion for normality denies or only provisionally grants nonwhites the benefit of believing in their own minds, senses, and experiences—in short, their humanity.[15] For this criterion functions in effect as the final authority (in determining, for example, truth, utility, or aesthetic value) beyond which there is no appeal. Indeed, for those who are the objects rather than the subjects of this criterion, life is lived not directly but analogously and with great hesitation, in nervous anticipation of the judgments of the dominant group. Where this anticipation proves to be too great to bear, the result is often a wholescale rejection of standards altogether. As the great Ibn Hazm of Muslim Spain once put it, "When anxieties reach a certain quantity, they simply disappear altogether (*idhā takāthurat al-humūm saqaṭat kulluhā*)."[16]

This situation is far more critical for blacks than for other nonwhites inasmuch as the southernmost border of American whiteness is a porous edifice through which other nonwhites might reasonably entertain the hope of entering and gaining the advantages of full participation, as happened, for example, with the Jews, the Irish, the Armenians, and others. To be sure, this does not occur without certain trade-offs. As Matthew Frye Jacobson has recently observed, among the aims of the "ethnic movement" (among non-Anglo Saxon whites) is the simultaneous preservation of the public benefits of whiteness (i.e., to be seen as normal) alongside the privilege and comfort of private ethnic idiosyncrasy (i.e., to indulge cultural difference or "abnormality").[17] Blacks, for their part, do not qualify for this public benefit. And this imputes an even greater penalty to their private difference. For it carries the subtle insinuation that their private difference is what justifies their public exclusion. Ultimately, the moral, practical, and even aesthetic hesitancy generated by this reality translates into a species of the above-cited "*fitnah.*"

Etymologically, the word "*fitnah*" is a verbal noun derived from the Arabic root *fa-ta-na*, whose basic meaning is "to test or try."[18] This testing and trying is akin to what we commonly refer to in English as a litmus test. *Fa-ta-na* refers to testing or trying for the purpose of seeing what a thing is made of or whether it can satisfy certain criteria or maintain a particular constitution in the face of various challenges. This basic meaning is captured in the standard example of *fa-ta-na* given in classical Arabic dictionaries: the putting of gold to fire in order to test its purity by seeing how many, if any, impurities come out.[19]

"*Fitnah*" and or its derivatives occur some sixty-six times in the Qur'ān in various contexts and with multiple applications. Generally speaking, these can be divided into two categories: (1) *fitnah* that entails God's testing and trying His servants; (2) *fitnah* that entails human beings testing and trying other human beings. Examples of the first would be the verse, "Every soul shall taste death; and We visit you with good and evil, as a test (*fitnah*) for you";[20] or the verse, "Your money and your children are simply a test (*fitnah*) for you."[21] Examples of the second category would be the verse, "And fight them until there exists no "fitnah" and religion is practiced solely out of devotion to God";[22] or the verse, "Verily those who test (*fatana*) the believing men and women and do not repent, their's shall be the penalty of Hell and a blazing fire."[23] This second usage of *fitnah* connotes a fairly broad range of contexts and strategies. As such, "*fitnah*" in this second manifestation has been variously translated as "oppression," "persecution,"[24] "sedition"[25] or "temptation."[26] In all of these applications, however, the basic meaning of the word remains intact: a test, trial, provocation, or act of oppression that seeks to draw on or expose human weakness. *Fitnah* from God seeks to expose human weakness for the purpose of nurturing a positive humility and a will to overcome. *Fitnah* from human beings is routinely based on self-interest and aims at exploitation.[27]

It is precisely this element of drawing on human weakness in order to exploit people that explains the Qur'ānic use of the term *fitnah*, as opposed to, say, *iḍṭihād* (oppression), *ta'dhīb* (persecution) or *inshiqāq* (sedition) in those instances where commentators take *fitnah* to refer to these things. These latter terms speak to the more superficial aspects of exploitation, that is, the transparent, causal relationship between the abuses of the powerful and the reactions of the powerless. The Qur'ān, however, appears to be more concerned with the deeper psychological/spiritual dimensions of exploitation, in short, with domination. For domination turns on the oppressor's success at reducing his victim to a state of self-contempt, whereby the latter internalizes a vague but inextricable feeling that redemption can only be achieved by living up to the criterion of his exploiter. This is the mechanism by which exploitation is "normalized," made "invisible," and placed beyond critique. For the feelings of triumph that occur as one approaches redemption habitually obliterate any recognition of the falseness of the criterion itself. In this context, ontological and even metacognitive truths that contradict this criterion are confronted agnostically, and individuals are given over to formalized ideologies, popular morality, or simply "the ways of the forefathers."[28] In the end, as Du Bois once observed, in pursuing a dignified social existence under a régime of *fitnah*, "The price of [full participation in the dominant] culture is a Lie."[29]

The Qur'ān's preoccupation with *fitnah* is grounded in the assumption that *régimes* of Unbelief (*kufr*)[30] (as opposed to individual *acts* of Unbelief)[31] require domination in order to sustain themselves. For, on the Qur'ān's depiction, if left to their primordial senses (*fiṭrah*),[32] humans are naturally inclined not only to worship God but to accept themselves—including their superior or inferior intelligence, strong or weak constitution—as the choice and handiwork of God. Through the process of normalized domination, however, even the most obvious truths can evade acknowledgment or be undermined: "If you ask them, 'Who created you?' they will exclaim, 'God!' How, then, are they given over to lies?"[33] "Say, [O Muhammad]: Who provides you with sustenance from the heavens and the earth? Is it He who dispenses hearing and sight?

And who draws life out of the dead and death out of the living? And who orders the affairs (of the universe)? They will say, 'God.' Will they not, then, be God-conscious?"[34] In sum, in a Qur'ānic context, the issue is not at all a simple one of knowledge or even belief. The Qur'ān speaks, rather, to a deeper psychological/spiritual matter of whether such knowledge and belief find their way to fruition and are permitted to run their course. And it here is that *fitnah* shows itself to be not only central to the Qur'ānic message but far more sinister than brute injustice (*ẓulm*), persecution, or even murder (*qatl*). For tyrants and murderers receive no psychological cooperation from their victims. Normalized exploitation, on the other hand, is an all-volunteer system. Whereas the victims of oppression and tyranny habitually fight against their abusers, the victims of normalized exploitation only fight against themselves. This underscores the true meaning and profundity of the Qur'ānic declaration, "*wa 'l-fitnatu ashaddu mina 'l-qatl* (domination is worse than murder)." White supremacy, for its part, may not always pursue the same ends as the Qur'ānic *fitnah*. But it is plainly a cognate institution, a consciously preserved system of normalized domination.

The Human Condition and the Uniqueness of Divine Transcendence

And yet, it seems pertinent to ask—and this is the question of all conservatives—what it is about the human condition that enables some to dominate others in this fashion to begin with? If one's humanity is indeed a divine fiat, how is it that one can be brought to doubt it in the first place? Are not individuals themselves responsible for sustaining belief in their own intrinsic worth? And might not domination itself be then a "natural" order, the Darwinian result of the interaction between those who assume their humanity and those who doubt it? Here I turn to the Muslim theological tradition, calibrated, as it were, to the realities of twenty-first century America.

Few issues in the history of Muslim theology have been more seminal than the question of God's transcendence versus God's immanence. This is at the heart of many of the great debates between the rationalist Muʿtazilites, Ashʿarites, and Māturīdites, on the one hand, and the antirationalist Traditionalists (often identified as Ḥanbalites), on the other. For the Muʿtazilites, God was too transcendent and self-subsisting to have attributes; for such attributes would either be eternal or temporal. If they were eternal, there had to exist a multiplicity of eternals. If they were temporal, God was subject to change. For the Muʿtazilites, both of these options constituted a violation of Islamic monotheism (*tawḥīd*). But the Muʿtazilites were unable to maintain this position in the face of criticisms by the rationalist Ashʿarites and Māturīdites on the one hand, and the antirationalist Traditionalists on the other. These latter are the three major Sunni theological schools that have come down to us in modern times. At the center of virtually all of the debates among them is the problem of how to affirm God's attributes and transcendence without falling into anthropomorphism, on the one hand, and without emptying God's attributes of concrete meaning, on the other. Whatever the approach taken to this dilemma (and metaphorical interpretation [*ta'wīl*] was among the most common), no school of Muslim theology has showed a willingness to compromise on the question of God's transcendence.[35]

This unwillingness to compromise on God's transcendence is the starting point of my approach to the question of human susceptibility to *fitnah*. On my approach, however, not only is God transcendent, God is emphatically *unique* in this transcendence. In other words, *only* God is transcendent. This transcendence entails, however, not simply a "vertical" beyondness but a beyondness that speaks to the complete noncontingency of God's "selfhood" and its imperviousness to the world "around" God. God is unique in this capacity inasmuch as God alone possesses a purity of being by virtue of which God remains God in all God's splendor and self-determined attributes, regardless of the conditions prevailing in the universe. This is not a new idea in Muslim theology. The traditionalist Ibn Taymīya points to a similar meaning when explaining the verse, "God is pure" (*Allāhu ṣamad*) in the 112th chapter of the Qur'ān.[36] It is similarly this aspect of imperviousness that the founder of the rationalist Māturīdite school, Abū Mansūr al-Māturīdī (d. 333/944), identifies with "godhood" (*ulūhīyah*).[37] I wish to emphasize, however, not simply the *fact* but, again, the *uniqueness* of God's imperviousness, as opposed to the utter perviousness of human beings. In other words, on my construction, the doctrine of divine transcendence is not merely a statement about God; it is equally, and in this context more importantly, a statement about human beings. Indeed, to the extent that what this doctrine says about human beings is compromised, so is what it says about God!

Humans enjoy nothing of the transcendence, purity of being, or "beyondness" that is uniquely characteristic of God. Human beings are, rather, a mere potentiality, ensconced in and informed by society and history. To deny this contingency is not merely to ignore the unearned advantages and disadvantages bequeathed to us by sociopolitical forces; nor is it simply to undermine the value and duty of civic responsibility. It is to assume, in addition to all of this, that our success or failure reverts to some inalterable essence within us that is so impervious as to preclude all other possibilities. From the vantage point of traditional Muslim theology, such obliviousness to human contingency may not be immediately recognized as a form of associationism or *shirk*. Upon reflection, however, such an oversight reveals itself to be nothing short of an act of attributing divine attributes—namely, transcendence—to other than God. Far from constituting a harmless theological deviation, such a position would number among the only unforgivable sins in Islam. As the Qur'ān states, "Verily God does not forgive that others should be accorded His status (or attributes), but other than that He forgives whomever He pleases" (4: 48; 4: 116).

In sum, *fitnah* is a play on the human condition. It is not aimed, however, at simple human weakness, as some sort of exceptional quality of certain groups or individuals. *Fitnah* is, rather, a play on the inalterable fact of human contingency. It proceeds and capitalizes on the knowledge that humans are susceptible to being disabused of their will to acknowledge even the most basic truths. Yet, the appropriate response to *fitnah* is neither to impugn nor to seek to deny human susceptibility. For to negate human contingency is, again, to commit oneself to associationism (*shirk*) in perhaps its most significant manifestation in modern times. Today, at least in the Western world, it is neither graven images nor idols that pose the greatest challenge to God's monopoly on divinity; it is false *mysterium tremendum*, second creators and the sociopolitical reality these produce. As such, it is against these, and not against idols, that modern men and women are likely to find the deepest meaning and resonance in Islam's foundational principle: "There is no god except God (*lā ilāha illā Allāh*)." And, on this understanding, the proper response to the problem of human contingency is not to seek to overcome it but to resist and oppose false *mysterium tremendum* and "re-creation," *both as subjects and as objects*.

In this context, it becomes clear that opposition to white supremacy—or, for that matter, any supremacy, including male supremacy or Arab supremacy[38]—is not the exclusive preserve of black nationalism. On the contrary, opposition to white supremacy should be embraced as a manifestation of ultimate allegiance to God and the preservation of God's status as the *only* noncontingent Definer of ultimate value. On this understanding, God, not "the man," becomes the true motivator and ultimate concern of resistance. Indeed, resistance in this context becomes part of the struggle to remain within the penumbra of primordial meanings where God occupies the center of human consciousness. In this light, resisting false *mysterium tremendum* and "second creators" acquires meaning not only for Blackamerican Muslims but for Muslims, period, whatever color they might be.

It has been argued that the human desire to believe in God provides no proof in and of itself that God does not exist; just because one is paranoid, it does not follow that one is not being followed. In a similar vein, just because Blackamericans are a protest people independent of religion, it does not follow that protest cannot be a religiously sanctioned activity in perfect harmony with divine intent and pleasure. Of course, at issue will always be the intention that motivates such activity. And this is why issues of personal piety and rectitude, which aim *inter alia* at training and directing intentions, are critical to the substance and practice of Blackamerican Islam.

Toward an Immanent Spirituality

Shedding false *mysterium tremendum* and second creators is also the starting point of spiritual health for Blackamerican Muslims. By "spiritual health," however, we need not restrict ourselves to the transcendental activity of mystical union with the Divine. Among the oddities of the black experience in the New World has been its failure to disabuse Blackamericans fully of a basic belief in God and an enchantment with creation. These continue to provide Blackamericans with teary-eyed moments of escape from the mundane and the practical. But these are constantly crowded out by the psychological energy expended on resisting false *mysterium tremendum* and the machinations of second creators. This has the cumulative effect of secularizing, or at least "despiritualizing," Blackamericans, inasmuch as the activity of fighting off false *mysterium tremendum* and second creators is rarely recognized as spiritual activity. This is certainly the case within contemporary Islam (and I suspect Christianity as well).

It is in this context that I propose that the masses of Blackamericans are apt to find meaning in what I shall characterize as an "Immanent Spirituality." Immanent Spirituality is not an end in itself but a means to the ultimate end of breaking through to the First Creator and a primordial enchantment with the first creation. Not only does it validate resistance as a spiritual activity, it valorizes it as part of the necessary psychological energy expended by Blackamericans in their effort to fend off the machinations of the fascinating trickster. Ultimately, it is this validating and valorizing potential that sets Immanent Spirituality off from the more common "transcendent spirituality." Stated differently, Immanent Spirituality recognizes as spiritual what transcendent spirituality tends to look upon as profane.

As mentioned earlier, "spirituality" in Islam has been dominated by the discourse and presuppositions of mystical Sufism. Sufism, to be sure, even in its mystical form, is not a monolith. The prescriptions of mystical Sufis have ranged from ascetic seclusion and renunciation of the world to social activism and anti-colonial jihad. At bottom, however, mystical Sufism is predicated on the belief that experiential knowledge is superior to conceptual knowledge and that spiritual fulfillment resides in the direct "experience" of God. Having absorbed certain Neoplatonic notions from Late Antiquity, alongside the Greek wisdom tradition, Persian dualism, and Indian traditions, much of this is grounded in a presumed dichotomy between the body and the self and the idea that ultimate good resides in transcending both. Much of mystical Sufism constitutes, as such, a spirituality of transcendence, according to which transcending the body and annihilating the self and the ego are prerequisites for directly experiencing or achieving union with the Divine.[39]

Whatever appeal Sufism's transcendent spirituality may have had among its ancient and modern proponents, it is easy to see how it might hold little meaning for a people who, to borrow the depiction of Dr. King, have been harried by day and haunted by night by a nagging sense of nobodyness, who have had to struggle to hold on to physical life in the face of psychological death. On the criterion of classical Sufism, the American experience should have transformed Blackamericans into a race of mystical wonders, splendidly annihilated in both body and self. But this is hardly the meaning that Blackamericans would impute to their New World odyssey. And such annihilation is hardly what Blackamericans would value in any spiritual tradition.

For Blackamericans, who are largely alien to both Enlightenment rationalism and the traditions of Late Antiquity, the issue has never been one of escaping the tyranny of the body, reason, or the ego in order to find God. The issue has been, rather, what to do with an inextricable faith in God in the context of a civilization that consistently cast aspersions on the hearts and minds in which this faith and enchantment is housed. The problem, in other words, has not been one of belief in God; the problem has been sustaining the value and validity of that belief based on belief in *self*. Stated differently, it was not so much the *spirit* as it was the *psyche* of Blackamericans that came under assault in the New World. As such, their issues are far less "spiritual" than they are sociopsychological. In this context, any spirituality that is to prove meaningful and efficacious for Blackamericans will have to come to terms with the psychological dimensions of the Blackamerican experience. This is the starting point of Immanent Spirituality.

Contrary to what might be assumed at first blush, Immanent Spirituality does not compromise the doctrine of divine transcendence. In fact, the concept of Immanent Spirituality actually reinforces that doctrine by affirming that spiritual well-being need not entail any "ascent" of the spirit to divine precincts, which, if taken seriously, would seem to contradict the idea of God's transcendence. As in the case of my construction of the doctrine of divine transcendence, the primary focus of Immanent Spirituality is on the human rather than the divine side of the religious equation. It is to affirm that spirituality can reside in the activity of "walking *with*" as opposed to "ascending *to*" God. Its locus is neither the convent nor the mosque but the everyday trials and tribulations of human existence. It comes primarily of (1) perseverance in the face of hardship and disappointment, and (2) resisting the pressure to substitute the values and "vision" of second creators for those of the First.

I should like to make it clear that my point in proposing this Immanent Spirituality is *not* to imply that transcendent spirituality in all its forms is substantively invalid. My aim is merely to counter the presumption that transcendent spirituality is *universally* enabling and that all spiritually minded people find meaning and efficacy in this mode of religiosity. This is necessitated by the fact that many, if not most, people identify spirituality so closely with transcendence that they assume there to be no other forms of spirituality. As a result, those who find little or no meaning in transcendent spirituality are often seen (and often see themselves) as being aspiritual.

Perseverance and the Enhancement of Spirituality: "Īmān *Increases and Decreases*"

If there is one category in Qurʾānic discourse that functions as the template for spirituality, it is most certainly that of "*īmān*." After God (Allāh in Arabic), *īmān* (or derivatives, i.e., verbs, active participles) is the most oft-cited term in the Qurʾān. Standard translations of *īmān* include "faith" and "belief." Philologically speaking, however, there is a dimension of *īmān* that is not always captured by these translations. *Īmān* is derived from the Arabic root *a-m-n*, which means "safety," "security," "tranquility." *Īmān*, however, is the *causative* form of *a-m-n*, which is to say that its basic meaning is "to *cause* to be safe, secure, or tranquil." When speaking of faith or belief in God, the Qurʾān generally uses *īmān* in construct with the preposition "*bi*" (through, by, in). Thus, the true meaning of *īmān* is actually "to cause or bring about safety, security, tranquility *through* (one's relationship with) God."

Early on, a debate developed among Muslim theologians over whether *īmān* was a static entity (like pregnancy) or a dynamic one that was subject to varying degrees of intensity or perfection. Various groups among the Muʿtazilites and Kharijites held *īmān* to be static and constituted by one's deeds. For these groups, anyone who committed a grave sin was denied the status of a Believer. Among the Kharijites, such persons were condemned to Hell forever.[40] The founders of Muʿtazilism, meanwhile, deemed unrepentant sinners to be neither Believers nor Unbelievers. Instead, they came up with the famous doctrine according to which such persons were assigned "a status between these two statuses (*manzila bayna al-manzilatayn*)."[41] At the other end of the spectrum was a group called the Murji'ites. They also held *īmān* to be static but insisted that it was made and unmade not by physical deeds but by such psychological states as knowing (*maʿrifah*), giving assent (*iqrār*) and humbly submitting (*ʿadam al-istikbār wa al-khuḍūʿ*) to the existence of God and the fundamental truths of revelation. On the Murji'ite construction, deeds were irrelevant to the constitution of *īmān*. As the famous statement attributed to them put it: "Disobedience brings no harm to one who has *īmān*, just as obedience brings no benefit to one who does not have it."[42] One should not understand from this that the Murj'ites were libertines or lukewarm in their religious commitment. Their doctrine might be better understood, rather, as an attempt to preempt certain consequences of admitting deeds to be part of the constitution of *īmān*. For such an admission, on the one hand, would lend credence to the Kharijite position, and people who committed grave sins could be condemned as Unbelievers. On the other hand, people who neither believed in God nor the Prophet would have to be credited with at least some measure of bona fide *īmān*, if and when they committed religiously commendable acts.[43]

The orthodox Sunni majority, however, adopted what might be considered a middle position. They held that *īmān* consisted of both psychological/affective states and physical deeds. They defined it as "firm assent in the heart, acknowledgment by the tongue and actions with the limbs (*taṣdīq jāzim bi al-qalb wa iqrārun bi al-lisān wa ʿamalun bi al-jawāriḥ*)." Furthermore, *īmān*, according to them, was not static but dynamic, subject to increase and decrease, the former through obedience and laudable actions, the latter through disobedience and vice. At bottom, the orthodox majority agreed that *īmān* was *instantiated* by psychological/affective states. But in their view it could be brought to various levels of intensity or faintness, depending on one's actions. Actions, however, were rarely enough to obliterate *īmān*, and once a person was recognized as a Believer he or she could not be condemned as an Unbeliever based solely on his or her actions. As the common profession put it: "[W]e do not hold any professing Muslim to be an infidel because of sins committed."[44]

Among the proofs adduced by the orthodox majority are several Qur'ānic verses that explicitly mention the fact of *īmān* increasing. For example, Qurʿān 9: 124 reads: "And when a chapter (of the Qur'ān) is sent down, among them are those who say, 'Which of you is increased in *īmān* by this chapter?' As for those who have *īmān*, such chapters increase them therein and they are filled with positive anticipation." Qur'ān 48: 4 reads: "It is He who caused tranquility to descend upon the hearts of the believers in order to increase them in their *īmān*.

Beyond this, however, the Qur'ān includes several verses wherein the increase in *īmān* is explicitly linked to the psychological act of turning to and placing trust in God, particularly in times of suffering and hardship. At Qur'ān 3: 173, for example, we read of the gloom confronting the Muslims during one of their military confrontations where they were badly outnumbered and looking to suffer severe losses. Their response, however, resulted in an increase in *īmān*: "Those to whom the people said, 'Verily the people have all lined up against you, so be fearful of them.' But that only increased their *īmān,* as they said, Our affair rests with God, and He is the best Disposer of Affairs.' " Similarly, speaking of the crucible of the so-called Siege of Medina, we read on the one hand, "[T]hey approached you from above and from below and eyes darted (with fear) and hearts jumped into throats and you began to think vain thoughts about God" (33: 10). This becomes the occassion, however, for an increase in *īmān*: "And when the believers saw the Confederates (gathering against them), they said, 'This is what God and His Messenger promised us, and God and His Messenger have spoken the truth.' And that only increased them in *īmān* and submission" (33: 22).

To the extent that *īmān* is the template upon which spirituality rests, these verses clearly indicate that spirituality can be enhanced not by transcending terrestrial reality but by confronting it with trust in God and perseverance. In cultural, political, or socioeconomic contexts where it seems that the dominant group has "lined up against one," turning to God instead of indulging one's fear, anger, or bitterness can increase one's sense of security in the face of challenges whose resolution lie beyond reason, the senses or one's own devices. In this context, not only are those whose actions result in increased *īmān* endowed with greater security and an increased ability to endure subsequent difficulty, but an identifiably spiritual dimension is conferred upon their efforts to persevere with dignity and resolve in the face of the world's wrongs. On this understanding, all of the effort expended in overcoming dread and feelings of helplessness in order to be able to persevere in the face of false *mysterium tremendum* or the "quixotic manipulations of the fascinating trickster" can be recognized as both spiritual activity and a way to increased faith in God.

At first blush, many may see in this a Muslim version of Black Theology's "theodicy of the suffering servant."[45] It should be noted, however, that, on my approach, only where the causes of suffering are confronted, that is, with perseverance and reliance on God, are *īmān* and spirituality enhanced. To acquiesce in the face of unearned suffering is both to evince a paucity of faith in God and to forfeit the opportunity to increase it.

Spirituality Through Resistance

Beyond the act of turning to God specifically in times of difficulty, the Qu'ān also speaks of God granting spiritual enhancement to those who resist, as a general orientation, the urge to submit to the constellation of meanings instituted by second creators as the sole basis of their outlook on life and ultimate meaning. The emphasis here is not on morality or theology as matters of rational reflection. The focus is rather on morality and theology as visceral or psychological *orientations*.

It has been observed that "the Qur'ān is primarily concerned with the moral and religious orientation of the human soul."[46] By "soul," however, we need not restrict ourselves to that aspect of human beings that persists after death. In the Qur'ānic context, "soul" can be more broadly understood to include the human psyche, the driving force and fountain of a person's impulses, fears, hopes, and motivations. In Ancient Bible studies, the Greek term *psuché*/*psyché* is commonly translated as "soul," and this is obviously the word from which we get the modern term "psychology."[47] The Qur'ānic term most commonly used to denote the soul is "*nafs*."[48] And like English, modern Arabic reflects the connection between *nafs* and psyche in its translation of psychology as "*ʿilm al-nafs*," literally, "knowledge (or science) of the psyche."

Contrary to the notion that *īmān* resides primarily in a person's thoughts—hence the primacy of theology, literally *logos* (thoughts, thinking) on *theos* (God, Divinity)—it is the deeper recesses of the psyche, including the unthought and the unreasoned, that is the true locus of religious life. It is here, in the *nafs*, that attitudes are formed, wants and nonwants develop, and a person's vision about who he or she is or aspires to be takes shape. Depending on how accurately one identifies the causal relationship between one's actions and the realization of one's best self, actions may be consistent or inconsistent with one's quest for self-realization. Ultimately, however, it is the "vision" in the soul, not the thoughts in the mind, that determines a person's commitments. Indeed, as we now know—and this is *the* insight of postmodernist thought—reason can only operate in the interest of values or visions already present.[49]

From the perspective of the dominant group, be they white Americans or the Prophet's tribe of Quraysh, the aim is obviously to generate "visions" in the souls of individuals that render the latters' aspirations consistent with the former's interests. To this end, all manners of psychological sanctions will be employed, from praise and flattery to ridicule and scandal: "They say, 'O you upon whom The Reminder (Qur'ān) has been sent down, indeed, you are mad' " (15: 6); "We do not see anyone following you except those who are the lowest among us, primitive in their thinking" (11: 27); and "Indeed, they came close to disabusing you of what We had revealed to you, so that you might falsely attribute to Us something other than this, at which time they would have taken you as their close friend" (17: 73). To the extent that such efforts are successful, truth is certain to be bargained away in pursuit of false redemption. But not only is the truth of God lost in this process; truth of self is also sacrificed, for these efforts ultimately deny individuals a clear path to the self. In such a context, while everything the dominant group values may stir the emotions with promises of glory and public esteem, almost nothing seems to attach to the soul. Thus, the career one pursues, the spouse one marries, the neighborhood one chooses to live in, all of these turn out to be "choices" made in pursuit of what a "successful," "cultured," or even "pious" person is supposed to want rather than realizations of what the real person actually wants.

Against this threat of alienation from self and God, the Qur'ān prescribes spiritual/psychological resistance:

> You shall not find a people possessed of *īmān* in God and the Last Day trafficking in ingratiation with those who oppose God and His Messenger, even if the latter should be their fathers, their sons, their brothers or their cohorts. These are the people in whose hearts God has inscribed *īmān* and enhanced them with a spirit from Himself. (59: 22)

In this post-9/11 world, two things about this verse must be noted before going on. First, such verses do not preempt friendship, fellowship, or even love between Muslims and non-Muslims. The Qur'ān itself states, "God does not forbid you to have amicable and just relations with those who do not fight you because of your religion and do not drive you out of your homes" (60: 8). The Qur'ān even insists that, "God may cause love to emerge between you and your former enemies" (60: 7). Similarly, Islam flatly forbids the severing of family ties (*qaṭʿ al-raḥim*), even between Muslim and non-Muslim members. And marriage between Muslim men and non-Muslim women is permissible. Clearly, love and fellowship lie at the core of these relationships, some of which Islam not only allows or encourages but absolutely obliges.

Second, in the context of seventh-century Arabia, the tribe (to which "fathers, sons, brothers, and cohorts" is a synecdochic reference) was the "dominant group" beyond whose value judgments there was no appeal. The focus of the verse is thus not interpersonal relations, regarding which the Qur'ān advises, "O you who believe, verily among your spouses and your children are enemies of yours, so beware. And if you excuse, pardon, and forgive (them), verily God is forgiving, merciful" (64: 14). Nor is the focus of the verse intertribal relations. The focus is, rather, sociopolitical relations, where individual conscience comes up against group morality and "the way of the forefathers," a ubiquitously negative category throughout the Qur'ān. Given the pagan Arabs' institutionalized judgments about God, morality, and related matters, the point of the verse is that one cannot seek to ingratiate oneself with that order and at the same time entertain faith in God and the Last Day. Having said this much, while there are several instances in which the Qur'ān prescribes physical fighting as a means of preserving the physical integrity of the Muslim Community,[50] the proper response to this particular challenge is identified not as *fighting* the pagan Arabs but as *resisting* being pulled into their universe of meanings. In other words, where a particular sociopolitical order threatens one morally or theologically but not physically, the proper remedy is not at all organized violence but spiritual/psychological resistance!

It is in response to this commitment to psychological resistance that God promises in this verse to confirm *īmān* in the believers' hearts and to enhance them with a "spirit" from Himself. Given its role in the early polemics with Christians, Neoplatonic (Muslim) philosophers and certain Sufi groups, the term "spirit" (*rūḥ*) was a source of controversy among classical scholars. Ibn Qayyim notes that in the Qur'ān the term carried several meanings, including (1) the angel of revelation (Gabriel); (2) revelation itself; (3) the human soul; (4) the spirit associated with Jesus; and (5) a certain "inner strength, aid, and steadfastness."[51] Regarding the verse in question, however, there appears to be a general consensus among exegetes from across the ideological spectrum. They affirm that the term "spirit" here refers to an inner strength that God grants believers for psychologically resisting the urge to surrender unquestionably to the dictates of the reigning paradigm as a substitute for truth.[52] Psychological resistance, in other words, is identified as a means to receiving *spiritual enhancement* from God.

For a people whose psychological universe has been circumscribed from the time of their induction into the New World, such a perspective on spirituality would appear to be not only meaningful but absolutely crucial. At the same time, it would appear to be precisely this type of spiritual/psychological resistance that is needed to preempt the "bourgeoisification" of Blackamerican Islam that may otherwise result from the indiscriminate appropriation of American middle-class norms and institutions. Sociopolitical resistance may be the antidote to a dominant group's self-serving laws and policies; but spiritual/psychological resistance is required to prevent their self-serving values and meanings from striking roots in the soul. It is perhaps their lack of attention to this distinction that has seen none other than the Nation of Islam "bourgeoisify" over the years into Black Afro-Saxon protestants who nurse a subtle contempt for "low-type coons," who equate success with rivaling the material achievements of the dominant culture, and who have become almost wholly detached from the mellow but uncompromising fervor of the religious tradition of the folk.

Personal Piety, God-Consciousness and the Imperceptible Advance of American Secularism

The problem of having to negotiate the boundary between religion and spirituality on the one hand, and secular nationalism on the other, is not exclusive to Blackamericans, nor to Muslims. It is part of a broader challenge facing all religious communities, perhaps most especially in America. Ultimately, the problem reverts to the threat of eudaemonism and the ease with which it can be substituted for bona fide religion. The Black Theologian James Cone warned of the pull and power of this enticement when, at the height of his effort to devise a Christian Theology of liberation, he expressed his concern with being seduced by the temptation to conflate "our wishes" with "God's will":

> Unless we black theologians can make an adequate distinction between divine revelation and human aspirations, there is nothing to keep Black Theology from identifying God's will with anything black people should decide to do at any given historical moment.[53]

At bottom, Professor Cone is describing the power and seductiveness of what one might refer to as the "new anthropomorphism." This new anthropomorphism seeks to superimpose not the *form* but the *wishes* of humans onto God. Religion, on this approach, ceases to be about service to God and is converted into an enterprise wholly devoted to the self-service of man. This goes beyond the mere attempt to *discover* in God's commands and prohibitions benefits or even pleasures that accrue to humans here and now. It even goes beyond the attempt to *reconcile* God's commands and prohibitions with human wants and aspirations. Instead, the new anthropomorphism *begins* with a non-negotiable insistence that what humans want, God wants, and what humans do not want, God cannot (or certainly should not) want. At bottom, it is the ultimate rejection of heteronomy ("other-law") and the ultimate affirmation of autonomy ("self-law"), reinforced by the insistence that individuals and societies should only submit to the latter and never the former.

This religious orientation is easily reconciled with the pragmatism, individualism, and diffidence toward tradition that have long characterized the American spirit. Back in the early nineteenth century, Alexis de Tocqueville (a Catholic) noted in his description of American religiosity, "I do not see a trace of what we generally consider faiths, such as customs, ancient traditions, and the power of memories."[54] More recently, Charles Long has suggested that the American religious disposition has little appetite for the old-fashioned fear and trembling of *mysterium tremendum*. In his view, the dominant culture is much more comfortable with a *mysterium fascinosum*, that is, a congenial fascination with a "harmless" God who is to be assimilated and snuggled up to, having been denuded of all awe and total otherness.[55] In this regard, America appears as an extension of Europe but with a patently different response to the problem of religion. Whereas the European response resulted in the "death of God," the American reaction has tended toward the "death of Satan," drowning the Evil One in a torrent of *fascinosum* powerful enough to extinguish the fires of Hell. This radically alters the meaning of religion. For at the very least it undermines the notion of salvation—salvation from what?—and worship loses much its urgency, except as a means of soliciting earthly favors from God. In the end, death itself is rendered an end rather than a beginning, and "going it alone"—autonomy—becomes the only "reasonable" (read desirable) approach to life, at least for most of us most of the time.

This is the broader context within which Blackamerican Islam is situated. Indeed, the greater Blackamerican Muslim success at appropriating middle-class and genteel American values, the more deeply embedded in this universe of meaning they are subject to become. In the meantime, the perduring stigma of race threatens to lock them into a struggle that only recognizes external enemies. Here is where Blackamericans' religion becomes most susceptible to being converted into a protest instrument strictly for use against an external foe. And, given that external adversary's continued circumscription of Blackamerican life (socially, politically, legally, economically), even morality can take on the appearance and feeling of capitulation, a "false heteronomy," so to speak. In the potential for getting lost in these concentric contexts of American blackness and the dominant culture's *fascinosum*, the situation confronting the Blackamerican Muslim is reminiscent of the Qur'ānic verse that speaks of "layers of darknesses one heaped upon the other; (so dark that) when he stretches forth his hand, he can hardly see it" (24: 40).[56] In a real sense, both success and failure equally threaten the very essence of what Blackamerican Muslims are supposed to be about: an Islam that God would recognize as Islam.

It is here that the personal piety side of learned or "high-mosque" Sufism[57] may help to strengthen the vision and steady the course of Blackamerican Islam. To begin with, this dimension of Sufism is squarely dedicated to the struggle against the inner adversary. At the same time, it fully embraces (true) *mysterium tremendum* and is inextricably bound to an unwavering commitment to the principle that religion is, first and foremost, about salvation, and salvation is ultimately about service to God. All of this culminates in a régime of critical self-analysis, discipline, and character building that is independent of one's grievances against the world. In this capacity, what has often been deemed one of Sufism's greatest weaknesses, namely its apoliticism, turns out to be among its strengths. God, not "the man," emphatically occupies the center of its religious consciousness.

Beyond its substance (to which I shall turn momentarily) learned Sufism confers the additional advantage of attaching its participants to a *tradition* of personal piety and moral refinement. Tradition, of course, is the repository of tried and tested wisdom, heroes and heroines, and a deep sense of belonging that defies the tendency of modern society to break down community and isolate individuals. Without tradition, each generation begins almost anew, deeply distrustful of its predecessor and having to learn old lessons all over again. This is all the more critical in the case of Blackamericans. For the loss of the African past, on the one hand, and the deep distrust of the European past, on the other, have denied Blackamericans the luxury of being able to look back for trusted insights and answers that they can embrace as their own. This has essentially forced them into a posture of perpetual on-the-job training, especially as regards religion and the life of the spirit.

Yet, traditions are also notorious for growing old, foolish, and blind, losing sight of the historical contexts and forces that produced them, imagining themselves to have come down like revelation from heaven, inalterable in every aspect. Sufism, even if we restrict it to its personal piety side, has shown the extent to which it is subject to this. Indeed, it has ranked among the most expedient of all expressions of Islam as a front for religious chicanery, guru-charlatanism, and cultlike exploitation. Blackamerican Muslims must be careful and discriminating in the manner in which they approach this legacy. And they must be not be afraid to ignore what they deem to be irrelevant or harmful and add what they deem to be useful or necessary. Rather than restrict themselves to a single order, a single figure or a single Sufi text, Blackamerican Muslims should avail themselves of the best from the entire tradition of Sufism, in a spirit of autodidactic license and responsibility. Even here, however, the goal should be the concepts, emphasis, and accumulated wisdom of learned Sufism, not the institutional structures, romantic exaggerations, or fossilized liturgical practices. Especially to be avoided, moreover, are the religiously fraudulent excesses and escapades of the Muslim world's popular Sufism along with Modern Islam's often blind and virulent prejudices against Sufism in all its forms.

As a tradition, Sufism is more than a thousand years old, a vast reservoir of spiritual/psychological wisdom as variegated as the peoples of Islam. Neither space nor my expertise will allow for more than an adumbrated glimpse into its substance.[58] Perhaps the most effective and expedient means of achieving this would be through a sampling of some of its wares. For the sake of space, I will contradict my earlier suggestion and restrict myself to a few aphoristic excerpts from a single work by a famous Egyptian Sufi, Ibn ʿAṭāʾ Allāh al-Iskandarī (d. 709/1309).

On arrogance:[59]

> Nothing repels provisions (from God) like arrogance. Indeed rain settles on the plains, not on the mountain tops. Such is the likeness of the hearts of the arrogant. Mercy rolls off of them and falls upon the hearts of the humble. And by the arrogant, we simply refer to those who reject the truth, not those who have fine clothing. Indeed, arrogance is nothing more than disregard for the truth—that is, pushing it aside—and contempt for people. And do not think that arrogance can only reside in persons of power or wealth. Nay, it may reside in one who does not have enough provisions for a single night. Yet he spreads corruption instead of good, because of his pride.[60]

On false piety:

> How disgraceful it is to find cowardice in a soldier; how disgraceful it is to hear solecisms from a grammarian; and how disgraceful it is to find one who feigns asceticism pursuing the vanities of this world.[61]

> One who feigns pursuit of the Afterlife to achieve worldly gain is like one who uses an emerald spoon to scoop feces.[62]

On loving God:

> God is not satisfied with the fact that you love Him; the important thing is that He love you.[63]

On manly strength:

> A man is not simply one who is able to raise his voice against people at gatherings. To be a man is to be able to raise one's voice against one's self and turn it back towards God.[64]

On secondary causes:

> One who sees the ultimate source of his problems in creatures is like a dog whom a man strikes with a brick; the dog then goes and bites the brick, because it is unable to see that the brick is not a primary cause. And one who sees the ultimate source of his advantage in creatures is like a horse who, when its trainer approaches, wags its tail (in happiness); but when its owner approaches it pays him no attention.[65]

On humility:

> Disobedience in a spirit of humility and penitence is superior to obedience in a spirit of glory and arrogance.[66]

On knowledge without practice:

> One who has knowledge but does not live by it is like a candle that lights the way for others by burning itself out.[67]

On seeking honor and glory:

> You seek honor and glory from people, but you do not seek it from God. One who does this has simply lost his way. And one who loses his way will only be taken farther from his (desired) destination the longer he travels.[68]

On being trapped between worship and disobedience:

> Do not be like the sick person who says, "I will not treat my illness until I find a cure." For it will be said to you, "You will not find a cure until you treat your illness." There is no sweetness in jihad; there is but the jagged edges of swords. So prosecute the jihad against your passions. This is the greatest jihad.[69]

On character:

> When felicitous people see a person engaged in disobedience, they rebuke him while secretly praying for his rehabilitation. Miserable people, on the other hand, rebuke him in pursuit of self-gratification; and they may even assassinate his character. The Believer is one who is sincere to his fellows in public and seeks to cover their faults in private. Miserable people are the opposite: when they see a person engaged in disobedience, they slam the door (of repentence) in his

> face and scandalize him. Such people's inner vision is shrouded in darkness and they are far removed from God.[70]

On envy:

> It is enough ignorance that you should envy people with money and allow your heart to become preoccupied with this. This makes you more ignorant than they, because while they are preoccupied with what they have been given, you are preoccupied with what you have not.[71]

On true friendship:

> If you are looking for a Qur'ān-reciter, they are countless in number; if you want a doctor, they too are many; if you are looking for a jurist, they are equally numerous. But if you are looking for someone who will direct you to God and disclose your faults to you, such people are few in number. So if you find such a person, hold fast to them with both hands.[72]

On trusting God:

> There is no manifestation of obedience more loved by God than trust in Him.[73]

On religious ostentatiousness:

> Shall you reform your outward appearance while your inner reality remains in shambles? Your likeness is that of a leper who wears fine clothing while pus and matter flow underneath. Shall you reform that which the people observe but not your heart which is for your Lord (to observe)?[74]

On halfhearted repentance:

> One who continually sins and makes repentance is like one who continually drinks poison and follows it up with its antidote. It is said to him, "You may not make it to the antidote one day and death may rush upon you."[75]

On maintaining one's focus on the life to come:

> One who is preoccupied with the vanities of this life with no concern for the life to come is like a person who is about to be eaten by

> a lion but then is bitten by a flea, at which time his preoccupation with the flea diverts his attention away from the lion.[76]

On self-defeatism:

> Do not say, "What benefit shall I derive from attending religious gatherings, while I remain steeped in sin and unable to leave it?" The archer must continue to shoot! If he does not hit his target today, he will hit it tomorrow.[77]

None of this contradicts the value or propriety of protest and resistance, assuming that there are justifiable reasons for engaging in these. Nor does it reduce God and religion to mere tools and handmaidens in the quest for secular "success" and opulence. Nor, indeed, are protest and resistance left to pose as substitutes for bona fide religious devotion and God-consciousness. Rather, personal piety and reflection, moral responsibility, and concern for the Afterlife occupy the center of this universe. All of this is executed, moreover, in a tone that is homiletic without being preachy. Indeed, among the important intangibles of this discourse is that many Blackamericans are likely to detect in it a palpable strain of "color." This feature alone qualifies it to go places that works such as William Bennett's *Book of Virtues* could never go. For such works as the latter, despite their lofty aims, are routinely dismissed out of hand by the Blackamerican masses as just another chapter in the book of manipulations by the fascinating trickster.

There are those who would argue that Blackamerican life is so circumscribed by white supremacy that Blackamericans are essentially objects who only "choose" to go where they are permitted or told to go. Others maintain that even in this context Blackamericans remain actors possessed of real and effective choices. Whether one subscribes to one or the other of these views, the actions, inactions, choices, or pseudochoices that Blackamericans exercise—as fathers, wives, daughters, friends, and neighbors—critically affect the lives of those around them, most especially those closest to them. And in the end, the shape that their actions and inactions assume will depend on the fortitude of their souls, the purity and magnitude of their hearts and the strength of their psyche. If Blackamerican Islam is to maintain its efficacy as a source of inner strength, a builder of human character, and a bridge to salvation, commitment to God-consciousness and personal piety will have to maintain their place above and beyond the revolt against second creators and false *mysterium tremendum*. Ultimately, if God is to remain the center of Blackamerican Muslim consciousness, the final result of their existential struggle will have to be left in the hands of God. Otherwise, Blackamerican Islam is destined to degenerate into yet another thinly veiled eudaemonistic contradiction in which a God who has been denuded of all absolute and unilateral prerogative is beseeched to exercise His irresistible choice to intervene on behalf of His suffering servants and grant them salvation and felicity in an Afterlife in which they themselves hardly believe.

Notes

INTRODUCTION

1. The National Origins Act of 1924 was explicitly designed "to confine immigration as much as possible to western and northern European stock." The "Asiatic Barred Zone" rendered all persons from Asia ineligible for U.S. citizenship. See I. F. Haney-Lopez, *White By Law: The Legal Construction of Race* (New York: New York University Press, 1998), 38.

2. For a discussion and description of Black Religion and its shared status with Blackamerican Christians, see pp. 29–38, Chapter 1. On its influence among Blackamerican Jewish groups, see H. M. Brotz, *The Black Jews of Harlem* (New York: Schocken Books, 1970).

3. This was really what was at stake in the Salman Rushdie affair. For an insightful treatment of both the Satanic Verses and the doctrine of Prophetic infallibility, see S. Ahmed, "Ibn Taymiyya and the Satanic Verses," *Studia Islamica* 87, no. 2 (1998): 67–124, esp. 70–74, 86–90, 100 passim.

4. This would become the major difference between Sunnism and Shiism, at least during the latter's formative period, during which the living Shiite Imams were deemed infallible.

5. See Stanley Fish, "Postmodern Warfare: The Ignorance of Our Warrior Intellectuals," *Harper's Magazine*, July, 2002.

6. The case with judicature was, of course, different. But, while a judge's decision bound the two parties to the dispute, it did not extend beyond them to the rest of the community.

7. For a sense of the seriousness with which this was taken, see I. K. Nyazee, *The Distinguished Jurist's Primer* (a translation of Ibn Rushd's *Bidāyat al-mujtahid wa nihāyat al-muqtaṣid*) (United Kingdom: Garnet, 1995), where the views of numerous medieval interpretive communities are catalogued.

8. A. Bloom, *The Closing of the American Mind* (New York: Simon and Schuster, Inc., 1987), 92.

9. K. A. Appiah, "The Uncompleted Argument: Du Bois and the Illusion of Race," in *"Race," Writing and Difference,* ed. H. L. Gates Jr. (Chicago: University of Chicago Press, 1986), 35. Appiah continues and expands on this thesis in *In My Father's House: Africa in the Philosophy of Culture* (New York: Oxford University Press, 1992), esp. 28–46.

10. I am especially indebted in this regard to Lucious Outlaw's *On Race and Philosophy* (New York: Routledge, 1996), esp. Chapters 5 and 6, and Maboga P. More's "Outlawing Racism in Philosophy: On Race and Philosophy," in *The African Philosophy Reader,* ed. P. H. Coetzee and A.P.J. Roux (New York: Routledge, 1999), 364–373.

11. On their rationalist and scientific racism, see Outlaw, *On Race,* 160–174.

12. Cited in H. R. Niebuhr, *The Social Sources of Denominationalism* (Gloucester, Mass.: Peter Smith, 1987), 29. I should add here that Ibn Taymīya was an inveterate enemy of the syncretism and superstition of "popular religion."

13. See, for example, *Majmūʿ fatāwā shaykh al-islām aḥmad ibn taymīya,* 37 vols., ed A. M. b. Qāsim (Rabat: Maktabat al-Maʿārif, n.d.), 9: 52–53.

14. W. B. Hallaq, *Ibn Taymīyya Against the Greek Logicians* (Oxford: Clarendon Press, 1993), xxii–xxiii.

15. For Ibn Taymīya, this was actually part of a larger response to a theological doctrine influenced by Plato's notion of Forms. On this doctrine, "existence" (*wujūd*) was viewed as a sort of sempiternal blank canvas onto which God inscribed created beings by endowing each with its individual essence. On this understanding, all existing things could be said to consist of this sempiternal existence plus created essence. From here, however, it would be only a short step to blurring the distinction between the Creator and the created via the assertion that both were "related" by their common participation in this shared, sempiternal existence. For more on this point, see, for example, *Majmūʿ fatāwā,* 5:332.

16. Akbar Ahmed, speaking on the topic of his book, *Islam Under Seige,* on NPR's The Dianne Reem Show, August 16, 2003.

17. W. E. B. Du Bois, "The Conservation of Races," in *Negro Social and Political Thought, 1850–1920,* ed. H. Brotz (New York: Basic Books 1966), 485.

18. J. P. Sartre, *Anti-Semite and Jew* [*Réflexions sur la Question Juive*], trans. G. J. Becker (New York: Schocken Books, 1948), 57. The original first appeared in French in 1946 and parts of it go back as far as 1944 (see, e.g., the note at the bottom of p. 71).

19. Sartre, *Anti-Semite,* 57.

20. M. F. Jacobson, *Whiteness of a Different Color: European Immigrants and the Alchemy of* Race (Cambridge, Mass.: Harvard University Press, 1998), 143.

21. I do not intend to imply here that such social problems are unheard of in immigrant Muslim communities in America. I would argue, however, that outside places like New York City or East Dearborn, Michigan, where immigrant Muslims swell the ranks of taxi drivers and have representation on the welfare role, respectively, the *image* of both "immigrant Muslim" and "the Muslim world" is far more

tied to the profile of immigrant Muslim professionals than it is to their socioeconomic inferiors.

22. I was invited to speak to the Muslim communities in Melbourne, Perth, and Sydney, where I delivered lectures to large audiences. I am not claiming that there are no indigenous Muslims in Australia. But, while I had ample occasion to meet them (it is common to showcase Western converts to other Westerners), I met none. One factor perhaps contributing to this apparent paucity might be that, unlike Muslim immigrants to the United States, who are (or have been) generally considered white or at least "nonblack," Muslim immigrants in Australia (like England) are routinely considered black.

23. On Salafism and the Salafis, see pp. 48–49, 83–84.

CHAPTER 1

1. On these figures, see F. Nuʿman, *The Muslim Population of the United States: A Brief Statement* (n.p.: American Muslim Council, 1992), 11–13.

2. See, for example, C. E. Lincoln, *The Black Muslims in America*, 3rd ed. (Grand Rapids, Mich.: W. B. Eerdmans Publishing Company, 1994), 27ff. and passim; G. Usry and C. Keener, *Black Man's Religion: Can Christianity Be Afrocentric?* (Downer's Grove, Ill.: Intervarsity Press, 1996), 21–44 passim. Such claims are not wholly without basis, as Elijah Muhammad's *Message, to the Black Man* and numerous editions of the Nation's newspaper, *Muhammad Speaks*, plainly demonstrates. But there is also a clear ideological element at work, which delivers these authors into some fairly stark anachronisms. For example, neither Elijah Muhammad nor any of the early twentieth-century proto-Islamic groups (e.g., Moorish Science Temple) were the *originators* of this view. Rather, it goes back more than a century and a half to Blackamerican Christians, beginning, perhaps with David Walker (d. 1912) (see Chapter 3). Bishop Henry McNeil Turner (d. 1915) would insist that whites had commandeered Christianity and infected it with their racial biases. Edward Wilmot Blyden (d. 1912) would make a similar claim in his classic *Christianity, Islam and the Negro Race.* Even the late C. Eric Lincoln would state in his later years that African slaves brought to America "would eventually meet *the white man's God.*" See his *Race, Religion and the Continuing American Dilemma* (New York: Hill and Wang, 1999), 31 (emphasis added). The redoubtable James Cone openly spoke of "the white man's religion"; see *Martin and Malcolm and America: A Dream or a Nightmare* (New York: Orbis, 1993), 9. And William Jones would go so far as to refer to Christianity as "Whiteanity"; see his *Is God A White Racist? Preamble to Black Theology* (New York: Doubleday, 1973). In all of this, we should distinguish between essential and historical claims and note that any contention that Christianity is *inherently* "the white man's religion" must buy into the reification of whiteness (and blackness) as a transcendent and permanent reality, failing to appreciate that Christianity was on the scene long before whiteness as a racial category had even been invented. On the invention of whiteness as a racial category, see T. Allen, *The Invention of the White Race*, 2 vols. (New York: Verso, 1994), 1: 1–51.

3. See J. van Ess, "From Wellhausen to Becker: The Emergence of *Kulturgeschi-*

chte in Islamic Studies, *Islamic Studies: A Tradition and Its Problems,*" ed. M. Kerr (Malibu, Calif.: Undena Publications, 1980), 48–49.

4. A. Mazrui, *World Culture and the Black Experience* (Seattle: University of Washington Press, 1974), 92, 94 passim.

5. C. H. Long, "Interpretations of Black Religion in America," in *Significations: Signs, Symbols, and Images in the Interpretation of Religion* (Aurora, Colo.: The Davies Group, 1995), 152–153 (emphasis not added).

6. See, for example, A. Raboteau, *Slave Religion: The "Invisible Institution" in the Antebellum South* (Oxford: Oxford University Press, 1978), 47ff; E. F. Frazier, *The Negro Church in America* (New York: Schocken Books, 1974), 9–14; C. E. Lincoln, *Race, Religion and the Continuing American Dilemma* (New York: Hill and Wang, 1999), 23–59.

7. J. Baldwin, *The Fire Next Time* (New York: Dell, 1963), 40.

8. L. Jones (Amiri Baraka), *Blues People: Negro Music in White America* (New York: Quill, 1999), x. This is a reissue of this book which was first published in 1963.

9. W. J. Cobb, *The Essential Harold Cruse* (New York: Palgrave, 2002), 290–291.

10. Contrary to the popular stereotype that Islam spread so quickly because it was imposed by the sword, it took literally centuries for places like Egypt, Syria, greater Iraq, and Iran to become majority Muslim. On this point, see R. Bulliet, *Conversion to Islam in the Medieval Period: An Essay in Quantitative History* (Cambridge, Mass.: Harvard University Press, 1977). Interestingly, some of these early communities became Arabs along with becoming Muslim (e.g., Egypt, Syria, parts of Iraq), while others did not (e.g., Iran, parts of North Africa).

11. On this orientation, see the informative work of J. Mbiti, *African Religions and Philosophy* 2nd ed. (Oxford: Heinemann, 1989).

12. F. Mernissi, *Islam and Democracy: Fear of the Modern World* (New York: Addison-Wesley, 1992), 111.

13. One wonders, however, how the hegemonic expansion of Americana, in the form of globalization, will affect this situation. Will globalization also support the spread of the Blackamerican perspective to other black and colored peoples of the world?

14. Interestingly, in places like England, black is not simply a color but connotes a social standing or political alliance. It applies not only to Africans but to all non-whites, including such groups as Indians and Pakistanis. See, for example, S. P. Mohanty, *Literary Theory and the Claims of History: Postmodernism, Objectivity, Multicultural Politics* (Ithaca, N.Y.: Cornell University Press, 1997), 17. On a recent trip to Australia, I learned of a similar phenomenon there.

15. See F. Esack, *Qur'ān, Liberation and Pluralism: An Islamic Perspective of Interreligious Solidarity Against Oppression* (Oxford: Oneworld Press, 1997), 31.

16. Esack, *Qur'ān,* 32ff.

17. Blacks in South Africa, incidentally, had far more access and exposure to Islam and Muslims than did Blackamericans in the early twentieth century. Indeed, South Africa boasted standing mosques, religious scholars, schools of law (*madhhabs*), the public practice of Islamic liturgies, Muslim educational institutions, etc. In North America, meanwhile, prior to the twentieth century, all of these were either eradicated or forced underground.

18. These organizations include, *inter alia*, CAIR (Counsel for American Islamic Relations), AMC (American Muslim Counsel), and MPAC (Muslim Political Action Committee). My point here is simply that these organizations acted in apparent defiance of the wishes of the Blackamerican Muslim community, not that it is un-Islamic or even against the interests of Blackamerican Muslims to support the Republican Party nor that the Democratic platform is necessarily in their best interest. Indeed, one could argue, as I shall below, that the marriage between Liberalism and the Civil Rights establishment has had a devastating effect on Blackamericans over the past quarter century.

19. C. H. Johnson, *God Struck Me Dead: Voices of Ex-Slaves* (Cleveland: The Pilgrim Press, 1993). This is actually a reprint of the work first published in 1969.

20. Johnson, *God Struck Me*, 160.

21. Johnson, *God Struct Me*, 160.

22. Johnson, *God Struck Me*, 161.

23. For an overview of Thurman's thought, see *A Strange Freedom: The Best of Howard Thurman on Religious Experience and Public Life*, eds. W. E. Fluker and C. Tumber (Boston: Beacon, 1998).

24. H. Thurman, *The Luminous Darkness: A Personal Interpretation of the Anatomy of Segregation and the Ground of Hope* (New York: Harper and Row, 1965), x.

25. A. Cerillo, "The Beginnings of American Pentecostalism: A Historic Overview," in *Pentecostal Currents in American Protestantism*, eds. E. L. Blumhofer, R. P. Spittler and G. A. Wacker (Chicago: University of Chicago Press, 1999), 235. The quoted segment is taken from R. Anderson's *Vision of the Disinherited: The Making of American Pentecostalism.*

26. This is certainly the opinion of I. MacRobert, *The Black Roots and White Racism of Early Pentecostalism in the USA* (London: Macmillan, 1988). See also Cerillo, "Beginnings," 231, 235, and 237.

27. See, for example, B. Jackson, "The Other Kind of Doctor: Conjure and Magic in Black American Folk Medicine," *African-American Religion*, eds. T. E. Fulop and A. Raboteau (New York: Routledge, 1997), 415–431.

28. See, for example, Frazier, *Negro Church* 82–85 (published with C. E. Lincoln's *The Black Church Since Frazier.*)

29. Frazier, *Negro Church*, 62–67.

30. A. Raboteau, *Canaan Land: A Religious History of African Americans* (Oxford: Oxford University Press, 2001), ix.

31. See, for example, C. H. Long "Perspectives for the Study of African-American Religion in the United States, in Fulop and Raboteau, *African-American Religion*," 21–35; Lincoln, *Race, Religion*, xviii–xxv, 52–59 passim; J. R. Washington Jr., *Black Religion: The Negro and Christianity in the United States* (Lanham, md.: The University Press of America, 1984); and M. Karenga, "Black Religion," in G. S. Wilmore, ed., *African American Religious Studies* (Durham and London: Duke University Press, 1995), 271–300.

32. Lincoln, *Race Religion*, 31.

33. Speaking of the invisible institution of slave religion, Raboteau writes, for example: "The slave preacher had to be careful not to mention freedom or equality for

black people in this life, but only in Heaven—at least in the presence of whites." *Canaan Land*, 46.

34. Even the so-called Black Theology that emerged in the 1960s on was an effort limited to Blackamerican Christians thinking on the data of Christianity. As such, Black Theology was really a Black Christian theology and not a theology of Black Religion per se.

35. C. H. Long, "Freedom, Otherness and Religion: Theologies Opaque," *Significations*, 212.

36. H. A. Baker, *Afro-American Poetics: Revisions of Harlem and the Black Aesthetic* (Madison: University of Wisconsin Press, 1988), 7 (emphasis added).

37. H. L. Gates Jr. and C. West, *The Future of the Race* (New York: Vintage Books, 1998), 82–83 (emphasis added).

38. C. West, *The Cornel West Reader* (New York: Basic *Civitas* Books, 1999), 436. All emphases added.

39. Mbiti *African Religions and Philosophy*, 1.

40. A. Austin, *African Muslims in Antebellum America: Transatlantic Stories and Spiritual Struggles* (New York and London: Routledge, 1997), 22. As concrete figures, these numbers are problematic. The U.S. Census of 1900 put the total number of blacks at nine million (see below). Still, Austin's percentages are likely good approximations, which is sufficient to make the point at hand.

41. There is, I believe, no longer any need to apologize for a religious orientation. Indeed, if nothing else, postmodernism has exposed the fallacy of the "belief vs. knowledge" dichotomy of the (French) Enlightenment. The difference between a religious and nonreligious orientation can now be seen to be not between belief and unbelief (or nonbelief) but rather between belief in different things, that is, religion, science, or the power of reason. Belief, in other words, is, in the end, all that any of us have.

42. C. West, *Prophesy Deliverance: An Afro-American Revolutionary Christianity*, (Philadelphia: The Westminister Press, 1982), 44.

43. On Blackamerican tragedy, see West, "Subversive," in *The Cornel West Reader*, 437–438.

44. While traditional African religion posited the existence of God, God was actually marginal in everyday religious practice. At the center of this practice stood, rather, the ancestors and the "living dead." On this point see Mbiti, *African Religions and Philosophy*, 74–89.

45. On these and other basic features of traditional African religion, see Mbiti, *African Religions and Philosophies*, 58–89.

46. Raboteau, *Slave Religion*, 87.

47. D. W. Wills, "The Central Themes of American Religious History: Pluralism, Puritanism, and the Encounter of Black and White," in Fulop and Raboteau, *African American Religion*, 14.

48. Eds. S. A. Brown, A. P. Davis, and U. Lee, *The Negro Caravan* (New York: Arno Press and The New York Times, 1969), 422.

49. G. Wilmore, *Black Religion and Black Radicalism: An Interpretation of the Religious History of African Americans*, 3rd ed. (Maryknoll, N.Y.: Orbis Books, 1999), 26.

50. It is true that not all those who revolted against American slavery in the name of Christianity were Blackamericans. The name John Brown comes immediately to mind as a white American who mounted violent protests. Yet, inasmuch as American slavery in particular was the raison d'être behind these revolts, they can be considered products of Black Religion, in the same way that blacks embraced and practiced aspects of white Christianity.

51. See Long, "Perspectives," 32.

52. Wilmore, *Black Religion and Black Radicalism*, 30.

53. The term "fundamentalism" comes from a set of twelve volumes entitled *The Fundamentals*, published by a group of conservative Christian scholars and theologians between 1909 and 1919 in response to liberal re-interpretations of Christianity. There were five main fundamentals: (1) the inspiration and infallibility of Scripture; (2) the deity of Christ (including his virgin birth); (3) the substitutionary atonement of Christ's death; (4) the literal resurrection of Christ; and (5) the literal second coming of Christ. For a good introduction to fundamentalism, see E. Dobson, E. Hindson, and J. Falwell, *The Fundamentalist Phenomenon* 2nd ed. (Grand Rapids, Mich.: Baker Book House, 1986).

54. The leading figures in this enterprise are, without question, James Cone and J. Deotis Roberts.

55. On Noble Drew Ali, see E. E. Curtis IV, *Islam in Black America* (New York: State University of New York Press, 2002), 56–61. On Elijah Muhammad, see Z. I. Ansari, "Aspects of Black Muslim Theology," *Studia Islamica* 53 (1981): 137–176.

56. Showing the extent and depth of this conservative impulse, one survey taken as late as 1985 revealed that most Blackamericans favored the death penalty and school prayer (while most Blackamerican politicians opposed these), most Blackamericans opposed school busing (while most Blackamerican elected officials favored it), and three times as many Blackamericans opposed abortion as did their leaders. See Gates and West, *The Future of the Race*, 35.

57. Gayraud Wilmore, for example, refers to it as "black folk religion." See his *Black Religion and Black Radicalism* 48, 258 passim.

58. Wilmore, *Black Religion and Black Radicalism*, 276.

59. See, for example, A. Austin, *African Muslims in Antebellum America* (New York: Garland Publishing, Inc., 1984); S. Diouf, *Servants of Allah: African Muslims Enslaved in the Americas* (New York: New York University Press, 1998); and M. Gomez, "Muslims in Early America," *The Journal of Southern History* 40, no. 4 (1994): 671–710.

60. See T. Allen, *The Invention of the White Race*, 1:14. Meanwhile, scholars like Oscar Handlin imply that many peoples now thought of as white, for example, Jews, Italians, Armenians, and even Swedes and Germans, were not inducted into whiteness until the middle of the twentieth century! See his *Fire-Ball in the Night: The Crisis in Civil Rights* (Boston: Beacon, 1964), esp. 24–25.

61. See, for example, N. Daniel, *Islam and the West: The Making of an Image* (Oxford: Oneworld Press, 1997).

62. M. Koszegi and J. G. Melton, *Islam in North America: A Sourcebook* (New York, Garland, 1992), xi, report that the white American convert, Muhammad Alexander Russell Webb, established the first mosque in North America in New York in

1893. Sulayman Nyang speaks of Ukranian Muslims conducting services and classes in their "place of worship" in New York city at the end of the nineteenth century. See his *Islam in the United States of America* (n.p: ABC International, Inc., 1999), 16.

63. It is true that any mosques the African Muslims might have built did not have to be formal structures; they could have been simply sacred spaces closed off by rocks or twigs marking the circumference. The existence of such mosques would assume, however, that African Muslims in North America, like African Muslims in other parts of the Americas, enjoyed the luxury of engaging in communal worship. This is doubtful. And even if they did build "makeshift" mosques, none of these appear to have survived as places of worship.

64. See Austin, *African Muslims*, 146–151.

65. Among the four Sunni schools of law, the Ḥanafī school, traditionally the largest, is dominant in Turkey, India, Afghanistan, Pakistan, Iraq and the Balkans and has representation in Egypt and parts of the Fertile Crescent. The Mālikī school, traditionally the second largest, predominates among North and sub-Saharan Africans, Spain (before expulsion) and Sicily (before expulsion), and has representation in Egypt and parts of the Gulf. The Shāfiʿī school, now perhaps the largest, predominates among Malaysians, Indonesians, South Africans, and Somalis and also has followers in the Fertile Crescent and Egypt. The Ḥanbalī school, numerically the smallest, predominates in Saudi Arabia and the Gulf region.

66. S. Diouf, *Servants of Allah*, 179.

67. Diouf, *Servants of Allah*, 206–207.

68. E. Blyden *Christianity, Islam, and the Negro Race* (Baltimore: Black Classic Press, 1994), 14.

69. *Christianity, Islam*, ii.

70. *Christianity, Islam*, 44.

71. Gates and West, *Future*, 126–27.

72. See p. 10. "Bourgeoisification" is meant to capture the phenomenon of religious groups' quest for upward mobility moving them away from their folk roots. Niebuhr introduces the basic concept but does not use this term.

73. Baraka, *Blues*, 142. See also Wilmore, *Black Religion and Black Radicalism*, 170–172.

74. Frazier, *The Negro Church in America* (with C. E. Lincoln, *The Black Church Since Frazier*), 77–79.

75. Claude McKay's "Enslaved," *The Black Poets*, ed. D. Randall (New York: Bantam Books, 1971), 62.

76. Washington, *Black Religion*, 37.

77. Interestingly, this was also the period during which Judaism established a short-lived relationship with Black Religion, a relationship in the forging of which a certain "Wallace Ford" appears to play a key role. See H. M. Brotz, *The Black Jews of Harlem* (New York: Schocken Books, 1970). The book was first printed in 1974.

78. Washington, *Black Religion*, 235.

79. See, for example, Lincoln, *The Black Muslims in America*; A. B. McCloud, *African American Islam* (New York, Routledge, 1995); R. B. Turner, *Islam in the African Ameri-*

can Experience (Bloomington: Indiana University Press, 1997); Curtis, *Islam in Black America.*

80. See, for example, Turner, *Experience,* 94.

81. Unless he availed himself of the often crudely misleading nineteenth-century European translations of the Qur'ān, Noble Drew Ali (who died in 1929) would only have had access to the translation by Muhammad ʿAlī, which appeared in 1917. As for Elijah Muhammad, who took over the Nation of Islam in 1934, he cites in *Message to the Black Man* both the Muhammad ʿAlī and the ʿAbd Allah Yūsuf ʿAlī translations.

82. This is not to mention some of the crude and blatant indiscretions found among Muslim immigrants to the United States in the twentieth century. Speaking, for example, of activities commonly observed at immigrant mosques all the way up to the 1960s, G. M. Ahmad writes: "Daily prayers were not observed. Friday prayer either was not organized or was held on Sunday. Mixed dances were held in the mosques accompanied by lavish parties where liquor was freely served. Belly dancers were invited to fund-raising events organized in mosque basements." See "Muslim Organizations in the United States," in Y. Y. Haddad, ed., *The Muslims of America* (New York: Oxford University Press, 1991), 12.

83. Abū al-Ḥasan ʿAlī b. Ismāʿīl al-Ashʿarī, *Maqālāt al-islāmiyīn wa ikhtilāf al-muṣallīn,* 2 vols., ed. M. M. ʿAbd al-Ḥamīd (Cairo: Maktabat al-Nahḍah al-Miṣrīyah, 1389/1969), 66–67.

84. Al-Ashʿarī, *Maqālāt,* 1: 69–72.

85. Al-Ashʿarī, *Maqālāt,* 1: 76–77.

86. Al-Ashʿarī, *Maqālāt,* 1: 214.

87. Al-Ashʿarī, *Maqālāt,* 1: 170.

88. I do not mean hereby to legitimize the Nation's theology. My point is simply that when Nation members walked down the street they were both immediately recognized as "Black Muslims" and conscious of this.

89. By "dual appropriation," I am referring here to the manner by which they simultaneously appropriated Islam and aspects of white American culture. For more on this point, see Chapter 4, pp. 157–158.

90. Turner, *Experience,* 109–146.

91. See pp. 74–77.

92. Reflecting his own affinity for the "Protestant approach," even Imām W. D. Muhammad would affirm his belief in *sola scriptura*: "They say, 'Well, what do you have, Brother Imām, that makes you so special?" The Qur'ān, the Word of God,' he replied. 'You mean to tell me that just you and the word of God? That's right. Just me and the word of God.' " See Curtis, *Islam in Black America,* 124.

93. For more on the Dār al-Islām movement, see R. Mukhtar Curtis, "Urban Muslims: The Formation of the Dār ul-Islam Movement," in *Muslim Communities in North America,* eds. J. Smith and Y. Haddad (New York: State University of New York Press, 1994), 51–74; S. Nyang, *Islam in the United States,* 143–147; R. Dannin, *Black Pilgrimage to Islam* (New York: Oxford University Press, 2002), 67–80; A. B. McCloud, *African American Islam,* 64ff, 85ff; and J. I. Smith, *Islam in America* (New York: Columbia University Press, 1999), 97–98. Smaller though similar to the Dār were the

Islamic Party, the International Islamic Brotherhood, and the *Fuqrah* Movement, actually a militantly mystical spin-off from the Dār. The Islamic Party was formally dissolved in 1977 (Dannin, *Black Pilgrimage*, 76); the International Islamic Brotherhood appears to have simply withered with time and to have been absorbed by other groups. On all of these groups, see R. Dannin, *Black Pilgrimage*, 57–83.

94. The American Society of Muslims has gone through several name changes from the time of the death of Elijah Muhammad. Included among these are American Muslim Mission, The World Community of Al-Islam, The World Community of Al-Islam in the West, and the Muslim American Society. For more on the group, see McCloud, *African American Islam*, 72–78; Turner, *Experience*, 223–227: and Smith, *Islam in America*, 89–93.

95. On August 31, 2003, at a speech in Chicago, Imām W. D. Muhammad announced his formal resignation as leader of the ASM. Time will only tell if this resignation is reversible and, if not, whither the movement is headed in terms of leadership and ideology.

96. This is not to deny the various *formal* ties between the ASM and the Muslim world. My point, however, is simply that these have not resulted in any *ideological* transfer of any significant degree.

97. For more on this group see McCloud, *African American Islam*, 72–78; Smith, *Islam*, 89–93; Turner, *Experience*, 223–231.

98. For more on these Sufi groups, see McCloud, *African American Islam*, 88–94.

99. For more on this dichotomy between Modern and Modernized Islam, see chapter 2.

100. Washington, *Black Religion*, 229.

101. That is, given their intimate relationship with their Eastern co-religionists. For more on this, see pp. 70–77.

102. For more on this point, see pp. 135–136.

103. I wish to emphasize *dominant* here in response to those who tend to view "the West" as an intellectual, cultural, and even civilizational monolith. There are not one but many "Western traditions," that is, traditions produced by people who are Westerners, including Blackamericans, Native Americans, Hispanic Americans, and even various "dissident" white Americans. What generally passes as "Western tradition," however, is simply that voice that has succeeded in dominating the national master–narrative and in substituting itself for the whole.

104. See pp. 37–38.

105. Lincoln, *Race, Religion*, xxiii.

106. R. Niebuhr, *Moral Man and Immoral Society* (New York: Charles Scribner's Sons, 1960), xv.

107. J. R. Washington, "Folk Religion and Negro Congregations: The Fifth Religion," *African American Religious Studies: An Interdisciplinary Anthology* (Durham, N.C.: Duke University Press, 1989), 56.

108. For an explanation of this distinction, see chapter 2.

CHAPTER 2

1. Imām Muhammad's name has gone through a number of permutations, from Wallace D. Mohammed to Warith Deen Muhammad to Wārithuddīn Muhammad.

2. See, for example, A. McCloud, *African American Islam* (New York: Routledge, 1995), 72ff; on Farrakhan's dissent see McCloud, 78ff.

3. Indeed, prior to the "immigrantization" of American Islam, terrorism, for example, was never associated with American Muslims. Even the radical posture of the proto-Islamic Nation of Islam was not generally portrayed by the national media as a terroristic threat.

4. See, for example, McCloud, *African American Islam*, 21–24.

5. For example, the Islamic Society of North America (ISNA), the Islamic Circle of North America (ICNA), the Council on American Islamic Relations (CAIR), the American Muslim Council (AMC), the Muslim Public Affairs Council (MPAC). On these and other Muslim national organizations see J. I. Smith, *Islam in America* (New York: Columbia University Press, 1999), 167–176; Q. Ahmed, "Muslim Organizations in the United States," *The Muslims of America*, ed. Y. Y. Haddad (New York: Oxford University Press, 1991), 11–24.

6. See A. J. Robinson Jr., "American Colonization Society," in *Africana: The Encyclopedia of African and African American Experience*, ed. K. A. Appiah and H. L. Gates Jr. (New York: Basic *Civitas* Books, 1999), 79. Meanwhile, Gayraud. Wilmore places the origins of the idea of the ACS with the Reverend Samuel Hopkins, a white minister and former slaveholder, in 1759. See G. Wilmore, *Black Religion and Black Radicalism: An Interpretation of the Religious History of African Americans*, 3rd ed. (Maryknoll, N.Y.: Orbis Books, 1999) 127. See also E. Blyden, *Christianity, Islam, and the Negro Race* (New York: New York University Press, 1998), xii–xv.

7. See L. C. Robinson, "Blyden, Edward Wilmot," *Africana*, 275.

8. Blyden, *Christianity, Islam*, xiv.

9. Blyden, *Christianity, Islam*, 379.

10. "Africa and the Africans" and "The Mohammedans of Negritia" carry no date. The other directly relevant essays, including "Mohammedanism and the Negro Race," "Christianity and the Negro Race," "Christian Missions in West Africa," "Mohammedanism in West Africa," and "Islam and Race Distinctions" were all written between 1871 and 1876.

11. In several places in this essay, Blyden quotes sources that were published in 1886. See, for example, *Christianity, Islam*, 369.

12. Blyden, *Christianity, Islam*, 382.

13. See G. E. Shankle, *American Nicknames: Their Origin and Significance* (New York: The H and W Wilson Co., 1937), 452–453. I am thankful to Prof. Sulayman Nyang for this reference.

14. Blyden, *Christianity, Islam*, ii.

15. Cited in H. R. Niebuhr, *Christ and Culture* (New York: HarperCollins, 2001), 30. In a similar vein, R. A. Markus writes of the sixteenth-century Spanish Dominican, Diego Durán, working in Spanish America, that he was "always suspicious that beneath the outward conformity with the newly imposed Christianity rites and an-

cient beliefs might linger, and aware that rituals and festivals could be ambiguous enough to allow Indians 'to introduce their ancient beliefs into our ceremonies,' Durán insisted that 'If any recollection of the ancient religion exists among the natives, it is necessary that it be uprooted.' " See his *The End of Ancient Christianity* (Cambridge: Cambridge University Press, 1990), 1–2.

16. Blyden, *Christianity, Islam,* 44

17. Blyden, *Christianity, Islam,* 58.

18. Blyden, *Christianity, Islam,* 66.

19. Blyden, *Christianity, Islam,* 24

20. Blyden, *Christianity, Islam,* 75.

21. Blyden, *Christianity, Islam,* 75–76.

22. Blyden, *Christianity, Islam,* 92.

23. Blyden, *Christianity, Islam,* 44.

24. Blyden, *Christianity, Islam,* v.

25. Blyden, *Christianity, Islam,* 354.

26. Blyden, *Christianity, Islam,* 14.

27. See, for example, M. Gardell, *In the Name of Elijah Muhammad: Louis Farrakhan and the Nation of Islam* (Durham, N.C.: Duke University Press, 1996), 102.

28. Gardell, *Name,* 102.

29. See, for example, R. Dannin, *Black Pilgrimage to Islam* (New York: Oxford University Press, 2002), 61, 71, 73.

30. On these two smaller movements, see note 77 in chapter 1.

31. See Gardell, *Name,* 4. See also C. Stone, "Estimates of Muslim Living in the United States," *Muslims of America,* ed. Haddad, 25–36.

32. Ahmed, "Muslim Organizations in the United States," 14.

33. Ahmed, "Muslim Organizations," 15.

34. Ahmed, "Muslim Organizations," 15–18; see also Smith, *Islam in America* 170–171.

35. Smith, *Islam in America,* 171.

36. Among the major translated works in this regard are Sayyid Quṭb's *Milestones,* Abū al-Āʿlā al-Mawdūdī's *Towards Understanding Islam* and his *Tafhīm al-Qur'ān* (*Explaining the Qur'ān*), Sayyid Sābiq's *Fiqh al-Sunna* (*Jurisprudence Based on the Prophetic Practice*), Yūsuf al-Qaraḍāwī's *The Permissible and Impermissible in Islam,* and the *fatwās* (legal opinions) of ʿAbd al-ʿAzīz b. Bāz. This list is by no means exhaustive, and there is a steady stream of translations and books written in English by immigrant and overseas Muslims flowing into the Blackamerican Muslim community.

37. *Black Theology* 2 vols., ed. J. Cone and G. Wilmore (New York: Orbis, 1993).

38. J. H. Cone, *God of the Oppressed,* (New York: Orbis, 1997).

39. C. West, *Prophecy Delverance!: An Afro-American Revolutionary Christianity,* (Philadelphia: The Westminster Press, 1982).

40. C. E. Lincoln, *Race Religion, and the Continuing American Dilemma* (New York: Hill and Wang, 1999), a revised version of the book first published in 1984.

41. Exceptions to this might be Imām W. D. Muhammad's *As the Sun Rises from the East* or Imām Jamil al-Amin's *Revolution by the Book.* However, neither of these

works show the clarity of thought or the relevance of Islam to the existential realities of Blackamericans in the way that black Christian writers of the period did with Christianity.

42. On this and related points, see the masterful essay by Charles Long, "The Oppressive Elements in Religion and the Religions of the Oppressed," *Harvard Theological Review* 69, no. 3–4 (July–Oct. 1976): 397–412. This essay was reprinted in Long, *Significations: Signs, Symbol, and Images in the Interpretation of Religion* (Aurora, Colo.: The Davies Group, 1995), 171–186. Black Religion is, incidentally, a religion of the oppressed.

43. Blyden, *Christianity*, ii.

44. Million Family March, *The National Agenda: Public Policy Issues, Analyses, and Programmatic Plan of Action, 2000–2008* (Washington, D.C.: Million Man March, Inc., 2000).

45. See, for example, S. E. Ahlstrom, *A Religious History of the American People* (New Haven: Yale University Press, 1972), 830, on the attitude of Catholic and Lutheran immigrants from Germany.

46. It should be noted in this context that there are some *in the West* who do not believe that Judaism or Christianity is completely compatible with the dominant culture in the West.

47. See his *Mustaqbal al-thaqāfah fī miṣr* (*The Future of Culture in Egypt*), 2 vols. (Cairo: Dār al-Maʿārif, 1993), 1:30–52 passim. This was a re-issue of the original published back in the 1930s. Ṭaha Ḥusayn's foreward to this edition carries a date of 1938.

48. See his famous *Gharbzadegī* (*Weststruckness*), trans. J. Green and A. Alizadeh (Lexington, Ky.: Mazdā Publishers, 1982). The work first appeared in Persian in 1962. Meanwhile Daryush Shayegan would more bluntly refer to this phenomenon as "cultural schizophrenia." See *Cultural Schizophrenia: Islamic Societies Confronting the West*, trans. from the French by J. Howe (New York: Syracruse University Press, 1992).

49. Ṣalāḥ ʿAbd al-Faṭṭāḥ al-Khālidī *Amrīkā min al-dākhil bi minzār sayyid quṭb* (*America From Within From the Perspective of Sayyid Quṭb*), 2nd ed. (Jeddah: Dār al-Minārah, 1406/1986), 115.

50. al-Khālidī, *Amrīkā*, 116.

51. al-Khālidī, *Amrīkā*, 136. Quṭb has an entire chapter entitled, "Our Primary Enemy: The White Man (*Adūwunā al-Awwal: al-Rajul al-Abyaḍ*), ibid., 135–140.

52. R. Dyer, *White* (London, New York: Routledge Press, 1997), 19–20.

53. Muslim Modernism, essentially an attempt to vindicate Islam and reform Muslim society on the basis of Western values, and Sufism (mysticism) are also orientations found among immigrant Muslims. These, however, have had a minimal influence on Blackamerican Islam. I shall thus omit them from the present analysis.

54. On the genesis and original definition of fundamentalism, see note 53 in chapter 1.

55. Scholars differ in their descriptions of the Salafīs. J. Voll, for example, in *Islam: Continuity and Change in the Modern World* (New York: Syracuse University Press, 1994), 298, refers to them as Fundamentalists, while O. Roy, *The Failure of Political Islam* (Cambridge, Mass.: Harvard University Press, 1996), refers to them as

Neofundamentalists. I prefer the designation of Roy in that it connotes a departure of sorts, which I locate in the palpable shift in the texture of Salafism from the time of its founders Muhammad ʿAbduh and Rashīd Riḍā to its establishment as the dominant hegemony in Saudi Arabia. I would not agree with applying the term "fundamentalist" to either ʿAbduh or Riḍā.

56. Roy, *Failure*, 22.

57. See Muḥammad b. Isḥāq b. Khuzaymah, *Kitāb al-tawḥīd wa ithbāt ṣifāt al-rabb*, ed. M. K. Harrās (Cairo: Maktabat Kullīyāt al-Azharīyah, 1387/1968), 197–229.

58. See Abū Bakr b. Muḥammad b. Ibrāhīm b. al-Mundhir, *Al-Ijmāʿ* (Riyadh: Dār Ṭība, 1402/1982).

59. For a description of this work, entitled *Ikhtilāf al-fuqahā'* (Disagreements Among the Jurists), see Y. al-Ḥamawī, *Muʿjam al-udaba'* (aka *Irshād al-arīb ilā maʿrifat al-adīb*), 8 vols., ed. D. S. Margoliouth (London: Luzacs and Co., 1929), 6: 447.

60. For more on the neologism, "Islamic," see Chapter 4, pp. 154–156.

61. See Roy, *Failure*, 196–197, esp. 196: "What the Islamists advocate is not the return to an incomparably rich classical age, but the establishment of an empty stage on which the believer strives to realize with each gesture the ethical model of the Prophet."

62. Cited in D. R. Roediger, ed., *Black on White: Black Writers on What it Means to be White* (New York: Schocken, 1998), 14.

63. Ironically, there is some recognition of this in the Arab world. While in Cairo on August 1, 2000, I heard and saw the commentator Faysal al-ʿAlawī on the popular television program, *al-Ittijāh al-muʿākis* (*The Opposite Direction*) aired on the *al-Jazīrah* channel state to his guests, Ṣabrī Saʿīd and Muḥammad al-Miqdādī, that one of the problems of the Arabs is that they are no longer world players, culturally, as well as otherwise. He contrasts the Arabs in this context with the blacks, whom he says the Arabs generally think of as "backward" but who have produced the likes of Bob Marley, whose music has mesmerized the world and is part and parcel of the hegemonic expansion of globalization.

64. Roy, *Failure*, 35–36.

65. On the *madhhabs*, see note 51 in chapter 1.

66. Y. al-Qaraḍāwī, *Fatāwā muʿāṣirah*, 2 vols. (Beirut: al-Maktab al-Islāmī, 1421/2000), 2: 383–384.

67. al-Qaraḍāwī, *Fatāwā*, 2: 384–389 (for his full response).

68. R. Niebuhr, *Moral Man and Immoral Society* (New York: Charles Scribner's Sons, 1960), xv.

69. See Esack, *Qur'ān, Liberation and Pluralism: An Islamic Perspective of Inter-religious Solidarity Against Oppression* (Oxford: One world Press, 1997), 78.

70. This is the real meaning behind Imām Warithuddin Muhammad's advocacy of a new "American school of Islamic law." See Curtis, *Islam in Black America*, 124–127.

71. P. Gilroy, *The Black Atlantic: Modernity and Double-Consciousness* (Cambridge, Mass.: Harvard University Press, 1993).

72. Premodern and even early modern jurists spoke quite casually of the "non-Muslim wife" (*al-zawjah al-kāfirah*), the "non-Muslim mother" (*al-umm al-kāfirah*),

and "non-Muslim parents" (*al-wālidān al-kāfirān*) as human beings worthy of respect as such. For example, in *Bulghat al-sālik li agrab al-masālik ilā madhhab al-imām Mālik* 2 vols. (Cairo: Muṣṭafā al-Bābī al-Ḥalabī, n.d.) (an authoritative Mālikī text still used on the graduate level at al-Azhar seminary today), after indicating that a Muslim must be good to his parents regardless of their religion, al-Dardīr (d. 1201/1786) writes, "and he should guide the blind parent, even if he or she is a *kāfir*, to church, and deliver him or her thereto and provide him or her with money to spend during their holidays" (2: 523). Also, the Mālikī and Ḥanafī schools unanimously agreed that a non-Muslim mother (*umm kāfirah*) had a primary right to custody of her Muslim children in cases of divorce from a Muslim husband, assuming that she would not attempt to steer the children away from Islam. For more on this point see my "Kramer Versus Kramer in a Tenth/Sixteenth Century Egyptian Court: Post-Formative Jurisprudence Between Exigency and Law," *Islamic Law and Society* 8, no. 1 (2001): 33–36. It should be noted that the Mālikī school bore the brunt of the atrocities inflicted by the Christians upon their expulsion of the Muslims from Spain and Sicily and the Hanafī school bore the brunt of the Mongol invasions. Still, these views on non-Muslim relatives remain standard in the Mālikī and Hanafī schools right down to the present day. On another note, the tendency of certain Muslim "liberals" to deny essentially that *anyone* is a *kāfir* reflects their subscription to this same notion of a *kāfir* being some sort of subhuman species.

73. This is not a call to physical arms; indeed, even a physical victory on the ground would most likely result in either the substitution of one *regime* of domination for another or the substitution of one *agency* by which the values and ideals of the dominant culture are pursued and concretized for another. The authority of white supremacy can be undermined only by exposing the falseness of its claims to transcendence. For example, anthropology as a field tends to assume the transcendence and normalness of white idiosyncrasies and then to judge the "primitives" from this perspective. Rarely, however, are there any anthropological studies of whites. Such studies could establish, however, that whites are no less ensconced in history and idiosyncrasy than anyone else and thus not deserving to serve as any universal standard. What we need, in other words, is an "Anthropology of Whiteness." Perhaps this is related to the meaning of the verse in the Qurʿān that states: "We have created you from a single male and female and turned you into peoples and tribes that you may come to know one another."

74. See bell hooks, *Killing Rage: Ending Racism* (New York: Henry Holt and Company, 1995), 186: "The term 'white supremacy' enables us to recognize not only that black people are socialized to embody the values and attitudes of white supremacy, but that we [black people] can exercise 'white supremacist control' over other black people."

75. In his famous Drum Major Instinct sermon, the Reverend Dr. Martin Luther King Jr. recalled a conversation he had with some of his jailors in Alabama. When they responded to his inquiry about how much they earned, King told them, in a tone of empathy and near disbelief, "You know what, you all oughta be out there marchin' with us!"

CHAPTER 3

1. For instances of this critique and influence, see 46–47.

2. Bernard Lewis's *Race and Color in Islam* (New York: Harper and Row, 1971) and then his *Race and Slavery in the Middle East: An Historical Enquiry* (Oxford: Oxford University Press, 1990) appear to be essentially reactions by a nonblack Jew to the Muslim populations' rising potential as political players who can possibly affect U.S. foreign policy, particularly regarding Israel. Being the keen observer of American trends that he is, one may note that the appearance of Professor Lewis's books parallel the rise of crude Black Orientalism and its evolution into more sophisticated scholarly forms.

3. E. Said, *Orientalism* (New York: Penguin Books, 1987), 11.

4. The group was originally made up of the poets Alafia Pudim (later Jalaluddin Mansur Nuriddin), Umar bin Hassen, Abiodun Oyewole, and the percussionist Nilija. According to Yusuf Nuriddin, tension developed within the group because Pudim and bin Hassen were Muslim, while Oyewole and Nilija were practioners of Yoruba. The group went through personnel changes between 1969 and 1974. And in 1974 their new album reflected changes in ideology. This album, significantly entitled *At Last*, had a cover decked out in stylized calligraphy to resemble or convey the impression of Arabic script. According to Nuriddin, "The obvious message in the title is 'at last the Last Poets are all Muslim.' " The group now consisted of Jalaluddin Mansur Nuriddin, Sulaiman El-Hadi, and Umar bin Hassen. See Y. Nuriddin, "African-American Muslims and the Question of Identity Between Traditional Islam, African Heritage, and the American Way," in *Muslims on the Americanization Path?* eds. Y. Y. Haddad and J. Esposito (Atlanta: Scholars Press, 1993), 309, note 20.

5. According to Nuriddin, examples of this are reflected in: C. Williams, *The Destruction of Black Civilization* (Dubuque, Iowa: Kendall/Hunt, 1971); S. Maglangbayan *Garvey, Lumumba, Malcolm: Black Nationalists-Separatists* (Chicago: Third World Press, 1972); Y. ben Jochannon, *African Origins of Major Western Religions* (Baltimore, Md.: Black Classic Press, 1970); H. Madhubuti (Don L. Lee), *Enemies: The Clash of Races* (Chicago: Third World Press, 1978); J. H. Clarke, *Africans at the Crossroads* (Trenton, N.J.: Africa World Press, 1991). See his "African-American Muslims," 282–287. Most important of all, however, were the works of M. K. Asante, beginning in the 1980s (see below).

6. 'Abd al-Raḥmān b. Khaldūn, *al-Muqaddimah* (Beirut: Dār wa Maktabat al-Hilāl, 1986), 45.

7. See Muhammad al-Amīn al-Shinqīṭī, *Aḍwā' al-bayān fī īḍāḥ al-qur'ān bi al-qur'ān*, 10 vols. (Beirut:Dār al-Kutub al-ʿIlmīyah, 1421/2000), 1: 330. Al-Shinqīṭī refutes the position of Ṭā'ūs by referring to several marriages contracted by the Prophet between a black and a white, for example, Zayd b. Ḥāritha (white) with Barakah, the mother of Usāmah (black), or Usāmah b. Zayd (black) with Fāṭima bt. Qays (white, from the "royal" tribe of Quraysh), or Bilāl (black) with the sister of ʿAbd al-Raḥmān b. ʿAwf (white).

8. al-Shinqīṭī, *Aḍwā'*, 1: 330. Al-Shinqīṭī, himself a Mālikī, refutes this view and cites several poems in praise of the beauty of black women.

9. Ahmad al-Dardīr, *al-Sharḥ al-kabīr*, 4 vols. (Beirut: Dār al-Fikr, N.d.) 4: 309 [on the margin of Muhammad al-Dasūqī, *Ḥāshīyat al-dasūqī ʿalā al-sharḥ al-kabīr*, 4 vols. (Beirut: Dār al-Fikr, n.d.)].

10. Cited in ʿAbduh Badawī, *al-Sūd wa al-ḥadārah al-ʿarabīyah* (*Blacks and Arab Civilization*) (Cairo: al-Maktabah al-ʿArabīyah, 1396/1976), 191–192. Al-Ḥayqaṭān responded with a scathing satirical poem of his own.

11. This is obviously not the place for a full treatment of slavery in Muslim history, though the subject certainly deserves a full study, especially given the tendency on the part of Blackamericans to assume American slavery to be the norm that all other sytems of slavery followed, making no distinction, for example, between slavery in a capitalist society and slavery in a noncapitalist order, slavery that was race based and slavery that was race neutral, or slavery that drew slaves under the full orbit of law and slavery that denied slaves any legal rights. This makes objective discussions of Muslim or African or Polynesian slavery virtually impossible. And it obscures the fact (in my view at least) that it was not slavery but white supremacy that was—and remains—the author of black subjugation in America.

12. I. Berlin, *Many Thousands Gone: The First Two Centuries of Slavery in North America* (Cambridge, Mass.: The Belnap Press of Harvard University Press, 1998), 8. Emphasis added.

13. See M. E. Dyson, *I May Not Get There With You: The True Martin Luther King, Jr.* (New York: The Free Press, 2000), 193–194.

14. Cited in W. J. Moses, *Afrotopia: The Roots of African American Popular History* (Cambridge: Cambridge University Press, 1998), 80.

15. Cited in Moses, *Afrotopia*, 69.

16. R. Hernstein and C. Murray, *The Bell Curve: Intelligence and Class Structure in American Life* (New York: Free Press, 1994).

17. Ibn Khaldūn, *al-Muqaddimah*, 89.

18. Ibn Khaldūn, *al-Muqaddimah*, 63. He actually states that al-Masʿūdī took this fallacious notion over from Galen through the Arab philosopher al-Kindī.

19. Ibn Khaldūn, *al-Muqaddimah*, 61.

20. Ibn Khaldūn, *al-Muqaddimah*, 60. But see the entire discussion from p. 44ff for a full exposé on the theory of climate. This is confirmed, incidentally, by St. Clair Drake in his *Black Folks Here and There*, 2 vols. (Los Angeles: Center for Afro-American Studies, 1990), 2: 157–159. Drake relies on the French translation of Ibn Khaldūn. In my view, Drake was *not* a Black Orientalist. Indeed, the fact that he relies exclusively on Orientalist writings but is still able to avoid Black Orientalism shows the extent to which this phenomenon is far more conscious than unconscious. Black Orientalists, in other words, tend to see only what they are looking for.

21. For example, see Drake, *Black Folks*, 2: 77–184.

22. See Shāfiʿ b. ʿAlī, *Ḥusn al-manāqib al-sirrīyah al-muntazaʿah min al-sīrah al-ẓāhirīyah*, 2nd edition, ed. ʿA. Khowaytar (Riyadh, 1410/1989), 79. There are numerous other instances of black rulers in the central lands of Islam where Arabs predominated.

23. See I. Goldziher, *Muslim Studies*, 2 vols. (London: Allen and Unwin, 1967), 1: 268.

24. Cited in H. A. Jughām and M. Banīs, *al-Jins fī aʿmāl al-imām jalāl al-dīn al-suyūṭī* (Tunis: Dār al-Maʿārif li al-Ṭibāʿah wa al-Nashr, 2001), 262.

25. Jughān and Banīs, *al-Jins*, 266.

26. From his hit single, "Baby Got Back," on the album, *Mack Daddy* (Universal, 1992).

27. For more on this theme, see my discusssion of *fitna* and "second creators" in chapter 5.

28. Ashis Nandy, *The Intimate Enemy: Loss and Recovery of Self Under Colonialism* (Delhi: Oxford University Press, 1983), 26–27, note 35.

29. As W. J. Moses points out, Afrocentric thought dates back at least to the nineteenth century and was even championed in the twentieth century by a number of white scholars, most notably Melville Herskovitz in his famous work, *Myth of the Negro Past*, and Martin Bernal in his seminal work, *Black Athena*. The term "Afrocentrism" itself was used by W. E. B. Du Bois as early as 1962. See *Afrotopia*, 1–2, 11–12.

30. Molefi Kete Ashante, *Afrocentricity* (Trenton: Africa World Press, 1988), 2.

31. *Afrocentricity*, 3.

32. *Kemet*, 131.

33. On this point, see I. F. Haney-Lopez, *White By Law: The Legal Construction of Race* (New York: New York University Press, 1998), 1.

34. On this concept, which basically speaks to the *prima facie* eligibility of every group in America except blacks to join American whiteness, see M. F. Jacobson, *Whiteness of a Different Color: European Immigrants and the Alchemy of Race* (Cambridge, Mass.: Harvard University Press, 1998), 109–135.

35. S. Diouf, *Servants of Allah: African Muslims Enslaved in the Americas* (New York: New York University Press, 1998), 204. She goes on to observe: "In this mind-set, to celebrate the so-called real Africa, or what is perceived as being the real Africa, Islam and the Muslims have to be denied or minimized." Ibid.

36. Williams, *Destruction*, 23.

37. See H. Modarresi, *Crisis and Consolidation in the Formative Period of Shiite Islam* (Princeton: Darwin Press, 1993), 63, note 38.

38. See Muhammad ʿAlī b. Ḥusayn al-Mālikī, *Tahdhīb al-furūq wa qawāʿid al-sanīya fī al-asrār al-fiqhīya* (on the margin of Shihāb al-Dīn al-Qarāfī, *al-Furūq*), 4 vols. (Beirut: ʿĀlam al-Kitāb, N.d.), 1: 3, note 1: "One of the trusted notables said to me that the author of this statement is our master Ahmad Bābā al-Timbuktī, author of *al-Ibtihāj* and other original works, whom Shaykh Mayyāra mentioned in *Sharḥ takmīl al-minhāj* as the *mujaddid* of the tenth [sixteenth C.E.] century after al-Suyūṭī."

39. Williams, *Destruction*, 17.

40. Williams, *Destruction*, 23.

41. Asante, *Afrocentricity*, 57–58.

42. Asante, *Afrocentricity*, 5.

43. B. Lewis, *Race and Color in Islam* (New York: Harper and Row, 1971), 102.

44. R. Stephen Humphreys, *Between Memory and Desire: The Middle East in a Troubled Age* (Berkeley: University of California Press, 1999), 40.

45. I should add here that Gates completely overlooks the extent to which Nas-

ser's policies affected non-Nubians in Egypt. I recall, when my youngest son was born, sitting in the maternity unit at Salām Hospital in the Cairene suburb of Muhandisīn. An Arab-Egyptian man approached the counter and then burst into a tirade against the nurses: "My God, who are you, the government? Is she the government? How despicable! (*Allāh, anti tib'ī min, al-ḥukūmah? Hiya dih al-ḥukūmah? Ḥājjah ti'rif bi 'ṣ-ṣaḥīḥ*)." The man had wanted to give his son both his last name and the patronymic of his family. In order to break up the large landed families, however, Nasser's socialist government had outlawed this practice. When the nurse informed the man that he could give his son only one last name, he accused her of trying to destroy his heritage.

46. In note 7 of this chapter, for example, we saw how the Arabs identified certain members of their society as "white" and others as "black." These perceptions, however, would certainly not hold up in America, at least not their perception of who was "white." As I. F. Haney-Lopez notes in his *White By Law*, 2: "The courts ruled that applicants [for U.S. citizenship] from Mexico and Armenia were 'white,' but vacillated over the Whiteness of petitioners from Syria, India and Arabia." Similarly, the Blackamerican scholar, Adrienne K. Wing notes that in Brazil she is considered white, while in other parts of the world she and her darker-skinned partner are considered a mixed couple. See her "Polygamy From Southern Africa to Black Britannia to Black America: Global Critical Race Feminism as Legal Reform for the Twenty-First Century," *The Journal of Contemporary Legal Issues* 11, issue 2 (2001): 835.

47. This is why, incidentally, we have no mulattos in this community, only blacks, which explains such phenomena as the title to the popular book, *The Color of Water: A Black Man's Tribute to His White Mother.*

48. On this point see Jacobson, *Whiteness*, 280, where he refers to Rabbi Michael Lerner's assertion in 1993 that, "Jews can only be deemed 'white' if there is massive amnesia on the part of non-Jews about the monumental history of anti-Semitism." Even here, however, one notices how carefully Rabbi Lerner treads. By "non-Jews" he is certainly not referring to Hispanics, blacks, or Native Americans, who played no role in promoting regimes of anti-Semitism; he can only be referring specifically to white gentiles. His use of the more bland and inclusive "non-Jews," in other words, appears to be for the purpose of implying that non-Jewishness and whiteness are not synonymous, which preserves the alchemic character of the latter such that Jews remain eligible for admission.

49. R. B. Turner, *Islam in the African American Experience* (Bloomington: Indiana University Press, 1997), 5.

50. "Edward Wilmot Blyden and Pan-Africanism: The Ideological Roots of Islam and Black Nationalism in the United States," *The Muslim World* 87, no. 2 (April, 1997): 169.

51. See, for example, Turner, *Experience*, 34.

52. Turner, *Experience*, 17.

53. E. E. Curtis IV, *Islam in Black America* (New York: State University of New York Press, 2002), 53–56.

54. Jacobson, *Whiteness*, 83.

55. Jacobson, *Whiteness*, 90.

56. Jacobson, *Whiteness*, 73.

57. Jacobson, *Whiteness*, 152.

58. Curtis, *Islam in Black America*, 58.

59. The quotations from al-Ashʿari (see above, pp. 45–46) should not be misinterpreted here. Besides the fact that these were all heterodox doctrines, *none* of those who affirmed that God was a man *racialized* God.

60. See Wilmore, *Black Religion and Black Radicalism: An Interpretation of the Religious History of African Americans*, 3rd ed. (MaryKnoll, N.Y.: Orbis Books, 1998), 134–142.

61. Wilmore, *Black Religion and Black Radicalism*, 197. Wilmore was cited, incidentally, in the preface of *Experience* as one of Turner's teachers at Boston University.

62. Professor Turner makes one passing reference to Walker in *Experience*, 31.

63. Inside the tract he is more explicit, insisting that Blackamericans will find glory or happiness "but with the *entire emancipation of your enslaved brethren all over the world*." Walker, *Appeal to the Coloured Citizens of the World, but in particular, and very expressly, to those of the United States of America*, ed. S. Wilentz (New York: Hill and Wang, 1999), 29. Emphasis added.

64. Walker, *Appeal*, 71.

65. Walker, *Appeal*, 16–17.

66. Walker, *Appeal*, 9.

67. Walker, *Appeal*, 11.

68. Walker, *Appeal*, 21.

69. Walker, *Appeal*, 72 (in a footnote marked by an asterisk). Emphasis not added.

70. Walker, *Appeal*, 4. Emphasis not added.

71. Haney-Lopez, *White By Law*, 1.

CHAPTER 4

1. "Nouveau whiteness" in America yields two mildly contradictory tendencies. On the one hand, nouveau whites are some of the biggest defenders of white supremacy, referring to themselves, for example, as "Anglos" and functioning in effect as white supremacy's first line of defense, a task for which the reward appears to be a certain visceral reassurance of their place within American whiteness. At the same time, their nervous recognition of the precariousness of their status, it being historically and not biologically determined, draws them into a certain identification with blacks, this time as a first line of defense against any Anglo-Saxon nativist riposte.

2. See W. E. B. Du Bois, *The Souls of Black Folks*, 8th ed. (Greenwich, Conn.: Fawcett, 1969), 17.

3. S. Ahlstrom, *A Religious History of the American People* (New Haven, Conn.: Yale University Press, 1972), 828.

4. *History*, 835.

5. *History*, 837.

6. R. Niebuhr, *Christ and Culture* (New York: HarperCollins, 2001), 8.

7. R. Niebuhr, *Christ and Culture*, 52. It should be noted that Niebuhr is merely

cataloguing the various positions taken by groups of Christians. While acknowledging some of its merits, he neither holds up this view as the most authentically Christian nor as his own.

8. S. J. Carter, *God's Name in Vain: The Wrongs and Rights of Religion in Politics* (New York: Basic, 2000), 2.

9. Carter, *God's Name in Vain,* 2.

10. Carter, *God's Name in Vain,* 30.

11. Carter, *God's Name in Vain,* 2.

12. Carter, *God's Name in Vain,* 185.

13. Carter, *God's Name in Vain,* 31–32.

14. Cited in J. Cone, *Martin and Malcolm and America: Dream or Nightmare* (New York: Orbis, 1993), 1.

15. See his "The Conservation of Races," in *Negro Social and Political Thought, 1850–1920,* ed. H. Brotz (New York: Basic 1966), 488.

16. M. Walzer, *The American Intellectual Tradition,* 3rd. ed., 2 vols., ed. D. A. Hollinger and C. Capper (New York: Oxford University Press, 1997), 2: 437–449. Walzer's essay first appeared in 1990.

17. Far from naive or overly idyllic, Walzer notes the following in a lengthy footnote: "The current demand of (some) black Americans that they be called African-Americans represents an attempt to adapt themselves to the ethnic paradigm—imitating, perhaps, the relative success of various Asian-American groups in a similar adaptation. But names are no guarantees; nor does anti-nativist pluralism provide sufficient protection against what is all too often an *ethnic*-American racism. It has been argued that this racism is the necessary precondition of hyphenated ethnicity: the inclusion of successive waves of ethnic immigrants is possible only because of the permanent exclusion of black Americans. But I don't know what evidence would demonstrate *necessity* here. I am inclined to reject the metaphysical belief that all inclusion entails exclusion. A historical and empirical account of the place of blacks in the 'system' of American pluralism would require another paper." "What Does It Mean," 447 (emphasis not added). Incidentally, T. Allen's *The Invention of the White Race,* 2 vols. (New York: Verso, 1994), 1: 1–24, esp. 13–14, might be a good place to begin an account of the place of blacks in the system of American pluralism.

18. Walzer, "What Does It Mean," 441.

19. Walzer, "What Does It Mean," 443.

20. Walzer, "What Does It Mean," 441.

21. See his brilliant essay, "Trans-National America," *American Intellectual Tradition,* 2: 170–180.

22. "What Does It Mean," 444. Walzer actually draws here on the ideas of the Jewish-American theorist, Horace Kallen.

23. See again R. Bourne "Trans-National America," 173: "The Anglo-Saxon element is guilty of just what every dominant race is guilty of in every European country: the imposition of its own culture upon the minority peoples."

24. S. P. Huntington, "The Erosion of American Identity," *Foreign Affairs* 76, no. 5 (Sept.–Oct., 1997): 33.

25. On Fukuyama, see his *The End of History and the Last Man* (New York and

Toronto: Free Press and Maxwell Macmillan Canada, 1992). Fukuyama's thesis was essentially that the end of the twentieth century brought the decisive triumph of capitalism and liberal democracy as economic and political ideals. This marks the "end of history" in that it represents the end of humanity's ideological evolution in search of the optimal economic and political order. Humanity need not look any further.

26. See A. E. Mayer, *Islam and Human Rights*, 3rd. ed. (Boulder, Colo.: Westview, 1999), 197.

27. For a modern discussion on jihad, see my "Jihad and the Modern World," *The Journal of Islamic Law and Culture* 7, no. 1 (2002): 1–26.

28. The ʿAbbasid period was that during which the Muslim empire reached the height of its power and influence and during which the contours of "classical Islam" were established. In fact, the ʿAbbasids were not only a major Muslim dynasty but one of the world's most powerful and long-standing ones, lasting for over half a millennium, from 750 to 1258 C.E. After the fall of their capital at Baghdad at the hands of the Mongols, they continued to hold titular leadership until the caliphate passed to the Ottomans in the seventeenth century C.E.

29. See, for example, Abū Fidā' Ismāʿīl Ibn Kathīr, *al-Sīrah al-nabawīya*, 4 vols. (Cairo: 'Īsā al-Bābī al-Ḥalabī, n.d.), 2: 149–154; and A. M Hārūn, *Tahdhīb sīrat ibn hishām* (Cairo: Maktabat al-Sunnah, 1408/1987), 89–91.

30. Ibn Kathīr, *al-Sīrah*, 2: 155–172; Hārūn, *Tahdhīb*, 92–94.

31. Ibn Kathīr, *al-Sīrah*, 2: 158.

32. Ibn Kathīr, *al-Sīrah*, 2: 322; Hārūn, *Tahdhīb*, 117. This is the precise wording of the document, that is, it uses the word "*ummah*." The document goes on to state that the Jewish allies/neighbors of all the other Medinese clans are of the same standing as the Jews of Banī ʿAwf. For a fuller treatment of the Constitution of Medina, see R. B. Serjeant, "The Sunna Jāmiʿah, Pact with the Yathrib Jews, and the *Taḥrīm* of Yathrib: Analysis and Translation of the Documents Comprised in the So-Called 'Constitution of Medina'," *Bulletin of the School of Oriental and African Studies* 41 (1978): 1–42; and U. Rubin, "The 'Constitution of Medina' Some Notes," *Studia Islamica* 62 (1985): 5–23.

33. Ibn Kathīr, *al-Sīrah*, 2: 322; *Tahdhīb*, 117.

34. Ibn Kathīr, *al-Sīrah*, 1: 257–260.

35. For the entire discussion see Ibn Qayyim al-Jawzīya, *Aḥkām ahl al-dhimma*, 3 vols., ed. Y. al-Bakrī and A. A. al-ʿĀrūrī (Beirut: Dār Ibn Ḥazm, 1418/1997), 2: 764–769.

36. *Aḥkām ahl al-dhimma*, 2: 765

37. For more on this law–fact dichotomy in Islamic law, see below, pp. 161–162 and esp. my *Islamic Law and the State: The Constitutional Jurisprudence of Shihāb al-Dīn al-Qarāfī* (Leiden: E. J. Brill, 1996), 113–141.

38. See, for example, Aḥmad al-Dardīr, *al-Sharḥ al-saghīr* [on the margin of al-Ṣāwī's *Bulghat al-sālik li aqrab al-masālik ilā madhhab al-imam Mālik*, 2 vols. (Cairo: Muṣṭafā al-Bābi al-Ḥalabī, n.d.)], 2: 406–407.

39. See the record of this incident in Mālik b. Anas, *Muwaṭṭa'*, 2 vols., ed. Muhammad F. ʿAbd al-Bāqī (Cairo: Dār Iḥyā' al-Kutub al-ʿArabīyah, 1336/1918), 2: 543–544.

40. In fact, in his famous *al-Tāj al-ʿArūs,* the lexicographer al-Zubaydī states, on the authority of the earlier al-Rāghib al-Isfahānī, that "*maʿrūf*" refers to any act whose goodness is known on the basis of reason *or* revelation. See *Tāj al-ʿarūs min jawāhir al-qāmūs,* 10 vols. (Beirut: Dār al-Fikr, n.d.), 6: 192.

41. See, for example, Qur'ān, 79: 17 passim.

42. This is through the mechanism of analogy or *qiyās.*

43. See the discussion by Yūsuf al-Qaraḍāwī, "*Fiqh al-maʿrakah . . . fiqh al-awrāq,*" *Majallat al-ʿamal,* May–June (1991): 63.

44. See pp. 161–163.

45. On Western legal systems and their legal process, see A. Watson, *The Nature of Law* (Edinburgh: Edinburgh University Press, 1977), 20–22, 97 passim.

46. Some might argue that such rules do not constitute law at all, since they carry no sanction. On the other hand, it would be difficult to argue that rules that are deduced from the same sources and methodologies and by the same authorities as those governing marriage or homicide are not law, while the latter are universally accepted as law.

47. Traditionally, the majority has held abortion to be permissible through the first trimester (120 days), at which time, according to a Prophetic hadith, ensoulment takes place and the fetus becomes a human. All of the schools impose a *prima facie* ban after 120 days.

48. On the limits of the Islamic legal process, see my *State,* esp. 185–224.

49. Traditionally, Muslims separated the jurisdiction of the executive power (i.e., the state) from that of the jurists, who evolved, incidentally, in conscious opposition to the state and whose exclusive preserve it was to determine what the law was. In theory, the state could only apply as law what the jurists sanctioned as such and only those portions of the law to which the jurists assigned a sanction. The jurists made certain exceptions for the executive under the provisions of discretionary punishments or *taʿzīr.* For more on this point, see my *State,* 138–139, 221–222.

50. Cited in the introduction to H. R. Brown, *Die Nigger Die* (Chicago: Lawrence Hill Press, 2001), immediately following p. xxxviii. The present edition is a reprint of the classic work by Brown (now Abdullah Jamīl al-Amīn) which first appeared in 1969.

51. Hadith are the recorded sayings and deeds of the Prophet Muhammad. Unlike the Qur'ān, however, each hadith has to be scrutinized for the veracity of its attribution to the Prophet. Assuming that a hadith is authentic, there is virtually no difference between citing a hadith as an authority and citing the Qur'ān. In other words, not everything that Muslims believe or practice is necessarily found in the Qur'ān.

52. Interestingly, this hadith appears to be less than fully reliable. Its chain of narrators includes ʿAbd al-Raḥmān b. Thābit, whom both al-Bukhārī and Ibn Hibbān deem to be unreliable (*ḍaʿīf,* lit. "weak").

53. On al-Ghazālī's use, see his *al-Munqidh min al-ḍalāl,* ed. J. Salībā and K. Iyād (Beirut: Dār al-Andalus, n.d.), 98–99.

54. Muḥammad b. ʿAbd al-Karīm al-Shahrastāni, *al-Milal wa al-niḥal,* 2 vols. (Beirut: Dār al-Maʿrifah, 1417/1997), 2: 487ff. Ibn Taymīya makes a similar move in referring to al-Kindī as "the philosopher of Islam." Again, however, this had no pre-

scriptive power and was even descriptively misleading, a fact not lost on Ibn Taymīya himself. He writes: "Yaʿqūb b. Isḥāq al-Kindī, the philosopher of Islam in his time, I mean the philosopher who lived under Islam; otherwise, the (Neoplatonic) philosophers are not counted among the Muslims (*laysa al-falāsifa min al-muslimīn*)." See *Majmūʿ fatāwā shaykh al-Islām aḥmad b. taymīya*, 37 vols., ed. A. b. Muḥ b. Qasimī (Rabat: Maktabot al Maʿārif, n.d.). 9:186.

55. H. Cruse, *The Crisis of the Black Intellectual* (New York: Quill, 1984), 452. This was a re-issue. Cruse's work first appeared in 1967.

56. J. Baldwin, *The Fire Next Time*, (New York: Dell, 1963), 40.

57. This, incidentally, along with its failure to recognize Blackamericans' rootedness in a Protestant *religious* tradition, also explains the extremely limited success of the Afrocentric movement in America among Blackamericans.

58. In fact, at some point the entire Muslim world was non-Muslim.

59. For a brief summary of legal statuses, see my *State*, 117ff. For a more detailed discussion see B. G. Weiss, *The Search for God's Law: Islamic Jurisprudence in the Writings of Sayf al-Dīn al-Āmidī* (Salt Lake City: University of Utah Press, 1992), 93–109.

60. Franz Rosenthal has devoted a monograph to this controversy. See his *The Herb: Hashish Versus Medieval Muslim Society* (Leiden: E. J. Brill, 1971). On the legal discussion, see *The Herb*, 101–130.

61. See, for example, Ibrāhīm b. Mūsa al-Shāṭibī, *al-Muwāfaqāt fī uṣūl al-sharīʿah*, 4 vols., ed. A. Drāz, (Cairo: al-Maktaba al-Tijārīya al-Kubrā, n.d.), 1: 284.

62. Shihāb al-Din al-Qarāfī, *Kitāb al-iḥkām fī tamyīz al-fatāwā ʿan al-aḥkām wa taṣ arrufāt al-qāḍī wa al-imām*, ed. ʿAbd al-Faṭṭāḥ Abū Ghuddah (Aleppo: Maktabat al-Maṭbūʿāt al-Islāmīya, 1387/1967), 231.

63. Al-Qarāfī, *Tamyīz*, 231.

64. A. Qūtah, *al-ʿUrf: ḥujjīyatuhu wa atharuhu fī fiqh al-muʿāmalāt al-mālīyah ʿind al-ḥanābilah* (*Custom: Its Probative Value and Implications in the Islamic Law of Monetary Transactions According to the Ḥanbalite School*), 2 vols. (Mecca: al-Maktabah al-Makkīyah, 1418/1997), 1: 60.

65. ʿAbd al-Wahhāb Khallāf, *ʿIlm uṣūl al-fiqh* (Beirut: Dār al-Qalam, 1361/1942), 89.

66. See, for example, Abū Bakr al-Kishnāwī, *Ashal al-madārik sharḥ irshād al-sālik fī fiqh imām al-aʾimmah mālik*, 3 vols. (Cairo: ʿĪsā al-Bābī al-Ḥalabī, n.d.) 2: 342.

67. And even here, jurists have recognized numerous dispensations.

68. See his *Kitāb taḥrīm al-naẓar fī kutub ahl al-kalām*, trans. G. Makdisi, *Ibn Qudāma's Censure of Speculative Theology* (London: Luzacs Co. Ltd., 1962), xiv–xxiii.

69. See, for example, Abū Ḥāmid Muḥammad b. Muḥammad b. Muḥammad al-Ghazālī, *Iḥyā' ʿulūm al-dīn*, 4 vols. (Cairo: Dār Iḥyā' al-Kutub al-ʿArabīya, 1377/1957), 1: 22. Regarding the concept of communal obligation, according to classical jurisprudence, if sufficient numbers of community members undertake an activity deemed to constitute a communal obligation, all others are relieved of the responsibility. If sufficient numbers do not rise to this task, the entire community is considered to be in a state of sin.

70. See Ismāʿīl b. Ibrāhim al-Bukhārī, *Ṣaḥīḥ al-bukhārī*, 9 vols. (Beirut: Dār al-

Arqam b. Abī al-Arqam, n.d.), 3: 99. Actually, there are other reports to the effect that the Prophet used to fast this day even before his advent as prophet, in accordance with a practice followed by the pre-Islamic Arabs in Mecca. After he received revelation commanding the Muslims to fast the month of Ramadan, he continued to fast the day of ʿĀshūrāʾ as a superogatory fast, recommending to his followers that they do so as well. While these reports call into question the idea that the Prophet got the *initial* idea of fasting from the Jews in Medina, it does not contradict the idea that their attribution of this fast to Moses and the Exodus elevated its significance in his eyes and that he did not recognize any Jewish ownership over this fast, based on his own relationship to Moses. On all of this, see *Ṣaḥīḥ al-bukhārī*, 3: 98–99.

71. See C. West, *Restoring Hope: Conversations on the Future of Black America*, ed. K. S. Sealy (Boston: Beacon Press, 1997), 24. The quote is excerpted from an interview with Harry Belafonte.

72. As E. Franklin Frazier once put it, delusions of wealth and power are not enough to extinguish "the emptiness and futility of their existence." Indeed, according to Frazier, middle-class Blackamericans tend to suffer far more from feelings of "nothingness" than they do from persecution. See his *Black Bourgeoisie* (New York: Free Press Paperbacks, 1900, 237.

73. J. McWhorter, *Losing the Race: Self-Sabotage in Black America* (New York: HarperCollins, 2000), 66–67. McWhorter's depictions of the Nation of Islam are dated and naive, and he is often unable to conceal his double-standard. For example, on one and the same page (p. 67), he compares Elijah Muhammad to Al Capone but speaks of an "infectious charisma . . . that draws one irresistibly to the likes of . . . Richard Nixon."!

74. On these statistics, see Adrien Katherine Wing, "Polygamy From Southern Africa to Black Britannia to Black America: Global Critical Race Feminism as a Legal Reform for the Twenty-First Century," *The Journal of Contemporary Legal Issues* 2 (2001): 858.

75. See N. Cott, *Public Vows: A History of Marriage and the Nation* (Cambridge Mass.: Harvard University Press, 2000), esp. chapter 1 on "The Archaeology of American Monogamy," where she traces the federal government's steps in converting monogamy as a minoritarian sentiment into a signature of American national character.

76. The crowning scene in *1984* is one where the state wants to be assured that the protagonist, Winston, sees reality only and precisely as it wills. To this end, Winston is placed in a "pain-chair," and a state-official holds up four fingers. Then Winston is asked, "How many fingers am I holding up, Winston?" When he responds, "Four," the official insists that there are five. He then tweaks up the dial on the pain-chair and asks the question again. This continues until Winston finally exclaims that he is trying to abandon his senses and see five fingers!

77. Carter, *God's Name in Vain*, 3.

78. This distinction between recognizing deeply entrenched factual realities on the one hand, and attempting to invoke scripture in order to vindicate more inchoate, ideological would-be facts on the other, underscores a fundamental distinction between Muslim-Americans who seek to vindicate democracy in America and Muslim-Americans who seek to vindicate it in the Muslim world. The former are simply at-

tempting to process Islam on the basis of inextricable facts; the latter are attempting to use scripture to justify the *creation* of certain facts, as if such were a scriptural imperative. Moreover, beyond the congenial confusion between fact and law (read scripture), their tendency to equate American facts with universal facts is an exercise in invoking false universals.

79. The necessity of developing successful cultural expressions is a major reason for the transfer of religious authority from immigrant to indigenous hands. For more on this point, see my "Muslims, Islamic Law and Socio-Political Reality in the United States," *The American Journal of Islamic Social Sciences* 17, no. 2 (Summer, 2000): 4–8.

80. To take just one example of the inadequacies of present understandings of both pluralism and equality, Stephen Carter notes that he was told by a leading evangelist that Muslim inmates have no cause to complain because they have all the rights and privileges that Christian inmates have. Carter perceptively responds: "No doubt they do. But they would prefer to have the rights they need as Muslims. The right to do everything that Christians are allowed to do is not the same as the right to follow God in their own way." Carter, *God's Name in Vain*, 157–158. See also my "Shariʿah, Democracy and the Modern Nation State: Some Reflections on Islam, Popular Rule and Pluralism," *Fordham International Law Journal* 27, no. 1 (December, 2003): 102–107.

CHAPTER 5

1. W. E. B. Du Bois, *Souls of Black Folks*, 8th ed. (Greenwich, Conn: Fawcett, 1969) 149.

2. R. Otto, *The Idea of the Holy*, trans. J. W. Harvey (London: Oxford University Press, 1926), 18.

3. Otto, *The Idea of the Holy*, 31ff.

4. In C. H. Long, *Significations: Signs, Symbol, and Images in the Interpretation of Religion* (Auroro, Colo: The Davies Group 1995), 180.

5. J. Washington Jr., "Folk Religion and Negro Congregations: The Fifth Religion," in *African American Religious Studies*, ed. G. Wilmore (Durham: Duke University Press, 1989), 55.

6. Washington, "Folk Religion," 50.

7. Washington, "Are American Negro Churches Christian," in *Black Theology: A Documentary History*, 2 vols., ed. J. H. Cone and G. Wilmore (New York: Orbis Books, 1993), 1: 100.

8. Washington, "Are American Negro Churches Christian," 1: 96.

9. See, for example, J. H. Evans Jr., "Towards an African-American Theology," *Black Theology*, 2: 26.

10. By basics I am referring to belief in God and His oneness, belief in the prophethood and veracity of Muhammad, and belief in the reality of the Afterlife. The extrascriptural Aristotelian–Neoplatonic source of many of the details of Muslim theology was one of the main points of my book, *On the Boundaries of Theological Tolerance in Islam* (New York: Oxford University Press, 2002).

11. From E. Blyden, *Christianity, Islam and the Negro Race* (Baltimore, Md.: Black Classic Press, 1994), ii.

12. R. Dyer, *White* (London, New York: Routledge Press, 1997), 2.

13. Dyer, *White*, 1.

14. Dyer, *White*, xiv. Dyer, who is careful to note that he himself is white, has a stated aim of bringing people to see how the position of white authority is achieved and maintained in order to be able to undermine it.

15. Indeed, the Qur'ān itself equates the use of one's God-given faculties for knowing God with being human, referring to those who do not use these faculties as being on a lower level than beasts: "And We have filled the depths of Hell with many a human and jinn who had hearts that they did not use for understanding, eyes that they did not use for seeing and ears that they did not use for hearing. Such individuals are like beasts; nay, they are even more astray!" See 7: 179.

16. Abū Muḥammad ʿAlī b. Aḥmad b. Saʿīd b. Ḥazm, *al-Akhlāq wa al-siyar fī mudāwāt al-nufūs* (Beirut: Dār al-Āfāq al-Jadīda, 1398/1978), 26.

17. See M. F. Jacobson, *Whiteness of a Different Color: European Immigrants and the Alchemy of Race* (Cambridge, Mass.: Harvard University Press, 1998), 274–280.

18. See Ismāʿīl b. Ḥammād al-Jawharī, *al-Ṣiḥāḥ tāj al-lughah wa ṣiḥāḥ al-ʿarabīyah*, 6 vols., ed. Aḥmad ʿAbd al-Ghafūr ʿAṭṭār (Beirut: Dār al-ʿIlm li al-Malāyīn, 1376/1956), 5: 2175; Ibn Manẓūr, Jamāl al-Dīn Abū al-Faḍl Muḥammad b. ʿAlī b. Aḥ mad b. Abū al-Qāsim b. Ḥabqah, *Lisān alʿarab*, 6 vols. (Cairo: Dār al-Maʿārif, n.d.), 4: 3344; and Muḥibb al-Dīn Muḥammad al-Zubaydī, *Tāj al-ʿarūs min jawāhir al-qāmūs*, 10 vols. (Beirut: Dār al-Fikr, n.d.), 9: 297-298.

19. al-Jawharī, *Ṣiḥāḥ*, 5: 2175; Ibn Manẓūr, *Lisān al-ʿarab*, 4: 3344; and al-Rāghib al-Isfahānī, Abū al-Qāsim al-Ḥusayn b. Muḥammad, *al-Mufradāt fī gharīb al-qur'ān*, ed. Muḥammad Sayyid Kīlānī (Beirut: Dār al-Maʿrifah, n.d.), 371.

20. *Qur'ān*, 21: 35.

21. *Qur'ān*, 64: 15.

22. *Qur'ān*, 2: 193.

23. *Qur'ān*, 85: 10.

24. See, for example, the translation of Qur'ān 2: 191 by M. M. Pickthall (Karachi, Lahore: Taj Company Ltd., n.d.), 31. See also Muḥammad b. Jarīr al-Ṭabarī, *Jāmiʿ al-bayān ʿan ta'wīl al-qur'ān*, 30 vols. (Cairo: Muṣṭafā al-Bābī al-Ḥalabī, 1388/1968), 2: 191–192, 2: 349–351, and Muḥammad b. ʿAlī b. Muḥammad al-Shawkānī, *Fatḥ al-qadīr*, 5 vols. (Beirut: Mahfūẓ al-ʿAlī, n.d.), 1: 191, 1: 192 for various interpretations of Companions and Followers on the meaning of *fitnah* in various verses.

25. See, for example, M. H. Kamali, *Freedom of Expression in Islam* (Cambridge: Islamic Texts Society, 1997), 3, 4, 277–282 passim.

26. In this regard, the Prophet is reported to have said, "I have left no greater *fitnah* for men than women." See *Ṣaḥīḥ al-bukhārī*, 9 vols., ed. Sh. Qāsim al-Shamāʿī al-Rifāʿī (Beirut: Dār al-Arqam b. Abī al-Arqam, n.d.), 8: 16 (*bāb al-nikāḥ*).

27. On this point, see al-Isfahānī, *Mufradāt*, 372.

28. Among the many passages in the Qur'ān that attribute communities' refusal to follow the truth to their clinging to the ways of their forefathers, see 2: 170, 5: 104, 7: 28, 10: 78, 21: 53, 43: 22, 43: 23 passim.

29. Du Bois, *Souls*, 150.

30. I maintain, here, for the sake of convention, the common translation of *kufr* as "unbelief," "disbelief," the active participle, *kāfir*, being "unbeliever," "disbeliever." The Qur'ān, meanwhile, proceeds on the assumption that while humans can refuse to acknowledge the existence of or their debt to God, they cannot really disbelieve any of this, in the same way that one can refuse to acknowledge the existence of the sun but cannot truly disbelieve in it. It is this *refusal to acknowledge* that is captured in the Arabic word *kufr*, which in its original usage meant precisely "to cover up." In pre-Islamic times, the night, the ocean, and farmers were all referred to as *kāfir*, because they covered things up (in the case of the farmer the seeds he threw into the earth). In this light, perhaps a more accurate (but more awkward) translation of *kufr* would be "agnosticism," which refers more to a refusal or failure to acknowledge than to a refusal or failure to believe.

31. To some extent, this contrast of focus parallels the difference between the Qur'ān, on the one hand, and the theologians, on the other, the latter appearing to be far more concerned with defining specific acts of "heresy" or unbelief, with little attention to how or why these acts gain or sustain their currency.

32. For a brief discussion of *fiṭrah* in English, see Y. Mohamed, *Fiṭra: The Islamic Concept of Human Nature* (London: TaHa, 1416/1996).

33. 43:87. Similar statements appear at *Qur'ān* 10: 30, 29: 61, 31: 25, 39: 38, 43: 9 passim.

34. *Qur'ān*, 10:31.

35. For a brief survey on the main theological movements in Islam, see W. M. Watt, *Islamic Philosophy and Theology*, 3rd ed. (Edinburgh: Edinburgh University Press, 1995).

36. See, for example, Aḥmad Ibn Taymīya, *Tafsīr sūrat al-ikhlāṣ* (Cairo: Dār al-Ṭibā'ah al-Muḥammadīyah, n.d.), 13–17.

37. See Abū Mansūr al-Māturīdī, *Kitāb al-tawḥīd*, ed. Fathalla Kholeif (Beirut: Dar el-Machreq, 1986), 23. Al-Māturīdī's distinction between *rubūbīyah* (lordship) and *ulūhīyah* (godhood) should not be confused with this distinction as it was later articulated and popularized by Ibn Taymīya. Al-Māturīdī is almost certainly not Ibn Taymīya's precedent in this regard.

38. In both cases, however, it must be clear that the revolt is against constructs and values enshrined and dictated by second creators as opposed to those handed down by the First. Of course, the latter remain subject to interpretation, and the real issue lies in establishing "objective" standards of interpretation and objective qualifications for interpreters. At the very least, this means eliminating nonessential characteristics, such as gender and ethnicity, from the list of qualifications for admission to the community of recognized interpreters.

39. Like all generalizations, overstatement and overinclusiveness threaten the validity of this description. Still, while certain juridically minded mystical Sufis might take exception to aspects of this description, it is certainly characteristic of mystical Sufism as introduced to Blackamerican Muslims via Immigrant Islam.

40. For a brief summary of the Kharijite position, see W. M. Watt, *Islamic Philosophy and Theology*, 7–13. Not all Kharijites held strictly to this view of *īmān*. Some of

them endorsed Murj'ite views, and some even settled on the view of the orthodox majority (see below). As a whole, however, the Kharijites were fairly unanimous in their view that a person's status as a believer was undermined by his or her commission of a major sin. On the various groups of Kharijites, see al-Shahrastānī, *al-Milal wa al-niḥal*, 2 vols. (Beirut: Dār al-Maʿrifah, 1417/1997), 1: 131–161.

41. See, for example, Watt, *Philosophy and Theology*, 47ff; al-Shahrastānī, *Milal*, 1: 61–62.

42. al-Shahrastānī, *Milal*, 1: 162.

43. This raises some interesting questions regarding Farid Esack's recent attempt to redefine *kufr* (unbelief, i.e., the opposite of *īmān*) so as not to include, for example, Christians whose actions were consistent with Islam or the interests of Muslims, most specifically in the context of the struggle against South African apartheid. See his *Qur'ān, Liberation and Pluralism: An Islamic Perspective on Interreligious Solidarity Against Oppression* (Oxford: Oneworld Press, 1997).

44. See S. A. Jackson, "Ibn Taymīyyah on Trial in Damascus," *Journal of Semitic Studies* 39, no. 1 (1994): 58. The statement is excerpted from Ibn Taymīya's testimony.

45. The best summary of this theodicy is found in William Jones's critique of it in *Is God a White Racist? A Preamble to Black Theology* (New York: Doubleday, 1973). Even Jones admits, however, that not all suffering is bad, only what he calls "negative suffering," that is, "suffering that is either detrimental or irrelevant to one's highest good." Ibid., xxv.

46. See M. Marmura, "Soul: Islamic Concepts," *The Encyclopedia of Religion*, ed. M. Eliade, 16 vols. (New York: Macmillan, 1987), 13: 461.

47. On this point, see G. F. Hawthorne et al., eds., *Dictionary of Paul and His Letters* (Downers Grove, Ill.: InterVarsity, 1993), 765ff.

48. According to Ibn Qayyim, the Qur'ān only uses the word *nafs* to refer to the human soul. It is in hadith literature, according to Ibn Qayyim, that the term "spirit (*rūḥ*)" is used, alongside the term "*nafs*," to refer to the human soul. See his *Kitāb al-rūḥ* (Beirut: Dār al-Nadwah al-Jadīdah, n.d.), 153–154.

49. For more on this point, including the fact that Muslim thinkers such as al-Ghazālī made this insight almost a millennium ago, see my "The Alchemy of Domination? Some Ashʿarite Responses to Muʿtazilite Ethics," *International Journal of Middle East Studies* 31 (1999): 185–201.

50. For a contextualization of these, see my "Jihad and the Modern World," *Journal of Islamic Law and Culture* 7, no. 1 (2002): 1–26.

51. Ibn Qayyim, *Kitāb al-rūḥ*, 153–154.

52. See, for example, Fakhr al-Dīn al-Rāzī, *al-Tafsīr al-kabīr aw mafātiḥ al-ghayb*, 31 vols. (Beirut: Dār al-Kutub al-ʿIlmīyah, 1411/1990), 29: 241; al-Shawkānī, *Fatḥ al-qadīr*, 5 vols. (Beirut: Mahfūẓ al-ʿAlī, n.d.), 5: 193; Ibn Kathīr, *Tafsīr al-qur'ān al-ʿaẓīm*, 4 vols. (Cairo: al-Maktab al-Thaqāfī, 2001), 4: 329; and al-Qurṭubī, *al-Jāmiʿ li aḥkām al-qur'ān*, 10 vols. (Beirut: Dār al-Fikr, 1420/1999), 9: 224–226.

53. *God of the Oppressed*, 77.

54. Cited in Long, "Interpretations of Black Religion in America," *Significations*, 150.

55. Long, "Interpretations," 154–155.

56. Not insignificantly, the verse ends by stating, "And to whomever God does not provide light, no light shall they have."

57. I should like to reiterate, for the sake of clarity, that I am speaking only of that aspect of Sufism that is dedicated to the inculcation of personal piety, not the mystical side dedicated to the annihilation of the self, denial of the world, or pantheistic or monistic union with the Divine.

58. One might consult as useful introductions to learned Sufism, A. Knysh, *Islamic Mysticism: A Short History* (Leiden: E. J. Brill, 2000); and A. Schimmel, *Mystical Dimensions of Islam* (Chapel Hill: University of North Carolina Press, 1975).

59. All subject headings are my own and do not come from the text.

60. Ibn ʿAṭāʾ Allāh, *Tāj al-ʿarūs al-ḥāwī li tahdhīb al-nufūs* (on the margin of *Kitāb al-tanwīr fī isqāṭ al-tadbīr*) (Cairo: ʿAbbās ʿAbd al-Salām Shiqrūn Press, n.d.), 14.

61. ʿAṭāʾ Allāh, *Tāj al-ʿarūs*, 15.

62. ʿAṭāʾ Allāh, *Tāj al-ʿarūs*, 26.

63. ʿAṭāʾ Allāh, *Tāj al-ʿarūs*, 6.

64. ʿAṭāʾ Allāh, *Tāj al-ʿarūs*, 15.

65. ʿAṭāʾ Allāh, *Tāj al-ʿarūs*, 27.

66. ʿAṭāʾ Allāh, *Tāj al-ʿarūs*, 4.

67. ʿAṭāʾ Allāh, *Tāj al-ʿarūs*, 48.

68. ʿAṭāʾ Allāh, *Tāj al-ʿarūs*, 27.

69. ʿAṭāʾ Allāh, *Tāj al-ʿarūs*, 8.

70. ʿAṭāʾ Allāh, *Tāj al-ʿarūs*, 12.

71. ʿAṭāʾ Allāh, *Tāj al-ʿarūs*, 12.

72. ʿAṭāʾ Allāh, *Tāj al-ʿarūs*, 28.

73. ʿAṭāʾ Allāh, *Tāj al-ʿarūs*, 31.

74. ʿAṭāʾ Allāh, *Tāj al-ʿarūs*, 25.

75. ʿAṭāʾ Allāh, *Tāj al-ʿarūs*, 44.

76. ʿAṭāʾ Allāh, *Tāj al-ʿarūs*, 15.

77. ʿAṭāʾ Allāh, *Tāj al-ʿarūs*, 10.

Index